The Rise and Fall of Colin Thatcher

Deny
Deny
Deny

SO-DPL-701

16170439 2

GarrettWilson
& LesleyWilson

James Lorimer & Company, Publishers
Toronto 1985

Cover design: Don Fernley
Illustrations are reproduced courtesy of: Miller Services (cover); Saskatchewan Archives (1); Regina *Leader Post* (2, 3, 7, 9, 15, 22, 33); Saskatchewan Liberal Association (4, 5); Saskatoon *Star Phoenix* (6, 18, 27-32, 34-39); Canapress/Regina *Leader Post* (14 upper right); Canapress/Moose Jaw *Times Herald* (8, 10, 14). Every attempt has been made to identify sources for photographs. The publisher would appreciate receiving information as to any inaccuracies for further printings.
Maps by David Hunter

Canadian Cataloguing in Publication Data

Wilson, Garrett, 1932—
  Deny, deny, deny

ISBN 0-88862-922-2 (bound)—ISBN 0-88862-921-4 (pbk)

1. Thatcher, Colin, 1938 —   2. Thatcher family.
3. Trials (Murder) — Saskatchewan — Regina.
4. Politicians — Saskatchewan — Biography.
5. Crime and criminals — Saskatchewan — Biography.
I. Wilson, Lesley, 1957— II. Title.

HV6535.C33R44 1985   364.1'523'0922   C85-099402-0

James Lorimer & Company, Publishers
Egerton Ryerson Memorial Building
35 Britain Street
Toronto, Ontario M5A 1R7

Printed and bound in Canada

5   4   3   2   1   85   86   87   88   89

Contents

Acknowledgements

In addition to acknowledging the kind assistance of so many of the participants, we would like to express our gratitude to several others whose encouragement and help carried this project through to completion.

Garrett's law partners and staff, particularly Gary J. Drummond, Donald Findlay and Eric Neufeld, were most understanding. Henrica van Lieburg, a friend for many years and a secretary of great skill, typed the manuscript, always against a deadline.

Many friends and associates from political days were helpful in recreating events of the past.

Lorimer editor Ted Mumford taught us the advantages of his discipline and brought order to the chaos of the early manuscript. His kindness and sure insight made this part of the process a pleasant experience.

Moral support came from Sheila and Bob McMullan, Taralyne and Kevin Wilson, and Florence Wilson. Jim Clark was also supportive. Faith came from several.

To Florence Wilson

Preface

"Why not you, Garrett?"

They were speaking to me. It was Friday evening, May 11, 1984. That week Colin Thatcher had been arrested on a charge of first degree murder for the killing of his wife, JoAnn Wilson; he had been arraigned, denied bail, and was in custody out at the Regina Correctional Centre. The members of the Regina City Police who had been involved in the fifteen-month-long investigation, the prosecutors, and some friends, were relaxing over a drink. Although I had had nothing to do with the investigation, or any of the civil litigation surrounding Colin Thatcher, I had been invited to attend, perhaps because of my long and close association with the Regina police as counsel. Besides, my office's boardroom had been chosen as the site of the gathering, and they felt obliged to include me.

Police investigators are more close-mouthed than lawyers about their work. During the lengthy investigation of the JoAnn Wilson murder, not a word had been uttered about its progress. Around the Regina police station no one knew a thing except a select few investigators. They were not talking, even to their colleagues.

Now, finally, with the arrest made and the evidence about to be revealed in court, the men who had been piecing together the clues in the puzzle were free to describe, albeit circumspectly, what they had encountered in their long pursuit.

All had many years in their profession and thought they had seen it all. But this case defied belief. Murder is the ultimate crime, and seldom uninteresting, but the story which began to unfold with the arrest of Colin Thatcher had all the elements of a classic case: power, money, sex, and, of course, violent death.

It was a story that cried out to be told. Someone, it was agreed, should write it. And they looked at me. Initially I brushed the idea away. But it kept returning, looking more reasonable every time. I knew practically everyone in the story, including Colin and JoAnn. (Tony Wilson, JoAnn's second husband, although a namesake, is no relation and we had only briefly met, on an introduction by JoAnn.) I had known Ross Thatcher, Colin's father, well and had worked closely with him politically during his years as premier. I had done some writing, had been a frustrated journalist since my days as a university newspaper editor, and, like many lawyers, felt that I would write a book — someday.

Lesley, who is developing a writing career, was intrigued. She attended the preliminary inquiry at the end of June and, on her return from a writing project in East Africa at the end of the summer, we outlined the story, divided the work, and set to it. Lesley covered the entire trial in October and November, both for this book and for a western newspaper.

The story grew, kept growing, and continues to grow a year later. Colin Thatcher was convicted, but an appeal has been heard by the provincial Court of Appeal; a decision is expected in the fall of 1985. Should the appeal be successful, a retrial may be ordered. Thatcher has consistently stated that he is innocent.

It became apparent to us soon after the trial that no book could cover every aspect of the Thatcher story, and we had to narrow the range of in-depth treatment to the criminal investigation and trial. We tried to delve into the personal lives of the participants only so far as we thought necessary to provide understanding.

While the idea for this book came from the people who brought Colin Thatcher to justice, this is in no way an "official" or "authorized" account. In fact, our thanks extend to the investigators and prosecutors on three counts: for suggesting the book; for answering our endless stream of queries; and for leaving us to write the book as we saw fit.

The people in this real-life story are our friends. We hope they will continue to be. We hope, also, that we have been reasonably successful in our attempt to be objective and fair reporters of a tragic event.

I
The Thatchers

"Go back to the ranch with the rest of the animals."
— Ross Thatcher to Colin, 1962

CHAPTER 1

May 1, 1984

Colin Thatcher was going to be a rancher that day, Tuesday, May 1, 1984. He had been down in California being a Palm Springs playboy since Easter and had returned to his home in Moose Jaw only the night before. Perhaps later in the week he would be a politician again and drop in on the Saskatchewan Legislature, but not today. There were new calves out on his Caron ranch and his men would be seeding his grain lands. It was spring and it was natural that he would rise early and drive the fifteen miles west to the shabby but serviceable buildings on the edge of the hamlet of Caron that served as his ranch headquarters. It would be natural also for him to stop first at the coffee shop at the Gulf service station at Caronport, on the north side of No. 1 Highway three miles east of Caron.

As Colin prepared to leave the family home at 1116 Redland Avenue that spring morning, he had no idea that quite a number of people were anticipating his movements. He was the quarry in the most sophisticated surveillance scheme ever staged in Saskatchewan, and a lot of adrenalin surged with every move Colin Thatcher made that May day.

Thatcher, who liked to hear himself described as a "millionaire rancher," had been a member of the Saskatchewan Legislature for almost ten years, had served as Minister of Energy and Mines in the current government, and was accustomed to receiving a lot of attention. He enjoyed it. But there was no adulation or envy in the eyes that were upon him that day, and there would be no opportunity for him to bask in the attention bestowed on him, for he would not be aware of it.

3

This was not the first time Colin's movements had been watched. Ever since his ex-wife, JoAnn Wilson, had been severely wounded by a gunshot out of the night three years ago to the month, and particularly since her murder in violent circumstances twenty-one months later, Colin Thatcher and his actions had been of acute interest to the police in Regina. He seemed to sense this, too. On several earlier occasions Colin had behaved as if he knew he was being observed; he had been extremely cautious and had even taken evasive action.

So, on this morning, extra care was taken to ensure that no alarm was given. For today, unlike earlier days, plans had been put in place down the road for Colin Thatcher. Today was critical.

At 8:15 a.m. Colin swung his ranch vehicle, a cream-over-brown GMC three-quarter-ton, from its customary place blocking the sidewalk at the bottom of his driveway, and drove the three short blocks east to Main Street. He did not notice his observers who had been in place waiting for him since 5:00 a.m. Confirmation of his movement went ahead of him by radio. At Moose Jaw municipal airport northeast of the city, a waiting aircraft, a single-engine, four-seater Piper Archer, immediately prepared for takeoff.

Main Street runs straight north from the CPR station in downtown Moose Jaw, crossing the Trans-Canada Highway outside the city, and then converts into No. 2 Highway. Colin turned up Main, heading for the Trans-Canada just one mile north. Half-way to the overpass he stopped for the traffic lights at Thatcher Drive, an industrial artery named after his father, Ross Thatcher, Premier of Saskatchewan from 1964 to 1971. That morning the son was being watched in a manner the father never had been.

Less than half a mile farther, Colin turned down the ramp and entered the westbound lanes of the Trans-Canada, heading for Caron. This portion of Saskatchewan's No. 1 Highway had also, in a fashion, once been named for Colin's father. Converting this busy route into a four-lane divided highway had been one of Premier Thatcher's election promises in 1964 and one of his early programs. It was reasonable that the most heavily travelled portion between Regina, the capital city, and Moose Jaw should

4

be constructed first. Coincidentally, the first contract let ran from Regina to just west of Caron, where the premier's ranch was located. Inevitably, Saskatchewan's first divided highway was promptly dubbed The Ranch Road.

This was Thatcher country that Colin was driving through that May morning. For almost all of the past forty years this part of Saskatchewan had been represented either in Parliament or the Saskatchewan Legislature by Ross Thatcher or Colin. Before that, Colin's grandfather had been a successful merchant in Moose Jaw and, in fact, had homesteaded near Caron where Colin was heading.

Colin Thatcher was very much on his own turf that spring day and feeling the confidence that flowed from his wealth and power. He had reason to believe that the investigation into his wife's murder was closing down and that the problem was evaporating. His political position seemed to be improving and the people around the premier's office were once again taking an interest in his opinions and advice. All in all, things were coming together nicely and it looked like a good day ahead. Certainly, it was a pleasant morning after a clear and crisply cold night. Some low, broken clouds were scudding along, but the sun was warming the land.

Seventeen hundred feet above the Trans-Canada two men in the Piper Archer found the weather ideal for their purposes. As they watched Colin's truck move west, they were able to use the clouds as cover. The plane's passenger, sitting in the back seat with four radios, spoke into the VHF channel on one. Colin Thatcher did not notice the slight change in the traffic as a car behind him dropped back and was replaced by another.

Colin Thatcher had not achieved quite the political prominence of his father, Ross, but there was still time. Certainly, he knew that he was almost as well known in Saskatchewan as Ross had ever been and, even if some of the publicity he had generated had arisen from his marital dispute with JoAnn, it had not done him any harm with the voters, where it counted. Sure, the premier had dismissed him from the Saskatchewan cabinet a week before JoAnn's murder, but the reasons for that would fade away, and he would be back.

It would not be impossible either, Colin considered, to

5

succeed or replace the premier some day, the way things were shaping up. People were beginning to notice that the man did not have the grip the job required. Certainly, there would not be much competition from the others currently in the play and what there was he could handle. The cattle and grain man with mud on his boots had won out over the lawyers and slickers from the city before and would do so again.

There were now a million people in Saskatchewan, but most of them still thought that farming was what made the province go. Ross Thatcher's conversion from a hardware merchant to a rancher had been a political plus for him, and Colin had done well playing his chosen role as champion of the country interests. Colin Thatcher still had a good future ahead of him.

Up ahead in the coffee shop at the Gulf service station a young couple, trained surveillance operatives made more unobtrusive by the woman's obvious pregnancy, ordered another coffee. In the parking lot, an acquaintance of Thatcher's named Garry Anderson sat in a blue Ford half-ton, wearing a bullet-proof vest and some sophisticated electronic equipment, awaiting instructions. In a deserted farmyard two miles north of the service station four very formidable looking Regina policemen, armed and camouflaged, stretched their cramped muscles and made themselves even more invisible in the sparse cover. They had been in their places more than three hours now. The men in the aircraft radioed more information, a relay was made, and again vehicles dropped in and out of early traffic moving west on the Trans-Canada.

A decision was made and signalled to the blue Ford. Anderson pulled out of the parking lot, crossed the highway, and drove west three miles down the grid road leading to Caron. He turned around and waited. Colin's truck arrived at the Caronport intersection and turned west towards Caron. No coffee this morning. On a signal, Anderson drove back towards the highway and, on meeting Colin's vehicle, raised his right forearm and passed it forward and down, hand edge foremost, in a long ago agreed signal for a meeting. Colin Thatcher pretended not to see and continued to the ranch at Caron.

Anderson drove back to the service station, turned around, returned down the grid road, and drove into the ranch yard. Here a few words were spoken with Thatcher, and Anderson once again drove back to and across the highway. This time he continued on to the deserted farm north of Caronport, where the hidden sharpshooters lay in wait. He was gasping with tension and controlled excitement. A few minutes later Colin Thatcher followed, this time driving a grey Ford car. He entered the yard, stepped out, and approached the bearded Anderson. The words "Mr. T. is here" were spoken into a microphone by one of the hidden men, and tension filled a mobile command post parked in a supposedly deserted campground six miles to the southwest. The carefully contrived chance contact, in which nothing had been left to chance, had been achieved.

Thatcher and Anderson wandered about the farmyard, deep in conversation, for twenty-eight minutes. The electronic equipment simultaneously transmitted and recorded. Their words, so very precious to the men in the command post, were preserved.

Thatcher and Anderson finished their talk and left, Colin driving west and south back to his ranch, and the other taking his blue half-ton to the east. The sniper rifles, equipped with telescopic sights, that had followed the men as they moved about the yard, were lowered and the arms holding them relaxed. But no one moved. The yard again appeared as calm and deserted as before. It was 9:25 a.m.

Anderson and his truck reappeared at the Gulf service station. After a ten-minute wait and a phone call, he drove west on No. 1 Highway to the deserted campground. Here the electronic equipment and the tape recording of the precious words were carefully removed from him.

That afternoon, in the Regina police headquarters, several senior members of the department and four Crown counsel, one of them a craggy-faced veteran, listened in silence as the tape was played for them. No words were needed to express the unanimous agreement that the four experienced prosecutors came to. The operation had been a success. The case was complete.

With the tape in hand, a few things remained to be done. On Friday morning, May 4, Colin Thatcher paid another visit to the deserted farmyard. Again he was watched. A package he left was soon after recovered — Colin's last unwitting contribution to his adversaries.

On Friday afternoon the craggy-faced prosecutor, Serge Kujawa, telephoned Gary Lane, the province's Minister of Justice and senior law official. The minister was informed that Colin Thatcher, the member for Thunder Creek, his colleague for nine years in the caucuses of two political parties and for nine months in the cabinet, had been charged with the first degree murder of his former wife, JoAnn Wilson. The prosecutor then went on to say: "If everything goes according to plan, Mr. Thatcher will be arrested early on Monday morning."

On Monday morning, May 7, on Redland Avenue, the team members were again in their places. At 7:52 a.m. Colin Thatcher climbed into his truck and headed for his ranch. Five minutes later, as he was on the ramp about to enter No. 1 Highway, he was stopped and, as he stepped from the truck, surrounded by members of the Regina City Police. Inspector Ed Swayze spoke first: "Wilbert Colin Thatcher, I have an information charging you with the first degree murder of JoAnn Wilson. You are under arrest."

Colin Thatcher's future, and his world, had stopped.

CHAPTER 2

The Thatcher Timing

The feud between Colin and JoAnn Thatcher was fuelled by money — money that was mostly the product of the foresight and frugality of two preceding generations. Colin's father Ross and his grandfather Bill had shown an excellent sense of timing in taking advantage of the growth of Saskatchewan, and built a substantial fortune. Colin, too, had been successful in the early years of his stewardship of the family estate.

Colin's grandfather, Wilbert Thatcher, came to Saskatchewan from Ontario in 1912, taking a homestead in the Caron district, where his son Ross located his ranching investment nearly half a century later. The given name "Wilbert" was carried into the next two generations by Wilbert Ross Thatcher and Wilbert Colin Thatcher. Although the name obviously had significance to the family, none of the bearers were known as Wilbert. The first Wilbert Thatcher in Saskatchewan was called "Bill."

Bill Thatcher was born of Ontario Methodist stock at Arthur, educated in Guelph, and came west at the age of twenty-four. He did not stay long in farming and was soon employed as a printer with the weekly Caron *Enterprise*. In 1915 he married another immigrant from Ontario and took employment with International Harvester, a farm implement firm.

In 1917, Bill Thatcher formed a partnership with Percy M. Prowse at Neville, Saskatchewan, about twenty-eight miles south of Swift Current, and the Thatcher name appeared for the first time above a hardware store. Thatcher & Prowse, Hardware & Harness carried on until 1920, when Bill Thatcher moved on and up, leaving the business at Neville to his partner.

Bill Thatcher then established Thatcher's Hardware at Limerick, Saskatchewan. He later opened branches at Lafleche, Melaval, Valor, and Wood Mountain. This was a prosperous period for those communities which served the large and still developing area fifty miles north of the American border. The opening of the CPR line to Wood Mountain in 1928 and on to Mankota in 1929 cut off much of this trade, but Bill Thatcher seemed to have anticipated this. In 1928 he sold out at Limerick and purchased Moose Jaw Hardware in Moose Jaw. Here the family roots stuck. This store was the cornerstone of the Thatcher family hardware business, which later extended to Saskatoon and Regina, until 1959.

Bill Thatcher's business journey through Neville and Limerick to Moose Jaw, although a minor odyssey geographically, displayed courage, perspicacity, and a shrewd placement of capital. In the 1920s, Moose Jaw had a population of over 20,000 and to Bill's customers in the south country it was a distant and imposing metropolis of great stature and wealth. The decision to compete in the commerce of this city showed upward mobility of a very high order for its time.

Bill and Marjorie Thatcher's first child, Wilbert Ross, was born at Neville on May 24, 1917. The family would become six with the arrival of Clarke, Ron, and Joan.

The Thatchers were well educated for the day, hard working, thrifty, and ambitious for their children. Marjorie was musical and taught piano for a time after their marriage. Ross studied piano and learned to play well, often winning his class at music festivals. The Thatcher parents expected their children to excel in all their undertakings, and Ross did, particularly in school where he usually led the class.

Ross received his early schooling during the family's stay in Limerick, but took his high school in Moose Jaw where he graduated from Central Collegiate Institute in 1932, just a month after his fifteenth birthday. Apart from his scholastic brilliance, the powerful personality which would later become known to all Canada, was already evident in the boy. At play with his friends he was dominant, the one who organized and directed the games, the one who was always the cowboy and never the Indian, the one who collected beer bottles like all small boys in Saskatchewan but who did so by system. The others gathered the bottles and delivered them to Ross who marshalled them, kept accounts, brokered their sale, distributed the proceeds according to productivity, and, of course, retained a small management fee.

In 1933, Bill and Marjorie Thatcher decided to risk granting Ross his desire to enter Queen's University at Kingston, Ontario. He wanted to study commerce. By good fortune another Moose Jaw lad was doing the same thing. Bill Gardner, son of a CPR locomotive engineer, had been at Central with Ross and, after being carefully vetted by Mrs. Thatcher, seemed a suitable and trustworthy roommate. Like a number of Ross's friends and colleagues, he would have very different dealings with members of the Thatcher family decades later.

The by now fifteen-year-old Ross Thatcher found the academic requirements of Queen's to be child's play. In May 1936, Queen's University conferred the degree of Bachelor of Commerce upon W. Ross Thatcher. He turned nineteen that month.

Ross Thatcher's classmates at Queen's remember him as a very positive youth with few convictions: that the free enterprise or capitalist system was the only dependable way; that, after the jewelry trade, the hardware business was the best available because of the mark-up; that politics was where his future lay; and that a girl in Moose Jaw, one Peggy McNaughton, was the only girl in the world. These convictions would neither change nor expand very much over the course of Ross Thatcher's career.

Ross's scholastic attainments earned him the offer of a position in the office of J. McLean, president of Canada Packers, in Toronto. He accepted and spent three years in the executive suites, learning about the practical application of the principles of modern finance and economics in which he had majored at Queen's.

Peggy McNaughton, Ross's only girlfriend, had been born in England and had moved to Moose Jaw where her father was manager of Western Ice Company. In those pre-refrigerator days, that was a position that gave immediate entry to the city's society where she and her equally attractive sister starred. Peggy waited awhile in Moose Jaw and then joined Ross in Toronto where they were married on January 20, 1938. He was twenty

11

and she was twenty-three. Their son and only child, Wilbert Colin, was born in Toronto on August 25, 1938.

In 1939, Ross and Peggy returned to Moose Jaw and his father's business. Ross began to take over the management of Moose Jaw Hardware from his father and, although there was the not uncommon friction in this regard, Bill Thatcher accepted an increasingly diminishing role.

Ross quickly established himself in the hardware business, but was presented with a problem by the advent of the Second World War. He was of the right age, and if he wanted a political career, military service was practically compulsory. But Ross failed the medical — four times, he claimed. It is generally assumed that his eyesight, which was weak, was the reason, but he is thought to have developed a slight heart flutter by then, too. The young executive stoically accepted Selected Service and, in 1944, assignment as a brakeman with the Canadian Pacific Railway.

Ross did not wait long in beginning his political career. In 1941 he entered the Moose Jaw civic election and on November 24, out of a field of fifteen candidates, was elected one of seven aldermen, ranking fifth with 1,275 votes. He won re-election two years later. Ross was also an active young man in the community, becoming president of the Moose Jaw Junior Canuck hockey club and president of the Saskatchewan Badminton Association.

Politically, Ross had been a Liberal and had served as secretary-treasurer of the Moose Jaw Young Liberal Association. But in 1941 he joined the Co-operative Commonwealth Federation (CCF), the forerunner of the New Democratic Party, founded in Regina in 1932. By 1942 he was vice-president of the Moose Jaw provincial CCF and a year later was president.

Ross had come under the spell of T.C. (Tommy) Douglas, leader of the CCF in Saskatchewan and soon to become premier of the first socialist government in North America. The young hardware merchant had a sincere desire, which stayed with him all his life, to improve the lot of Saskatchewan people by lifting the province out of a strictly agricultural economy. Douglas's theory that the way to do this was by creating Crown corporations to engage in secondary manufacturing was an attractive solution. Certainly, private industry was ignoring Saskatchewan.

Years later Ross explained his decision: "I joined the CCF in 1941 for the same reasons hundreds of thousands of others joined — as a protest against unemployment and because of the promise of a better future which they so convincingly offered. . . . But," he said, "I was never a real CCFer, even in those early days." That may well have been the reason. But it is also true that in Saskatchewan during the war the CCF was emerging as the only realistic ticket to Parliament, and Ross Thatcher was forever a realist.

On June 15, 1944, the CCF under T.C. Douglas overwhelmed the Liberal government of W.J. Patterson and took office, winning forty-seven of fifty-two seats, with 53 per cent of the vote. And on July 31, 1944, W. Ross Thatcher, "27-year-old Moose Jaw councillor," was nominated as the CCF candidate in the Moose Jaw federal constituency. The next year, in the federal election, he was elected to Parliament with 9,131 votes, 4,000 ahead of his nearest opponent, Liberal Gordon Ross. The CCF took eighteen of twenty-one Saskatchewan seats.

Ross Thatcher's ambition was not at all sated upon becoming a western Member of Parliament. He had more in mind and promptly set about preparing himself by becoming bilingual.

An impediment to Ross's aspirations was that he was not ideologically equipped to be a socialist, and was uncomfortable in the CCF caucus. He made his fellow CCFers uneasy, too. Because Ross often publicly ignored the party line, CCF leader M.J. Coldwell did not trust him with major responsibilities, and Ross chafed. The western businessman MP found his friends in the Liberal caucus. Liberal MPs, such as James Sinclair, Jack Gibson, and Fred Larson (whom Ross was later to appoint Saskatchewan Agent General in London, England), were all free enterprise thinkers and more Ross's kind of people.

In 1949, Ross gained re-election; in 1953 he took all deposits. But in spite of his electoral success the Moose Jaw member, because of his independence, did not enjoy the total allegiance of his CCF riding executive. By 1953 they were openly expressing concern about his failure to toe the party line.

13

Still, being a hardware and appliance merchant and a prominent CCFer was a good combination in Saskatchewan in the 1950s. Tommy Douglas's CCF government had embarked upon a program of rural electrification in Saskatchewan and there was a heavy demand for electric stoves, fridges, and other appliances. Ross Thatcher's hardware chain prospered.

Under Ross's management, Moose Jaw Hardware expanded. Bill Thatcher had retired in 1946, and brothers Clarke and Ron were brought into the business. They were sent off to Saskatoon and Regina respectively to operate new branches in those cities. By 1958, Moose Jaw Hardware Limited owned and operated the main store in Moose Jaw and, together with Ross personally, was the major shareholder in three other stores.

Ross Thatcher was more than just a carefully frugal businessman. He resented expenditures and any employee of his hardware business who found the temerity to speak of a raise never forgot the experience.

The dual responsibilities of Parliament and the hardware business did not leave Ross much time to spend with his son. Ross was an MP during a time when travel between the capital and distant constituencies was difficult and little provision was made for the expense of getting back and forth. A western Member of Parliament could expect to be in Ottawa from fall until early summer, returning home only for Christmas and Easter.

Ross Thatcher did not establish a family home in Ottawa. Peggy and Colin remained in Moose Jaw during most of the twelve years Ross served in Parliament.

Colin was seven years old when his father first went off to Parliament. When Ross returned from his long absences, he had difficulty in helping his young son over the emotional distance that would develop while he was away. A friend recalls Ross, on one of those reunions, teasing young Colin cruelly, asking, "Who is your daddy?" and denying that he was until the boy was in tears.

Ross was still sitting in Parliament when Colin graduated from his father's high school, Central Collegiate Institute, in June 1956. He played centre on the school football team, the

Cyclones, where he was known as "The Big T." His scholastic record was average.

In April 1955, Ross Thatcher left his colleagues in the CCF caucus and set up shop in the House of Commons as an independent. In explanation of this drastic career change he said:

> . . . .I regret to say recently there have been growing differences between myself and my colleagues on matters of major public policy. At one time I had hoped that these differences could be resolved. However, the present session of Parliament has convinced me that such a hope is futile. . . . .I feel that I have no alternative but to resign from the CCF party.

A better explanation came from Manitoba CCF leader Loyd Stinson, who said of Ross's departure, "He is a well-to-do young fellow who happened to get into the wrong party."

The month after Colin's high school graduation, Ross declared himself a Liberal again and joined the government caucus in Ottawa. When the 1957 election came on, he announced he would seek election as a Liberal, not in his home of Moose Jaw but in Assiniboia, a large rural riding immediately to the south. Assiniboia had been held since 1945 by Hazen Argue, who had been Ross's Centre Block office mate during his first eight years in Parliament.

It would be make or break. Argue would be hard to beat and Assiniboia was tough CCF country. The party Ross had abandoned was furious with him for his betrayal and determined to destroy him. Ross had made things worse when, in May 1956, a year after bolting the CCF, he had made a speech in Parliament castigating the CCF's Crown corporation experiment in Saskatchewan, calling it a complete failure.

Premier Tommy Douglas was enraged. Publicly branding Thatcher "a liar and a traitor," the articulate champion of the CCF vowed to follow his enemy wherever he went and "drive him out of the province." Douglas challenged Thatcher to a joint meeting to debate his accusations against Saskatchewan Crown corporations. Ross promptly accepted and, after some skirmish-

15

ing, the town of Mossbank was chosen as the site and May 20, 1957, as the date.

Douglas was at the height of his power and regarded as invincible in debate. This was therefore no small undertaking for Ross Thatcher and he was very much the underdog. The debate provoked tremendous interest all over the province. In spite of a heavy rain, Mossbank was inundated by partisan spectators. The proceedings were broadcast by radio. In the hall, Colin Thatcher stood on his seat and shook his fists in fury at CCF hecklers towards the back.

The contest itself was probably a draw, but Ross Thatcher emerged the clear winner because he had been able to accomplish this against the previously undefeated Douglas. Instead of suffering the political eclipse the CCF had confidently predicted for him, Ross established himself as a politician of provincial stature. That he lost the election to Argue, and did so again the next year in the Diefenbaker sweep of 1958, was almost insignificant. His reputation had been made.

The 1957 election in Assiniboia was so bitter and acrimonious that many feared for Thatcher's safety. A rumour developed that Ross was being protected by bodyguards. When a tall, surly young man appeared at the back of the meeting halls, the rumour gained credibility. Colin Thatcher was watching his politician father in action.

In 1959 the Saskatchewan Liberal Party began to lose faith in its leader, A.H. (Hammy) MacDonald. Ross Thatcher had been busy earning credentials within the party by organizing fundraising dinners and establishing a reputation for getting things done. When MacDonald resigned in July 1959, Thatcher was ready.

Ross was far from being the unanimous choice of the Saskatchewan Liberals. He had not been fully forgiven for his CCF years. But Ross's energy and organizational skills capitalized on the party's yearning for someone who could compete in the same arena with Tommy Douglas. At Mossbank, Ross had proven that he could do just that.

At the Liberal convention in Regina's Trianon Ballroom on September 24, 1959, Ross Thatcher secured 67 per cent of the first ballots, defeating three other candidates, and won the party leadership. Saskatchewan politics would be tumultuous for the next twelve years.

After becoming leader, Ross sold the Thatcher Hardware businesses to Ashdown's, a wholesale and retail chain out of Winnipeg. The sale displayed the Bill Thatcher touch of timing, for the bloom was off the rose for the hardware business. The Ashdown deal left Moose Jaw Hardware Limited, of which by then Ross was the only shareholder of consequence, in excellent financial health. A financial statement from 1962 (during the period of liquidation) shows that Ross held shareholder's equity worth $214,854.59. He wound up the company and it was discontinued.

Ross had developed an interest in purebred Hereford cattle in the early 1950s and had acquired some land near Tuxford, north of Moose Jaw. But he soon turned his attention to the Caron area where he had purchased 320 acres as early as 1953. The Thatcher Hereford Ranch had grown to 3,600 acres when Colin joined the operation in 1962.

These land acquisitions again displayed the excellent Thatcher timing. In the 1950s and 1960s, Saskatchewan farmland prices had not much recovered from Depression levels. A slow upward growth was seen in the 1960s, but the 1970s saw an explosive leap upwards. The land Ross Thatcher purchased for his Herefords was "light" land, mostly uncultivated grazing land not suitable for grain production. Land he had paid $56,300 for was appraised at $714,900 twenty years later.

Ross Thatcher knew he was on to a good investment, but even he did not foresee the mushrooming prices to come. In 1962 he gave Colin a quarter section he had bought five years earlier for $1,500 and, on sending the title to his son, said: "We paid $10.00 an acre. Hold it ten years and it will be worth $25.00 an acre." It was, but in 1980 it was worth five times that, or $125 per acre, a total of $20,000 for 160 acres of "dune sand with scattered brush, used for grazing," according to the 1980 appraisal.

Some members of the Saskatchewan Liberal Party, those with seats in the Legislature, had not even left the Trianon Ballroom on the day of Ross Thatcher's election as leader, before they learned that he intended to be in charge. Summoned to a "caucus" meeting in an upstairs room at the Trianon, while the convention was still in progress down below, the fourteen MLAs were greeted by Thatcher and Dave Steuart, Thatcher supporter and newly elected party president. When Mary Batten, the outspoken MLA from Humboldt, pointed out that, whatever the meeting might be, it was not a "caucus" because neither Thatcher nor Steuart were members of the Legislature, the new leader threatened to go right back to the delegates still assembled to have his mandate clarified if there was to be any question about the MLAs accepting him.

The rest of the Liberal party learned almost as quickly that an authoritative hand had taken over. Ross Thatcher believed in hard work for himself and for those around him. He recognized results only and was ruthless with members of the party "establishment" if their performance was lacking. He asked no more of anyone else than he was prepared to do himself, but Saskatchewan Liberals, somewhat complacent after fifteen years in opposition, were rudely awakened as Ross Thatcher prodded them into action or removed them if they resisted.

A provincial election was expected in 1960 and the new Liberal leader had to move quickly to put his creaky political apparatus into election trim. There was little thought of winning. Since the 1956 election the Liberals had been concerned only with survival. Social Credit had burst onto the Saskatchewan political scene in 1956, capturing more than 20 per cent of the vote and electing three members. The federal elections of 1957 and 1958 had wiped out all the province's Liberal MPs. Saskatchewan Liberals were worried that they would lose their position as the natural alternative to the CCF. Bringing with him some organizational techniques he had learned in the CCF, and a unique ability to motivate people, Thatcher revamped the Liberal party and put it to work. Within two months of Ross's election as leader, the Liberal party was back in business.

The selection of a seat was an easy choice for Ross. There was no sitting Liberal in the rural riding of Morse, just west of Moose Jaw, which formed part of his old federal constituency and contained his growing cattle ranch at Caron.

The election came as expected in June 1960. In contrast to his

18

usual solo style, Thatcher campaigned on behalf of the "Liberal Team." The centrepiece of his campaign was the "economic stagnation" Saskatchewan was suffering "under the iron heel of socialism."

The CCF and Tommy Douglas withstood the first onslaught from the defector, winning handily and increasing their seats by two for a total of thirty-eight. The Liberals won seventeen, an increase of three, including Ross Thatcher in Morse. Social Credit dropped to 12 per cent of the vote and lost all three of its seats. The Liberals were confirmed as the only opposition to the CCF. Ross Thatcher was now poised to move on to defeating his arch enemy.

The 1960 election never really stopped. By-elections kept it going for more than two years and Thatcher's momentum continued to swell, as each of the seats fell to his party. Notably, one of them was Weyburn, vacated by Tommy Douglas when he became federal leader of the newly founded New Democratic Party in 1962. The Saskatchewan government was turned over to Woodrow Lloyd.

While the Liberals and Ross Thatcher were on a roll, cracks were beginning to show in the socialist citadel. In the June 1962 federal election, Douglas, confidently running for Parliament in Regina, lost to the sitting Conservative. At the provincial level, the introduction of Medicare in 1962 produced a confrontation with the doctors of Saskatchewan that fused all political factions in opposition to Premier Lloyd's government. The resulting medical strike gave Ross Thatcher and the Liberal opposition an ideal opportunity to gather to their ranks all those who opposed the CCF/NDP.

In the Legislature, Ross Thatcher, the transplanted parliamentarian, handled himself well. At times, however, his zeal caused mortifying excesses. During the Medicare crisis, Ross demanded that the Legislature be called into session to deal with the impasse. To publicize his demand he approached the ornate main door of the Legislature, which was closed, accompanied by news photographers. A photographer suggested, "Give it a kick, Ross," and he did. The resulting picture of the Leader of the Opposition kicking at the doors of the Legislature like a small boy in a tantrum haunted him through the 1964 election, as the

CCF/NDP joyfully ran it in their advertisements.

In February 1962, Bill and Marjorie Thatcher embarked on a round-the-world cruise. On March 15, Ross's father died of a heart attack while sailing across the Indian Ocean. Mrs. Thatcher sent word to Ross at his office in the Legislature by a thrifty telegram which read: "Father died. Heart. Love, Mother." Bill Thatcher's body was returned to Vancouver by plane. Although Ross attended the funeral, he declared himself "too busy" to visit his mother at the Regina airport as the plane carrying his father stopped over.

The day after Regina learned of Bill Thatcher's death, Lachie McIntosh, the popular MLA for Prince Albert and Minister of Co-operatives, died suddenly. The Legislature adjourned to enable members to attend the funeral.

Two days later, while his own father's funeral was still pending, Ross Thatcher asked Premier Lloyd in the Legislature if he had yet "given any consideration to setting a date for the Prince Albert by-election." Both sides of the House groaned and the premier replied that "nothing could speak more eloquently of the insensitivity of the Leader of the Opposition than the question which he has just asked. We had the funeral just the day before yesterday." It was a strange side to Ross Thatcher that, in the midst of his own grief at the loss of his father, whom he dearly loved, he would attempt to mask his feelings by assuming a tough "life must go on" facade.

Bill Thatcher missed by two years his son's election as Premier of Saskatchewan. Leaving an estate valued at $200,000, his will made careful provision for Mrs. Thatcher, his sons Clarke and Ron, and his daughter Joan. Ross received only a very minor interest, but he was in a very much more secure financial position than his brothers and sister.

Later in 1962, Colin Thatcher, who had been studying agriculture at the University of Iowa, joined Thatcher Hereford Ranches as an employee of his father. Ross was on the verge of becoming premier of the province and needed a manager for his Caron cattle operation. It should have been another example of the happy coincidence of time in the Thatcher family, but the relationship of employer/employee between father and son was not to be a perfect success.

CHAPTER 3

Ross the Boss

On the evening of April 22, 1964, Ross Thatcher, Peggy, and two young aides sat in the den of 1116 Redland Avenue, in Moose Jaw, listening to election results as they came over the radio and television. Ross was discouraged. The early returns were bleak. He had fully expected to win but knew the realities of politics.

Liberal party workers and the press were waiting for him in the Trianon Ballroom in Regina, but Ross refused to drive over until the result was clear. Finally, one of the aides took a scrap of paper and performed some calculations that demonstrated the certainty of a Liberal victory. He handed them to Ross, saying, "You have won, Mr. Premier." Ross studied the numbers for a few moments with the total concentration he was capable of. Then he turned to Peggy and said, "Well, I guess we had better get going. Call Colin and see if he and JoAnn want to drive over with us." They did, and had been waiting at their home, hoping for the call.

It was typical that Colin would be excluded from the serious portion of the evening but invited to participate in the ceremony and success. The family left the home on Redland Avenue to drive to Regina and the lights and cheers in the Trianon. The house on Redland Avenue, left in darkness, would never again know its family in the same way.

The 1964 Saskatchewan election had been, in western parlance, a "barn-burner." The Liberals, galvanized as never before by Ross Thatcher and by events, had thrown themselves into the campaign with dedication and spirit. They were joined by many Conservatives and former Social Crediters, all determined to end twenty years of socialism in Saskatchewan. The New Democratic Party was, in spite of the obvious signals of unrest in 1962, guilty of some complacency and over confidence. Even so, the election was close.

As in 1960, when he introduced campaigning by light aircraft, Ross Thatcher brought innovations to Saskatchewan electioneering. He pepped up his meetings with bands and entertainment and engaged McLaren Advertising of Toronto to handle the Liberal public relations campaign.

Ross believed wholeheartedly that the mere existence in Saskatchewan of a government dedicated to socialist principles was an obstacle to industrial investment and preventing the province from enjoying the benefits of economic growth. That was his single message to the voters and had been since he became Liberal leader. He found it difficult to deliver that message in other than a negative way, and many voters, who were quite happy with the social programs initiated by the government he was castigating, were concerned that Ross Thatcher intended to throw out all the deeds of the CCF/NDP, the good with the bad.

Liberal campaign strategists had been quite unable to induce Ross to accept any advice on his public posture. "I've been in politics for twenty-two years," he reminded them so frequently that the phrase became the punch line among the campaign team.

It was even more difficult to overcome Ross's unbending honesty. "I am what I am," he insisted, refusing to act a role to improve his voter appeal. He stubbornly indulged his penchant for dark suits and black cigars, even though he conceded that it was not exactly Saskatchewan fashion in the mid-1960s.

The McLaren strategists discovered that if Peggy Thatcher could be convinced that a modification was in Ross's interest, it would not be long before Ross also began to see merit in the idea. Peggy was constantly at her husband's side during the wearying campaigning of the 1964 election. Gracious and decorative, a place was made for her on every meeting platform and a small girl assigned to present her with a bouquet of flowers. When they travelled by car, Peggy often drove and, during the late night returns to Regina from political events in outlying communities, she contributed greatly to the softening of Ross's political image.

The election was a tie in terms of popular vote: 40.31 per cent for the Liberals and 40.21 per cent for the NDP/CCF. But Ross Thatcher won thirty-two seats to Woodrow Lloyd's twenty-six. The Conservatives lagged behind with 19 per cent of the vote and one seat.

On election night the close results kept the Liberal party headquarters open until after two o'clock the next morning. The victory celebrations went on much later.

Ross did not relax. Participating mildly with his celebrating troops, he and Peggy returned to his Regina headquarters at the King's Hotel at 4:30 a.m. Over the next few hours he became Premier W. Ross Thatcher.

Shortly after 7:00 a.m. his secretary, Marj Totten, was telephoned into shocked awareness and instructed to call Ross's key advisers together immediately. A pitiful, hungover collection assembled in the Leader of the Opposition's office at the Legislature at 8:30 a.m. No time was spent savouring the victory of the night before. There was work to be done.

Later that morning the premier-elect laid off all party organizers and campaign staff, effective election day. People who had been working for months, and, in some cases, years, at subsistence-level salaries suddenly found that victory was hollow for them. No promises of government employment were made, and many did not secure positions with the new Liberal administration. Dave Steuart, Thatcher's closest confidant and most loyal supporter, was kept waiting for an hour and a half the day after the election until Ross felt that the message had been thoroughly understood that the old, casual way and open door were no more.

In the five years of his drive to the premiership, Ross Thatcher had been affable, approachable and quite open to suggestions, while never leaving any doubt that he was in charge. On the night of the election a metamorphosis had taken place, and "Ross the Boss" emerged.

Premier W. Ross Thatcher directed his imposing discipline and determination to running the Government of Saskatchewan in the way he had decided it should be. Waste and extravagance

23

would be eliminated and replaced with economy and efficiency. Government could and would be operated much in accordance with the principles of business.

The austerity drive included an immediate freeze on civil service hirings. The Liberals had complained for years of the size of the Saskatchewan bureaucracy and Ross planned a reduction by attrition. Vacancies could be filled only upon application to the Treasury Board, chaired by Premier Thatcher who had kept to himself the portfolio of Provincial Treasurer.

A few months into his term, displeased with the public service union agreement's restrictions on the hiring and placing of personnel, the premier decided that collective bargaining was not for him. "I don't think we'll have a union anymore," he said, exactly as if he had decided to get rid of the milk cow on the ranch. The shocked official to whom he was speaking, thinking of the political effect of wiping out the country's sole model of public sector bargaining, blurted, "You can't do that." That was a mistake. The premier growled, "Oh, can't I?" and issued a press release announcing his intention. However, the premier, having made his point, soon forgot about the matter.

As premier, Ross Thatcher became a confrontationalist in dealing with his ministers and officials. He believed that a sincere and constructive program proposal would survive his violent rejection and that a minister who believed strongly in its merit would defend it.

"It was very easy to withstand Ross's personality if you didn't mind having a row. But that was the only way you could do it. There aren't many people who like to have a fight every day of their lives, sometimes twice a day," is former Industry Minister Herb Pinder's description of the early days of the Thatcher cabinet. But there was no hostility in Ross's aggressiveness and he admired those who withstood him. When one MLA returned as good as Ross gave, the premier nearly appointed him to the cabinet on the spot.

The premier adopted the same style when dealing with prime ministers. With the gentle Mike Pearson he was generally successful in getting his own way, although Pearson once asked Steuart, "With Ross aren't there any minor issues where you just have a sane discussion and, perhaps, have a difference of opinion?'' Pierre Trudeau, however, was not impressed by Thatcher's bluster, and the Saskatchewan premier was reduced to reason in negotiations with the prime minister after 1968.

Contrary to the expectations of many, the Thatcher government did not slash social and health programs. Rather, the social service network was strengthened and hospital and nursing home facilities extended. Ross tried hard to mask his genuine humanitarian feelings but, occasionally, they showed. His eyes were full of tears when he saw first hand the primitive living accommodation of Saskatchewan's northern native population. Native housing and employment programs were promptly initiated. But the political gains of Ross's sincere desire to assist Saskatchewan's native people were somewhat diminished by the publication of his unguarded comment that ''they breed like rabbits.''

The highlight of the Thatcher government was industrial expansion. The showcase was the Prince Albert Pulp Mill, a development announced in 1965 and opened three years later. A $65-million project, it was a blend of public concession and the American capital of Parsons and Wittemore of New York. The government claimed it created 5,000 jobs in the mill, the bush, and support industries.

Ross Thatcher was convinced that he had been right all along, that ''removing the yoke of socialism,'' encouraging industrial expansion, and reducing the size and waste of government were all bringing economic good times to Saskatchewan. It only remained now to eradicate the NDP opposition. Claiming that he needed a fresh mandate, that investors, fearful of a return to power by the NDP, were still hesitant about Saskatchewan, Ross Thatcher called an early election for October 11, 1967.

The Liberal premier fully believed that he was headed for a landslide. The old professional who had never taken his eye off the essentials was this time almost completely careless about his campaign organization. He did not need one; he intended to win by himself. Only once during the entire election did he set foot in Liberal campaign headquarters, and then only by chance.

Ross Thatcher won, and even increased his majority, but it was a near-run thing. The Liberals elected thirty-five members to the NDP's twenty-four, but the popular vote was extremely close:

45.6 per cent to 44.3. The Conservative vote fell to under 10 per cent and they lost their one member.

On election night the barely victorious premier was late arriving at the campaign headquarters celebration being held in a Regina hotel suite. By the time Ross, Peggy, Colin and JoAnn arrived the bar had long since gone dry, except for a bottle of Ne Plus Ultra, a gift to the premier from the hotel manager that had been set aside. As the thirsty celebrants gathered around, Ross looked at the bottle, handed it to Colin and said, "That's good Scotch, Colin. See that it gets home safely." And into Colin's coat it went, to the amazement and dismay of those who had eagerly anticipated its opening.

When the narrowness of the win became apparent, Ross Thatcher was shocked and hurt. A redistribution of constituency boundaries had contributed as much to the survival of the government as any of its policies.

Although there had been faint signals in some of the premier's campaign speeches, no one in the Liberal party was prepared for the overnight transformation in Thatcher's attitude. Just as his first election victory had brought forth "Ross the Boss," the second produced something akin to "Ross the Tyrant."

Meeting with his cabinet the day after the election, Premier Thatcher announced that fiscal reality required cutbacks and severely controlled spending. And then began a short era of austerity and increasing confrontation that spelled the end of the Thatcher government.

Ross cancelled the Liberal party annual convention slated for later in the fall. He gave the explanation that Liberals were "too tired" after campaigning (an unusual thought for him), but the more likely reason was to avoid any disagreement with the unpopular health care and education cutbacks. More was to come in the 1968 budget, which Thatcher prepared and then turned over to Dave Steuart, who was appointed Provincial Treasurer in time to deliver it. Taxes were substantially increased.

Ross Thatcher suffered from diabetes, an ailment which affected his disposition when his insulin level went out of balance. Occasionally, he would require hospitalization for treatment of the condition. The persistent rumour that he was an alcoholic would increase with each hospitalization, and every cocktail party seemed to include at least one person who had a friend whose sister was a nurse on the ward where the premier was drying out. The rumour infuriated Ross's friends and associates, who knew how ridiculous it was.

In the late fall of 1968 Ross Thatcher was in Regina's Grey Nuns Hospital again. This time the problem was not diabetes. The premier had suffered a stroke and some temporary paralysis. It was a very well-kept secret. The party convention, cancelled the previous year, was under way in Regina and Ross missed it entirely, the only time during his leadership. The delegates learned nothing of the reason.

The setback did nothing to diminish Ross Thatcher's aggressive style or his determination to curtail public spending. He seemed, rather, to seek out opportunities for confrontation with communities and organizations wanting to advance their interests. The cabinet began a series of meetings outside of Regina, so they could hear first hand of local concerns. It should have been good politics, but some events were disasters. At Nipawin, when the chosen dignitary read a prepared text itemizing the town's problems and needs, Thatcher twice interrupted, requesting that the process be speeded up. Finally, the spokesman threw his brief to the floor in anger, asking why, if he had no time to listen, had the premier come at all, and stalked from the room. The spokesman was also the president of the local Liberal association.

Similar incidents marred other such meetings, as well as appearances before conventions of occupational and professional groups. As Dave Steuart later remarked, "If we missed making enemies of anyone, it was because we hadn't met them."

Ross Thatcher found apology difficult, although he sometimes recognized its need. At a cabinet meeting in Saskatoon, the premier had tongue-lashed Welfare Minister Dave Boldt, a gentleman of whom the premier was genuinely fond. The upset Boldt, a diabetic like Thatcher, had gone into insulin shock, collapsed, and had to be rushed to hospital. The premier took Dave Steuart with him to the hospital to apologize. "I see they are feeding you fine, Dave," he said to Boldt, inspecting the food tray beside the bed. "Well, don't stay here too long, Dave," he continued. "There is work to do, you know," and with that the visit was over.

Steuart stuck his head back into the room. "Oh, by the way, Ross says he's sorry." Boldt understood. Ross Thatcher's anger came and went like a summer prairie thunderstorm. Moments after an outburst he would be affable as if nothing had happened.

A frequent inspiration of Ross's wrath was his son Colin. A typical incident is recalled by one of Ross's political associates. One day in 1970 the two dropped in at the Thatcher ranch. Colin was discovered to have ignored some instructions and received another of the by-now-familiar verbal lashings from his father, in front of all present, including some ranch employees.

Back in the car Ross's companion asked, "Why don't you take him around the corner when you want to chew him out like that?"

"It's good for him," Ross replied.

A few moments later, Ross began to speculate upon his future. One more term of office would be nice, he thought, and then he would like to retire to the ranch.

"Back there? With that guy you just raised hell with?"

"Sure. Why not?" Ross seemed nonplussed.

"Why don't you buy him half a section of his own and let him run his own show?"

Ross snorted. "He couldn't handle it."

"He's married with two kids. Why couldn't he?"

"He couldn't handle it." The subject was closed.

A year later Colin was "handling" the entire operation.

Until then, Ross ran Thatcher Hereford Ranches from the premier's office. Books, cattle records, and correspondence were handled along with affairs of government. Frequently he would dictate letters of instruction to ranch manager Colin and, occasionally, these letters would be blistering with criticisms.

"Colin is too busy on the ranch," would be the reply to anyone who hinted that the premier's son might like to be involved in a political activity. But Ross liked to include Colin in some of his travels and associations with political and business leaders. The son, however, was clearly present in that capacity only. When Colin casually put a cowboy-boot-clad foot on a

28

coffee table on the patio of an American industrialist, Ross loudly berated him in the presence of the host and other guests.

The premier's staff were alert to the fact that JoAnn and grandson Greg had special status. They arranged air tickets when JoAnn and Greg visited the other grandparents in Iowa. Once, an executive assistant who had driven the two to the Regina airport was sent hurriedly back because the premier had neglected to give JoAnn "her spending money" for the two-week holiday. The assistant delivered twenty dollars to the daughter-in-law.

As the Liberal premier advanced towards his last election, he increasingly discouraged opposition to his policies. Party offices were filled with loyalists or, at least, non-complainers, and caucus and cabinet fell silent faced with the strong will of the leader. Warnings that his government's policies not only fell short of public expectation, but actually offended many sectors, were ignored.

The 1971 campaign contained no innovations. The techniques of 1964 and 1967 were applied one more time, and superficially seemed to be successful, but only the faithful were participating. As Dave Steuart described it, "It was like a dance without partners."

Ross Thatcher held the Liberal vote at 43 per cent, with just seven fewer votes overall than he had received in 1967, but it produced only fifteen seats as the Conservative vote collapsed and the NDP took 55 per cent of the popular vote with forty-five of the sixty seats in the Legislature.

On election night, June 23, Ross Thatcher stood for the last time in Regina's Trianon Ballroom. It was here he had been elected the Liberal leader in 1959 and had celebrated the victories of 1964 and 1967. Exhausted and ill, the defeated premier showed a graciousness and character that surprised even some who thought they knew him well. After publicly accepting full responsibility for the loss, and sharing consolations with defeated candidates, he went across town to the NDP headquarters and congratulated Premier-elect Allan Blakeney. It was an untraditional move that thrilled the NDP throng, which rose to the occasion with a round of "For He's a Jolly Good Fellow."

Ross returned to his Regina home with Peggy, Colin and JoAnn, and a few close Liberal friends. As they analyzed the

29

reasons for the loss, Peggy could not understand. "But it was such a perfect campaign," she said. "No, Peggy, it wasn't a perfect campaign," Ross replied quietly. "We lost."

Ross set about the business of transition in his usual crisp, businesslike way. Within a few days, he had turned over the premier's suite and was back in the opposition offices he had left seven years before. Staff was adjusted, the election aftermath cleaned up, and bills paid. The Liberal party council was called into session and told that Ross intended to continue as leader no more than a year.

Less than a month later, on July 22, 1971, Ross Thatcher was in a buoyant mood. In his offices, he chatted happily with several of his former cabinet members. A recent medical check-up had pronounced him fit. He had spent the day before at the ranch baling hay, and a slight pain in his chest he attributed to twisting on the tractor seat to look backward at the machinery. He had stopped on the way home at Redland Avenue for a swim with Colin, JoAnn, and his grandsons. Ross was not one bit contrite about the policies and actions that had led to his election defeat. Given the chance, he would not do one thing differently. "Well, one thing, perhaps. If I had to do it over again, I sure wouldn't call that damn election," he admitted.

The next morning, Ross Thatcher collapsed and died in his bathroom. The autopsy, usual in such cases, performed by pathologist Dr. Derrick Dexter, disclosed serious deterioration due to the chronic diabetic condition and the cause of death as massive cardiac arrest.

With his death, as with his life, Ross Thatcher provoked rumour and controversy. Perhaps because his death occurred exactly a month after the defeat of his government, the story of his suicide in despair at his loss crept throughout Saskatchewan. It slowly diminished with time but surfaced again with the publicity surrounding the arrest, trial, and conviction of Colin Thatcher in 1984.

An enigma even to those who were close to him, Ross Thatcher was, in spite of more foibles than most, a large and well-meaning man, sincerely dedicated to giving Saskatchewan the leadership and direction he deeply believed was right. He gave all of himself to his cause.

CHAPTER 4

Colin and JoAnn

On August 12, 1962, Wilbert Colin Thatcher and JoAnn Kay Geiger were married in the Methodist Church in Ames, Iowa. Colin was twenty-three, JoAnn a year younger. It was obvious to all that the cattleman and the high school teacher were very much in love, but the match was a mystery to many. Their interests and personalities were dissimilar, but JoAnn was most accommodating in adapting to Colin's lifestyle. Her parents, Betty and Harlan Geiger, had anticipated that she would leave Iowa, but they thought it would likely be for somewhere called New York, not Moose Jaw.

The pair met in 1960 as Iowa State University students, she in home economics and he in agriculture (animal science), two of the faculties which had brought esteem to the university. Even there they had little in common. JoAnn was an excellent student, as she had been in public and high school, and was heavily involved in extra-curricular activities. She was on the Dean's list every year, and in her graduating year received the Mortar Board, the university's highest honour, for outstanding leadership, scholarship and service to the university community. Colin, by contrast, was involved in nothing meriting mention in his yearbook listing, and even his photograph was missing.

Colin's one apparent interest was athletics. In high school he played basketball and was a centre on the football team. Moose Jaw's Central Collegiate yearbook observed that he was ''very fond of girls'' by Grade 9, a trait he would continue to demonstrate long after his betrothal to JoAnn.

In 1956 part of the comment alongside his graduation

31

photograph read " 'Le Gros T' can create quite a stir in French class when he gives his imitation of Elvis Presley." Three decades later, he would be known to the police as "Mr. T.," after "le gros" television character of the same name.

Colin spent the next year at the University of Saskatchewan in Saskatoon, did not excell, and then transferred in 1957 to the United States, graduating in 1960 with a Bachelor of Science in Agriculture. He met JoAnn on a blind date, ninety days short of his graduation. A year behind him, JoAnn would not graduate until 1961.

There are thirty-five fraternity and seventeen sorority houses at Iowa State, and they play a big part in university life. JoAnn lived at the Chi Omega sorority house, and Colin at the Alpha Tau Omega fraternity house. By the end of the school year she was wearing his fraternity pin.

In the summer of 1960 JoAnn's outstanding academic record won her a training position in a department store in St. Louis, Missouri, some 300 miles southeast of Ames. It was a step towards her goal of becoming a buyer. She had worked part-time in Younkers' department store in Ames during high school, and it was that experience which had led to her career choice. Colin headed 900 miles northwest to the family ranch. At the end of the summer, JoAnn went to Moose Jaw for a two-week visit.

On the evening of August 21, JoAnn's twenty-first birthday, she and Colin were out riding horses. Colin was thrown by his mount, severely injuring his shoulder and arm. After hospitalization, Colin faced the prospect of being incapacitated for the better part of a year, and the possibility of permanent loss of the use of his arm. He was obviously not going to be ranching for a while so chose to join JoAnn back at Iowa State, this time in a Master's program in animal breeding.

The pair spent Christmas 1960 in Moose Jaw, and became engaged. JoAnn surveyed the job prospects for a textiles and clothing merchandising major. The only option in the small community was teaching, so she made arrangements with the Board of Education to start in the fall of 1961 as a home economics instructor at the Technical High School.

Back at Iowa State, she had to pick up the necessary Education classes, so she altered her January class load and also attended the spring and summer sessions. In mid-August 1961, she arrived in Canada as a landed immigrant. JoAnn would retain her American citizenship for the duration of her life.

Teaching was not JoAnn's calling. Although she did her job to the best of her ability, her heart was not in it. It was a practical compromise, a good means of support at about $4,500 a year, but it was not her dreamed-of career.

In 1962, Colin graduated with his second degree. He claimed he had been offered a teaching position by Iowa State University, but instead returned to Canada, having recovered enough to ranch again. JoAnn returned to the United States to plan their summer wedding. By all accounts, August 12 was the happiest day of her life up to that point, but the two fathers, Harlan Geiger and Ross Thatcher, each made prescient comments which would be remembered many years later. "I sure hope Jo can handle him, because we never could," mused Thatcher while helping pack the wedding gifts. Colin's father-in-law was somewhat blunter, confiding to his wife, Betty, "If they ever fell out of love, he could kill her." Peers of the young couple also had reservations.

After their marriage JoAnn and Colin lived in Moose Jaw in a modest suite in a downtown store building owned by Ross, where JoAnn had already been resident for a year. The best that could be said about it was that the price was right. They lived exclusively off Colin's salary, in preparation for the day when JoAnn would not have one. Colin's came from his father, with a bit more from the fifty or sixty cattle he himself owned at the time of their marriage. However, most of the profits from the latter were ploughed right back into the herd. In the summer, Colin was on the cattle show circuit, and in 1963 and 1964 JoAnn went along and helped out with the animals.

There was mutual adoration between JoAnn and her parents-in-law. If Ross and Peggy Thatcher had ever regretted not having a daughter of their own, they certainly found the next best thing in JoAnn. Ross liked to include Colin and JoAnn in party conventions and other major activities, although only as guests. They were given no role.

The first convention the newlyweds attended in the fall of 1962 was a disaster. Entering the leader's hotel suite during the cocktail hour, Colin approached one of the Liberal MLAs, Alan Guy, a teacher who had just received a degree from the University of Saskatchewan. "I see you finally graduated," said Colin.

Insulting Guy was always a mistake. "Yes," the MLA happily replied, "glad I was able to do it here instead of having to go to some Mickey Mouse American college." The reference to Colin was clear.

Splash! Colin's Scotch went into Guy's face. The MLA lunged at Colin and the fight was on.

Ross stormed into the room as the two were separated. "What's going on?" he demanded.

"He insulted my mother," Colin replied instantly.

Ross was not deceived. He was furious with Colin and drove him from the suite, telling him to "go back to the ranch with the rest of the animals."

It was a shocking scene. It portrayed not only Colin's flash temper and Ross's brutal treatment of his son, but Colin's spontaneous lie also displayed an alarming tendency emerging in his personality.

Even in the early years of their marriage, Colin's ungentlemanly treatment of JoAnn at public functions was noted by many. Although the couple would arrive together, it was Colin's wont to immediately abandon his wife and leave her to find her own way. At political meetings, JoAnn would sit, often alone among strangers, while her husband attempted to mingle as an equal with his father's aides and associates on the sidelines.

With the 1964 Liberal election victory, life changed for the Thatchers. The family home on prestigious Redland Avenue in Moose Jaw, purchased in 1948, was sold to Colin and JoAnn for $7,500. It had a market value of $25,000.

In June, JoAnn left full-time teaching after three years on the job. She taught only as a substitute the next year.

On June 26, 1965, Gregory Ross was born. He was one of the most welcome babies ever to enter the world. The premier bestowed on his grandson all the affection he had never shown Colin. JoAnn would suffer two miscarriages before another child was born.

JoAnn and Colin were both active in the community. JoAnn

34

was particularly outgoing, loved people, and was always having someone over for coffee. She belonged to the Beta Sigma Phi sorority — a social and cultural fellowship — and to St. Andrew's United Church. Her predominant interest in the early years was upgrading and decorating her home. Cash was tight, but she coped well, doing a lot of the work herself, and buying furniture at auctions, which she would then re-upholster or refinish. Sewing was her other love, and in subsequent years these two creative outlets were augmented with oil painting classes and other artistic pursuits. Colin took little interest in what JoAnn did, but she had a circle of friends with common interests with whom she could share her pursuits.

Very much the supportive wife, JoAnn was terribly proud of Colin, and everything she said about him was glowing. There were accolades for how hard he worked, and for how well he took care of the family. If Colin was taking out the frustration he felt towards his demanding and verbally abusive father/boss on JoAnn, there was never a hint of it from her.

Ross was not one to instil a sense of worthiness in anyone, even his only son. Although Colin had both formal education and full-time experience in agriculture, he was treated like a hired man, given no authority, and was in fact junior to the foreman. Ross was not receptive to his son's advice about the cattle operation, although Colin did find ways of getting around his father, which usually consisted of acting behind his back. That, and his practice of not paying bills on time, incited many verbal lashings, in the presence of whatever ranch hands or political aides and colleagues happened to be around.

Politically, Colin was kept on the fringes to an even greater extent. Ross would at least discuss the cattle industry with him, but Colin was not even a superficial participant in the political arena. He was kept out of the way while campaign strategy sessions or the serious business of governing were attended to, but would be summoned, along with JoAnn, to participate in the social side of politics. Colin seemed to resent the roles of the premier's special assistants because they worked closely with his father and were confided in.

Yet, only two people, lawyer and executive assistant Ed Odishaw, and Colin, could get away with needling Ross. Colin

35

used to give it to his father regularly over "those dirty CCFers" and what his father was letting them get away with now. Sometimes the premier's colleagues would wish Colin was a little less successful at getting him riled up over accusations that they did not feel merited the follow-up the premier would then demand.

When baby Regan Colin finally came along on February 19, 1969, there was more rejoicing. A close colleague of Ross's would later tell him, in reference to his harsh treatment of Colin, that all his son would have to do to bring Ross to his knees would be to threaten to move away with his two grandsons.

Colin could not smoke a cigar in his father's presence and was required to go out on the porch or somewhere out of Ross's sight, even though Ross himself smoked cigars. This was the same ritual Ross had adhered to with his own father, and some couldn't help but wonder if he wasn't just passing the treatment down the genealogical line.

On the other hand, Ross did not usually object to Colin's having a drink. But one evening, as the premier left the headtable after a large fundraising dinner, he encountered Colin standing near the bar with a beer in his hand. Ross grabbed the bottle, growling "I told you not to drink."

A few minutes later in the parking lot, the still-angry Ross found Colin having trouble with the unfamiliar door lock on the premier's Chrysler. Ross snatched the keys away, gave them to Peggy, and sentenced Colin to sit in the back seat. Colin did not protest either incident.

It had been a successful evening and the premier was in good spirits, but his ebullience took a strange turn with his son.

In 1969, the Thatcher finesse for astute timing surfaced again, and Ross, at Colin's urging, got in on the ground floor of the Simmental cattle importation from Europe.

His stature may have been dubious in his father's eyes, but in the National Hereford Association, Colin was a national director. He was also a Moose Jaw director of the Saskatchewan Roughrider Football Club, chairman of the Moose Jaw Civic Centre Board, and a member of the local Kinsmen Club. In 1970 Colin let his name stand as a candidate in the June 3 election for one public school board trustee, and came fourth in a field of six.

Ross was angry that Colin had run in the first place, and that he had managed to lose. Had he been in the know, Ross probably wouldn't have permitted Colin's candidacy, but, if it was to be, he would have seen to it that Colin won.

In the spring of 1971 a small swimming pool was put in at the Redland residence. It was an instant hit as an unusual luxury, even in this upper-class neighbourhood. On July 22, a month after his party's devastating defeat at the polls, Ross was swimming in the pool and advising his family of what great shape he was in, according to a recent physical examination. It was that night that he died.

A friend said that Colin would not know whether to laugh or cry at his father's funeral. He had spent most of his thirty-two years trying to live up to the elusive expectations of a man he truly admired, and now, before any acknowledgements that he'd ever succeeded in proving himself, there was no chance left. Those close to Ross knew that he had great ambitions for Colin, and sincerely loved him, but that was manifested in strange ways.

Ross Thatcher's will made several specific cash bequests to family members, and set up the balance of his estate in two trusts to be maintained during his widow's lifetime. Colin received an equal interest with his mother in the first trust, and is to inherit the remainder of both upon her death.

The total estate of the late W. Ross Thatcher was valued for estate tax (then still in effect) purposes at $890,818.02. Under the terms of the will and codicil, Colin received the following benefits according to the values filed:

Cash bequest	$ 10,000.00
Land	110,654.00
Equipment	29,775.00
Cattle	32,650.00
Interest in Trust No. 1	70,295.61
	$253,374.61

With other lands he had secured during his father's lifetime Colin now had over five thousand acres, fully equipped and well stocked with good cattle. It could be fairly said in 1971 that Colin and JoAnn Thatcher were set for life. And, indeed, they were. But the very size of the inheritance would divide the couple in the long run.

Almost immediately following Colin's assumption of ownership of the Thatcher ranch, the explosion in Saskatchewan farmland prices struck. The averages advanced like a ticker tape on a bull market. From 1950 to 1960 the average price of Saskatchewan farmland had risen modestly from $26 to $36 per acre. This continued for ten more years, the price reaching $70 per acre in 1970. It remained stable during 1971 and 1972 and then took off in an escalation never before seen in the province. The per acre price shot up from $80 in 1973 to $279 in 1980.

Colin bought more land, four quarter sections in 1972, and six more in 1974, this time good grain land. It was again good Thatcher timing. Colin was in on the front end of a great land boom.

Colin Thatcher can be understood in his belief that he was successful in the years following his father's death, for he, like many other farmers and ranchers in western Canada during the same period, took into account the ever-rising value of his land holdings. At the time of his troubles with JoAnn he stated publicly that he "never had any trouble generating money." But, according to his tax returns he earned a net income of only $23,290.68 from his lands and cattle in 1977, incurred a loss of $3,910.84 in 1978, and had a net income of $269.71 in 1979. The gross returns were $200,000, $165,000 and $235,000, respectively. Like many of his western counterparts, Colin's wealth was in his land which never produced a return commensurate with its value. Or, as Colin later testified, "We were like many other agricultural people. We were big on paper but never had cash."

Two new worlds opened up to Colin on his father's death. He could now run the ranch with a free hand, answerable to no one, and he could also make his own way in provincial politics. Ross used to say that one Thatcher in politics was enough, and within a year both Colin and Peggy would make vain attempts at being the next one.

On the way home from Ross's funeral, a less than tactful

reporter asked Colin if he would run in his father's seat of Morse in the required by-election. Employing even less discretion than the journalist, Colin replied with some profuse profanity.

Colin stated years later that he had harboured no political ambitions of his own during his father's lifetime. "It must have been eating his heart out if he had some interest while his father was premier, yet was forced to remain on the sidelines," reflected an associate.

Without any encouragement from the Liberal party, Colin contested the Morse nomination. Peggy had former Chief Electoral Officer and Liberal party organizer par excellence, Jack Harrington, test the waters in the seat, and he reported back with a thumbs-down verdict. Colin went ahead anyway, and soundly lost the two-way race to Jack Wiebe, the constituency president, who most thought had earned the right to succeed to the seat. Colin himself conceded, years later, that "it was perhaps a dumb decision because I got massacred." Yet he surprised Liberals with his until-then hidden speaking ability.

At a provincial party council meeting dealing with the leadership problem after Ross's death, Colin gave an impromptu speech about the difficulties of living in his father's shadow. He voiced commiseration with Wilf Gardiner, son of former federal cabinet minister Jimmy Gardiner, and lashed out at certain party members he felt were not sufficiently honest about their indebtedness to or betrayal of his father. It was a surprise to his listeners, who had never heard him speak out before, nor suspected he felt these emotions.

Colin was also causing a stir in his position at the Civic Centre Board. He was a good chairman and put a lot of time into it, but in March he had lambasted City Council for cutting $8,100 from his budget without consultation. Then in August, he walked out of a board meeting in indignation over another issue, citing "certain unacceptable financial courses" taken by the board. It was Colin's way of resigning.

In 1972, the federal Liberals recruited Peggy Thatcher to represent them in Regina East, a riding she had resided in since 1964. She took the March 25 nomination by acclamation, and a former minister from Ross's cabinet, Don MacLennan, became her campaign manager. They mounted a serious campaign, and Peggy worked hard, excepting Saturday mornings, which she reserved to visit her late husband's grave at Moose Jaw.

Pierre Trudeau and the campaign slogan "The land is strong" were not vote-getters in western Canada. There had been high hopes in the spring, but by the time voting day, October 30, came along, the results were no surprise. Otto Lang, an MP since 1968, managed to hang on to his Saskatoon East seat, but no new Saskatchewan Liberals were elected.

There were six candidates in Regina East, three of whom each received less than 1,000 votes. Peggy Thatcher ran a distant third with 7,897 votes, incumbent John Burton of the NDP polled 15,175 votes, and Tory James Balfour won with 17,781. Peggy's candidacy had infuriated many Liberals, who felt that a faction within the party was exploiting the Thatcher name, with no regard for the best interests of Peggy herself.

With the exception of that campaign Peggy was in seclusion in the years following Ross's death. Aside from seeing her family regularly and working on scrapbooks of Ross's career, which would someday be given to her grandchildren, she was not very active and spent most of her time in her Academy Park Road home in Regina. It was not until the mid-Seventies that she started living again. She developed a close friendship with Beverley Banbury of Wolseley who had a cottage on Katepwa Lake near Regina. They spent much of the summers there and later wintered in Peggy's Palm Beach condominium.

On January 7, 1974, a daughter was born to JoAnn and Colin. Like her brothers, she inherited her mother's good looks, and charmed everyone she encountered.

After Ross's death, JoAnn had taken over the ranch's financial books, and was made secretary-treasurer of R.T. Holdings Ltd. In the fall of 1974, she took a first-year university accounting class, offered through the Saskatchewan Technical Institute in Moose Jaw, and received an "A."

Without exception, Colin and JoAnn spent every Christmas after their marriage with his family. JoAnn was close to her parents and would have liked to celebrate the occasional festive season with her own family, but Colin would not visit with the

Geigers at any time of year. JoAnn and the children travelled to Ames, but Colin never accompanied them, and, when her parents came to Moose Jaw every two years, he did not make them feel welcome. The Geigers had always felt well treated by Ross and Peggy, and could not understand Colin's behaviour. Whether he liked them or not, it was an exhibition of intolerance unbecoming a grown man.

Every Christmas, Ross and Peggy had given Colin and JoAnn substantial gifts of money, heirloom silverware or stocks and bonds. Occasionally there had been additional such gifts at other times of the year. The tradition continued after Ross's death. In 1974, Colin and JoAnn started making substantial gifts to their own children. They purchased a quarter section of land for each Greg and Regan, at a total cost of $44,000, with $20,000 coming from trust money willed by Ross to his grandsons.

Both boys developed an interest in farming and ranching, would own their own cattle while they were still in school, and spent summers and many weekends working on the ranch. "Interestingly enough, they appear to complement (each other) very nicely. Greg is primarily why I've kept any cattle around. Regan is very machinery-oriented, and I think the two of them are going to make an excellent team," Colin would observe in later years.

JoAnn and Colin had developed a regular circle of friends over the years, and socialized in a group of about five couples every Saturday evening. They often spent Friday nights out for dinner with Ron and Jane Graham. Ron and Colin had known each other since Grade 2. Like Colin, Ron had inherited his livelihood and wealth, in the form of Graham Construction.

As Colin and JoAnn came more into their own, she clearly enjoyed their new affluence and social status. Friends noticed that a touch of snobbery developed. JoAnn, as well as Colin, was capable of putting on airs. In a conversation with Jane Graham on the subject of Hawaii, one woman mentioned her "first" trip over and the other described her "last." In truth, each had visited exactly once at that time.

But JoAnn took her duties as mother of three children seriously. Intelligent and well-disciplined herself, she exercised a gentle and affectionate control over the bright and active Thatcher children. Neighbours and friends found the three to be well-behaved and happy.

Colin, however, was not one to dote on his children. In fact, JoAnn later reflected that he "was often distant and cold in his relations with our children to the point that the children frequently avoided him." She also stated in court that, when Regan was about six years of age, "my husband flatly told me that he really didn't feel anything for Regan and didn't particularly like him at that particular stage of his development."

Once when neighbours were taking Regan to Regina for the day, they stopped by the Thatcher house to pick up a piece of hockey gear the boy had forgotten. Colin insensitively referred to his son as the "family idiot" in his presence. Another friend recalled that "sometimes when I'd go to pick Stephanie up, it would bother me, the way Colin would mention he wished I would keep her. I often found that embarrassing, and I thought it was kind of detrimental for him to say things like that in front of the child." Another observer termed him "one of the worst fathers I've ever met." It would later become evident that Colin considered his children to be mere possessions, an extension of himself, whose best interests came after his own.

Colin resented and ignored authority and JoAnn complained of his passing this tendency on to their sons. Such things as the illegal use of farm fuel for personal driving, refusing to buy hunting licences, and even the improper parking of vehicles on Redland Avenue distressed her when Greg and Regan were encouraged in these ways.

Colin made it into the Saskatchewan Legislature in the first general election after his father's death, but not in Ross's old seat. There was a redistribution in 1974, moving Morse west, and creating the new constituency of Thunder Creek partially in its place. It was a large, roughly rectangular seat, with the Thatcher Ranch dead in the centre, and surrounding but not including the city of Moose Jaw.

Thunder Creek also included part of two other Liberal ridings, Gary Lane's old Lumsden seat, and the bulk of Cy MacDonald's constituency of Milestone. Thunder Creek was good Liberal territory, a safe place to run a weak or new candidate.

42

MacDonald, a strong, popular MLA, thus graciously moved to a seat that needed to be won over from the NDP. Lane, however, intended to stand firm, until Thatcher labelled him in the eyes of Liberals in the agricultural seat as another one of those city lawyers, with neither residence nor roots in the riding. Lane decided of his own accord that it would be astute to run elsewhere.

Home-grown rancher or not, though, Colin was not popular, and some believe Lane would have won the nomination if he had stayed in the race. As it was, Thatcher's competition in the February 23, 1974 nomination was not formidable. Area farmers Percy Lambert and Randy Devine could not project the sophisticated image Thatcher could, and he won on the first ballot. (Devine was the younger brother of the future Conservative premier.) In his victory speech, Thatcher told the 600 attending the Moose Jaw meeting that "my only regret is that my father could not have been here tonight."

On June 11, 1975, the Liberals under Dave Steuart won the same number of seats as they had under Ross Thatcher in 1971 — fifteen, in a Legislature of sixty-one members. Colin was just barely one of them, polling 2,640 votes. Don Swenson of the Conservatives received 2,348, and the NDP's Jim Murdock 2,036. Colin's plurality was only 292 votes.

As a member of the shadow cabinet, Thatcher did not become a team player, having perhaps left that skill behind on the football field. To the consternation of his colleagues, and especially the party whip, he would, at whim, not show up when he was scheduled to give a speech in the Legislature, or make statements contrary to party policy or to what his caucus colleagues had expected him to say on their behalf.

Colin prided himself on being a part-time politician, and, even when the Legislature was sitting, would spend mornings on the ranch. That meant being up and gone before the children were also up, as he had always done, but now he came home for a quick lunch, which he had not done before. Then after a shower and change, he would race down the highway to Regina, just in time for Question Period. The house often sat three evenings a week, and on Wednesday evenings MLAs would meet with various interest groups.

43

Thatcher's attendance in the Legislature was sporadic, and according to colleagues, "not extraordinarily effective." He was unpredictable, inconsistent, difficult to work with, and an outsider. One Liberal MLA "got the impression that he was really scared to let his guard down for a minute. You'd see him in a situation where he'd really sort of warm up to you, and then it would never continue. The next time you saw him, he'd be as cold as ice. If he'd been more open it would have made our jobs easier."

The Thunder Creek member cultivated a tough, no nonsense image but instead was perceived by some of his political associates as being "paranoid about everything," insecure, and having an inferiority complex which he compensated for in extreme fashion. Said one MLA, "when you're approaching middle age and you buy yourself a canary yellow corvette to race back and forth to Moose Jaw with, maybe you're putting the dog on a bit."

There was more than a little of the redneck in Colin Thatcher, a self-described "right-of-centre" Liberal. When there was a recorded vote in the House of Commons on the issue of capital punishment in June 1976, and Saskatchewan Liberal MP Dr. Cliff McIsaac voted against it, Thatcher declared that "McIsaac and his stand on capital punishment only deserve comtempt."

Thatcher's stated goal in politics was to get rid of the NDP, any way possible. As a free enterpriser, not only did he deplore socialism, but he also blamed the NDP for his father's death, due to the tough fight they had given him in the 1971 election which had destroyed the Liberal government. His father's successor, Dave Steuart, also was blamed for Ross's defeat, because Colin perceived him, as deputy premier, encouraging his father to call an election which he would lose, thus opening up the leadership for Steuart.

In 1976, Regina lawyers Ted Malone and Tony Merchant vied to succeed Steuart. Well into the campaign, Thatcher announced that, if neither of them obtained the confidence of rural party members, he would run as the rural candidate. He was probing for potential support, but did not find enough to run. Privately, Colin confided that he couldn't stand either of the candidates, and was credited with coining the line that it was a choice between "crazy (Tony) or lazy (Ted)."

Merchant, more practical than philosophical, proposed a coalition between the Liberals and the emerging Conservatives as a way of preventing the NDP from coming up the middle. That, and a too-slick campaign, spelled victory for Malone. Thatcher measured all men against his father, and Malone came out a weak leader in Colin's books, as had Steuart.

Thus Colin had an excuse to hold both Liberal party leaders he served under in contempt. Generally, no other facet of the provincial party impressed him either. There were, he claimed, no policies he could support. The federal Liberals he disowned, also on his father's account. He would not lift a finger in federal campaigns or even in provincial seats where federal Liberals were helping out.

In fact, in March 1977 he was even prepared to engage in public debate with a federal member of his own party. Agriculture Minister Eugene Whelan offered to debate anyone regarding the efficiency of marketing boards and how they would affect the beef cattle industry. When Thatcher accepted the challenge, it was vaguely reminiscent of the debate between his father and Tommy Douglas twenty years earlier. Colin's debate never came off, but, like his father, he was definitely changing his political stripe.

The 1975 election had produced seven Conservative MLAs, the first seen in the Saskatchewan Legislature for nearly ten years. With fifteen members the Liberals seemed confirmed as the alternative to the NDP, but they soon began to falter.

In the fall of 1976, Gary Lane, whom Colin had bluffed out of the Thunder Creek Liberal nomination, but who had secured election in the next riding east, Qu'Appelle, jumped parties and joined the Conservatives. Lane had been organizing a run for the Liberal leadership but succumbed to the realization that momentum and opportunity lay with the Conservatives.

Colin Thatcher was characteristically outspoken and critical of Lane's defection. It lacked class, he said. Within a year, however, Thatcher would be emulating Lane.

Lane's move made the score fourteen Liberals to eight

Conservatives. A senate appointment and a death caused vacancies in two Liberal ridings and the Conservatives won both 1977 by-elections. The score became twelve to ten. One more Liberal defection would produce a tie for the position of official opposition.

Conservative leader Collver fixed his sights on the Liberal MLA from Thunder Creek. If he could induce the son of the former Liberal premier to abandon his party, it would shatter the stumbling Liberals and signal to all of Saskatchewan that the Conservatives had become the anti-socialist alternative to the NDP.

Collver was a swashbuckling wheeler-dealer and much more Colin Thatcher's type than Liberal leader Ted Malone, whom Colin held in low regard. It was an easy seduction for Collver, who overwhelmed the Thunder Creek MLA. Colin was deeply impressed by Collver and the sly hint that the Conservative leadership might come to him when Collver gave it up was probably not necessary.

The timing and method of Colin's political transformation were critical. His majority was not large and it would make the transition more credible and acceptable to the voters of Thunder Creek if it was viewed as a group decision.

Colin took a closer look at the way in which Gary Lane had pulled off his switch. He found that Lane's manoeuvre, instead of lacking class as Colin had described it, had been very skilful indeed. Lane had taken his entire Liberal riding executive with him to the Conservatives. That made the defection look like a reasoned decision, a reluctant acceptance of the right thing to do, and much less like political opportunism. Colin set out to do the same.

Easily denying to Malone the rumours of his pending defection, Thatcher began manipulating the members of his Thunder Creek riding executive. Then in June 1977, he called a meeting in his Redland Avenue home.

Ted Malone got word of the meeting just as it began. At first he refused to believe that it was happening; only hours earlier Colin had again assured him that he had no intention of leaving the party. When Malone became convinced of Thatcher's purpose, he immediately gathered up Liberal party president

John Embury and the two drove from Regina to Moose Jaw where they knocked on the door at Redland Avenue.

Under the Liberal constitution, both Malone as party leader and Embury as party president were ex officio members of all riding executives and thus entitled to attend the Thunder Creek meeting. But Colin had thought of that. The meeting was in his home, and those in attendance were there by invitation, he pointed out to Malone and Embury. The invitation did not extend to them. The Liberal leader and president were denied entry to the Thatcher home and waited with a friend across the street until they were called back to receive the news. Their Thunder Creek MLA had switched parties, just a little over twenty-two years after his father had.

Colin did not succeed in inducing all of the Thunder Creek Liberal executive to cross parties with him. When one member, reminding him of his comment on Gary Lane's defection, suggested that he had not shown much class either, Thatcher agreed: "Yeah, that's right."

JoAnn was distressed, not only at Colin's decision but at his manner of implementing it. Her friends were in the Liberal party and it was her nature to be loyal. At the end of the Redland Avenue meeting, JoAnn had tears in her eyes. Some who were close to JoAnn felt that Colin's forsaking of his father's party was the point at which the marriage began to go sour.

Whatever the reason, it was certainly about that time that the deterioration in the relationship began. Later in that summer of 1977, Colin and his close friend, contractor Ron Graham, took some lady friends with them on a golfing holiday to Laguna Beach, California, the first of a series of "bachelor holidays." Adultery had struck the Thatcher marriage; it would later afflict both partners.

Thatcher seemed somewhat disappointed in the mild public reaction to his departure from the Liberal party. "My father built that party and I am not enthralled at the prospect of being the one who destroyed it," he said at the time. But a few months later he admitted that his move had been a "non-happening" compared to his father's similar action years before.

Collver appointed his new MLA as Conservative finance critic in the Legislature and set about to supplant the Liberals as

47

official opposition. Thatcher and Lane, although personally not fond of each other, became the stars in the Tory assault on the NDP government. Both were suspended from the Legislature for an unusual five-day period in December 1977, when Thatcher, with Lane backing him up, called the house committee on rules and privileges a "kangaroo court."

When Colin Thatcher felt a need to step away from reality, Palm Springs was the place to do it. The glittering desert oasis was nearly 2,000 miles from Saskatchewan, and offered a lifestyle a world away from almost anywhere, rising artificially out of the scorching desert and consisting of extremes only money can muster. Palm Springs life meshed well with Colin's loathing of restraints. Here he could be anything he said he was, and no one would be the wiser.

Colin went unnoticed in this hedonist mecca 110 miles southeast of Los Angeles, because here everybody is somebody. Half the postcards on sale are of celebrities' homes, and even the lesser-known residents overshadowed Colin. Palm Springs had earned the title of "the other Hollywood" by being the retreat, not only of film industry luminaries, but also of politicians (including several U.S. presidents) and those whose achievements were measured only in dollars.

It was JoAnn who first introduced Colin to "The Desert" — as the clustered communities of Palm Springs, Palm Desert, Rancho Mirage and Cathedral City are known — in the late Seventies. Colin claims he went against his will, loved it, and spent a total of sixty days there the first season. Early in 1977 the Thatchers acquired a condominium for $82,500 (U.S.) in the Cathedral Canyon Country Club, a private 450-acre walled community straddling the Palm Springs/Cathedral City border. Another of the nearly 700 residences in the complex already belonged to their friends Ron and Jane Graham.

There is a swimming pool right off the kitchen of their three-bedroom condo, on Paseo Real just inside the guarded security gates. A little farther down the meticulously landscaped street towards the nearby San Jacinto mountains is the 18-hole championship golf course. Colin, who considered himself a near scratch golfer, regularly played with Bob Gustav and Ron

48

Graham, Ron's father, Pete, nextdoor neighbour Jane Heron, or anyone needing a pick-up partner.

As in many of the "golf capital of the world's" more than ninety-five such country clubs, the sprawling clubhouse is the social centre. The only club that matters in the entire Desert empire, however, is the Raquet Club, founded in 1934. Colin was not a member, but he had friends who were, and he coveted invitations to this inner sanctum of high society, especially to its prestigious New Year's Eve bash.

In the next few years The Desert was one of the few constants in Colin Thatcher's life. He would certainly not lack for the company of Canadians. There are enough around to justify a Canadian column in *The Desert Sun*, a daily Canadian radio newscast, and, since 1983, a Canadian Club of Palm Springs. On the other hand, Colin later testified in his civil trials that he could enjoy himself there because no one knew him.

Ron Graham, a year younger than Colin, did not really begin to socialize with him until after university when they both returned to Moose Jaw, although they had known each other for most of their lives. Graham had been studying civil engineering at the University of Saskatchewan during the same years Colin had been at Iowa. The two were bonded by their wealth and Moose Jaw roots. Graham had married in 1961, a year before Colin and JoAnn, and he and Jane had three sons in the same age range as the Thatcher children who were their playmates.

Graham's main business venture was the family general contracting construction company, which carried on business in western Canada, Denver and Dallas. As president, he travelled frequently, and like Thatcher, also made regular visits to his Palm Springs residence. It was life in the fast track, with all the attendant perils.

Not long after Colin had added a political career to his already busy life, JoAnn had begun working part-time as an interior decorator. At first she provided the design for a few Moose Jaw houses. Then she was commissioned by Ron Graham to do the layout for his construction firm's new office building. That led to further Graham Construction contracts in Vancouver and Edmonton and a developing personal liaison between Graham and JoAnn.

Meanwhile, Colin found life in the Conservative caucus much more to his liking than with his former Liberal colleagues. Finally he was someone in his own right and no longer just "Ross's son." His new fellow MLAs were much more congenial in every way, and soon Colin began returning from night sittings of the Legislature well into the morning hours. JoAnn's protests were met with belligerence and, now, an occasional blow.

The support staff around the Conservative offices in the Legislature was more impressionable too, Colin found, particularly Janice Gardner, a public relations assistant in her early twenties. Colin discovered that he was attractive to some women and was not disappointed at the discovery.

Before the end of 1977 the flaws in their marriage became so obvious even to them that Colin and JoAnn occasionally discussed them. They took no corrective action, however, and their situation worsened. JoAnn, a proud woman, was almost entirely successful at concealing her bruises and unhappiness from her friends, but Colin's humiliating treatment of his wife in the presence of others was noticed.

As the unhappy JoAnn grew closer to Ron Graham, Colin's best friend found himself living a strained double life. He knew that Colin was having extra-marital affairs because he was participating with him and he was encouraging JoAnn to do the same. In the summer of 1978, Graham arranged to meet JoAnn in Des Moines, Iowa, while she was visiting her parents in nearby Ames. In the same summer he again went golfing to Laguna Beach with Colin where they shared a friend's condominium on the beach with two willing ladies.

Colin grew suspicious enough of JoAnn and Ron Graham that he began accusing her of an improper relationship. He developed a urinary infection and jumped to the conclusion that he had contracted a venereal disease. JoAnn was dragged from her bed late one night to explain.

Her husband's temper began to manifest itself so frequently and uncontrollably that JoAnn became fearful. Without warning a glass would be hurled against a wall, a door slammed and locked in her face, a chair seized from beneath her, throwing her to the floor. JoAnn's complaints met with indifference. Colin threatened to bring another woman into the house and embarrass JoAnn into leaving.

Colin and JoAnn disguised their crumbling marriage well enough to save his political career. Colin had to win nomination as a Conservative in Thunder Creek and it was no small undertaking. Don Swenson had been the Conservative candidate in 1975, had lost only narrowly to Liberal Thatcher, and did not intend to step aside in favour of the convert. Swenson, a local farmer, was highly regarded and well connected within the Conservative party. He would not be easily defeated, even by the high-profile Thatcher who had the quiet blessing of party leader Collver. Any hint of the trouble between Colin and JoAnn would have been disastrous to Colin's bid for the nomination.

Colin Thatcher won the close vote at a heavily attended nomination meeting held at a Moose Jaw high school in September 1978. The Conservative nomination was tantamount to election in Thunder Creek that fall, as the Liberal vote collapsed all across Saskatchewan and the anti-NDP vote coalesced around the Tories. In the October 18 election, Colin was easily returned, almost a thousand votes ahead of his NDP opponent.

In the province, the confident Conservatives fell short. They elected seventeen members to the NDP's forty-four. The Liberal party that Colin had left disappeared from the electoral map for the first time in Saskatchewan's history.

The election over, Colin and JoAnn carried on into their unhappy future. He became even more arrogant, volatile and uncaring, and, bluffing, told JoAnn he had consulted a lawyer about a divorce, although he would later claim that he had been working harder on his marriage than ever before. She became closer to and intimate with Ron Graham, making a cuckold of Colin with his best friend. JoAnn began to plan her escape from her misery while Colin carried on confidently unconcerned.

Collver appointed Colin as Conservative House leader in the Legislature following the 1978 election and, for a time, the Thunder Creek MLA took his responsibilities seriously. His attendance, particularly at committees, was the best of his years in the Saskatchewan Legislature. By the spring of 1979, however, legislative work began to pall for him. Still his party's finance critic, Colin missed most of the 1979 budget debate.

Colin had become close to Dick Collver, his third political leader after Liberals Steuart and Malone, and admired Collver's flamboyant style. But many in the Conservative party did not share Colin's view and Collver was held responsible for the failure to defeat the NDP the previous year. The dissent became sufficiently widespread to provoke Collver's resignation at the end of May. Colin was angry and depressed. By July he was openly suggesting that he might resign his seat. His family, he said, was well ahead of politics on his priority list.

CHAPTER 5

Breaking Up

Like Colin, JoAnn had fixed her priorities by July 1979. In April, during Easter week, she had again met Ron Graham in Des Moines. The two were now close enough that she was told of what went on during the California golfing holidays. The event had become an annual one and another was expected in August. JoAnn determined to make her escape from Colin, and Graham became party to her planning.

Timing and secrecy were critical. JoAnn was under no illusions about how Colin would react to her leaving. She was terrified of him and knew he would stop at nothing to have his way.

Colin's August golf-and-girls holiday would be the opportunity. JoAnn intended to be ready.

Where to go? JoAnn was intimate with Graham but knew that there was no future for her with him. The contractor would not be leaving his wife and she did not intend to be a woman waiting for a telephone call. She would go far enough to be free from both Colin and Graham, someplace where she could build a new life.

JoAnn turned to two close friends, United Church minister John Sullivan and his wife. Formerly of Moose Jaw, they now lived in Brampton, northwest of Toronto. In July, JoAnn visited Brampton and purchased a home there, with closing and possession to take place in August. She returned to Moose Jaw, carefully concealing her plans from Colin.

On August 9, JoAnn wished Colin a good holiday as he took off to Laguna Beach with Graham. Colin did not mention, but JoAnn knew from Graham, that Janice Gardner would meet him in Los Angeles.

On August 13, the day after her seventeenth wedding anniversary, JoAnn loaded her station wagon and, with Regan and Stephanie, left the Redland Avenue residence, forever she thought. The two children were told only that they were going on a holiday. It was not possible to tell them more until later. JoAnn made no attempt to take fourteen-year-old Greg with her. He was already too close to Colin and the ranch.

Only two people knew what JoAnn's plans and destination were, prominent Moose Jaw lawyer J.R. Rushford, QC, whom she had carefully instructed before leaving, and Ron Graham.

JoAnn drove to Winnipeg where she met Graham who, on a pretext, had left the golfing holiday early. The unsuspecting Colin had driven his wife's lover to the Los Angeles airport to catch the flight that took him to the rendezvous with JoAnn.

The four drove to Brampton where Graham assisted JoAnn with the financing for her house purchase. It was not ready for occupancy so Graham, who had business in the United States, took JoAnn and the two children on a combined business and pleasure trip. Their destination was an unintentional but prophetic signal of what was to come. They flew to Dallas.

After spending three days in Dallas with Graham, JoAnn and her children flew to Iowa and visited her parents for several more days and then returned to Brampton. There she enrolled Regan and Stephanie in school, Sunday school and, for Regan, hockey school. According to JoAnn the children settled into their new life perfectly. Regan, she said, never once asked about his father and Stephanie mentioned Colin only two or three times.

JoAnn knew that child custody was a matter of jurisdiction for the courts in the province where the children resided. She could not very well have asked the Saskatchewan courts for a custody order and it was her intention to do so in Ontario when things settled down.

All in all, it had been a well-planned and well-executed manoeuvre. JoAnn was free, and she and her two children had exciting new lives to live. JoAnn had just turned forty.

From his California bachelor holiday, Colin dutifully telephoned home on Monday, August 13, 1979, the day after his wedding anniversary. JoAnn had already left and Greg was able to tell his father little more than that. Colin assumed that JoAnn had taken Regan and Stephanie on an impromptu vacation trip.

Colin returned to Moose Jaw on Wednesday and, when JoAnn had still not called, he began to fear that an accident had befallen his missing family. Early Thursday morning he contacted the RCMP. By Thursday night the awful reality that JoAnn had left him became apparent when he discovered her clothing missing. The reality was confirmed by a telephone call to J.R. Rushford. Rushford told Colin that he was acting for JoAnn and declined to give him any further information.

The abandoned husband was distraught. He set about finding his wife and two younger children. From Jane Graham he learned of the involvement of her husband, but Ron was not due back in Moose Jaw for more than another week. He telephoned JoAnn's parents in Ames, learned nothing, but convinced them of his worry. When JoAnn reached Ames, her father induced her to at least call her husband and let him know she and the children were all right. JoAnn did call Colin and reassure him but refused to reveal her whereabouts.

The week after JoAnn had left, Colin wrote her through the office of Jack Rushford who undertook to forward his letters. He wrote three letters, clearly the words of a heartbroken and shaken man. "My Dearest JoAnn; words cannot describe the agony, emptiness and grief inside me. . . . Life has no meaning without you. You are my love and I will always love you." And: "My Dearest Jo; I deserve what you have done. . . . I feel guilty about many things, especially for the poor quality husband I have been for the majority of 17 years. . . . I *have* learned from this." Finally: "My Darling Jo; Time passes so slowly. It is terrible to wake up wishing this day was over. . . . A death in the family would be easier to handle than this. Still, I take all the blame for my intransigence in forcing this course of action upon you. . . . Please come home."

When Ron Graham returned home the second weekend, Colin arranged for a golf match which turned out to be an encounter of a different sort than the contractor had anticipated. Once the two men were upon the fairway, Colin demanded to know where

55

JoAnn was and threatened to beat the information out of Graham if it was necessary. It was not; Graham arranged for JoAnn to telephone Colin and some contact was re-established.

JoAnn attempted to keep her location a secret but, with the help of Jane Graham who found a telephone number in her husband's clothing, within a few days Colin had pinpointed his wife's whereabouts. But he did not allow JoAnn to know this.

During her calls back to Redland Avenue Colin assured JoAnn that he had no intention of trying to find her. When the school Regan and Stephanie were attending told JoAnn that an inquiry had been made about them, she became very concerned and promptly called Colin. Colin denied having made any inquiries. JoAnn was far from satisfied and told her husband that she was going to commence immediately legal proceedings in Ontario. Now Colin was concerned. "Please wait a week," he asked. "Don't do anything permanent. Don't do anything legal." JoAnn promised not to commence proceedings. It was to cost her dearly.

Colin and Sandra Hammond, the Thatcher baby-sitter, flew to Ontario and, on the morning of September 11, as Regan and Stephanie were on their way to school, their father picked them up and returned them to Saskatchewan. The next day Colin secured an interim court order approving of his custody of Regan and Stephanie. Colin had effectively pre-empted the situation by taking de facto custody of the children, a manoeuvre the law then permitted, and securing court approval until the matter was fully litigated. JoAnn now faced an uphill battle to recover custody of her children. Child snatching of that sort became more difficult with a change in the law three years later and, when Colin attempted the technique again, the results were very different.

Then began the litigation between Colin and JoAnn that boiled through the courts for the next two and a half years. Jack Rushford launched the custody application on behalf of JoAnn, and Colin's response signalled the flavour of the acrimonious dispute that ensued. He immediately filed an application to have Jack Rushford forced off the case on the grounds of a conflict of interest. The motion was spurious and went nowhere, but it disclosed Colin's attitude that anyone who was an ally of JoAnn's was an enemy of his.

Colin had retained E.F. Anthony Merchant, the Regina lawyer who had been a fellow MLA during the time Colin had sat in the Liberal caucus. Colin had derided Merchant as being "crazy" during the lawyer's run for the Liberal leadership in 1976, but now he found him entirely suitable for his purposes. Merchant had not run for re-election to the Legislature, opting to try for a seat in Parliament in the federal election expected in 1978. When the election did not take place until May 1979, Merchant had been running for office so long that his campaign offices were listed in the Regina telephone directory. Thoroughly defeated, he had ample time and energy to swing over to Colin's battle, although he was able to reactivate his campaign for one more failed attempt at the Regina East constituency in the unexpected February 1980 election.

Merchant was to be an entirely suitable choice for Colin Thatcher. In the eleven years Merchant had been practising in Regina, he had shown himself to be a lawyer who would go further than most in the service of his clients, and had encountered several brushes with the Law Society. A prominent Liberal and a brother-in-law of Otto Lang, who had been a minister in the Trudeau government until he, too, was defeated in the 1979 election, Merchant did not hesitate to capitalize upon his perceived political influence. He had hosted an open line radio talk show in Regina for three years, gaining a prominence that easily translated into a seat in the Legislature in the 1975 provincial election. He was to welcome the publicity the Thatcher case brought him.

The trial of JoAnn's custody application was heard in early November 1979 by Mr. Justice M.A. MacPherson, Jr. of the Saskatchewan Court of Queen's Bench. "Sandy" MacPherson was the senior member of the court and had earned the reputation as a judge with very strong views, one who did not fear to adjudicate.

After hearing two days of testimony from Colin and JoAnn and their friends about who was the better parent, Mr. Justice MacPherson reserved his decision, handing it down on November 27. In a mild judgment, mentioning Colin and JoAnn's mutual adultery and "child grabbing," Mr. Justice MacPherson "scored them even" on those matters and then determined that, although both were adequate parents, JoAnn was the better. He had been more impressed with JoAnn's personality than with Colin's. Custody of Regan and Stephanie was granted to JoAnn. Greg, since he clearly would not live with his mother, was allowed to stay with Colin.

Merchant immediately launched an appeal, the effect of which was to stay or put in limbo Mr. Justice MacPherson's judgment until the matter was considered by the Saskatchewan Court of Appeal. That would not be until spring and in the meantime Regan and Stephanie would remain with Colin.

In spite of the bitterness and intimate accusations each had hurled at the other during the custody trial, something happened that led Colin to believe that JoAnn was willing to be reconciled and come back to him. He began making arrangements for a trip to Hawaii for the two of them, but a day or so later cancelled them in a fit of fury when he learned that it was not to be. He later testified that even at Christmas that year he had hopes that JoAnn might accompany the family to Palm Springs and had an airline ticket purchased for her. The ticket was instead used by Blaine Mathieson, boyfriend of baby-sitter Sandra Hammond. During the holiday, Colin and his entourage drove over to Wickenburg, Arizona, to spend New Year's with his former leader and mentor, Dick Collver.

JoAnn, however, was increasing the pressure on the litigation front. In December 1979, she launched an application under The Matrimonial Property Act. That application would first come before the Saskatchewan courts on January 9, 1980, eight days after new and sweeping changes to the law governing the distribution of property between husband and wife had taken effect.

In April 1979, Colin Thatcher, the member of the Saskatchewan Legislature for the constituency of Thunder Creek, had joined his Conservative caucus in supporting Bill No. 68, which bore the cumbersome title "An Act Respecting The Possession And Distribution Of Property Between Spouses." When he did this, Colin could not have considered, even fleetingly, that his assets would be almost the first to be brought under this new

58

legislation. The Bill, better known as The Matrimonial Property Act, was enacted on May 3, 1979, and proclaimed in effect January 1, 1980.

The Matrimonial Property Act replaced earlier and similar legislation that had first been enacted in 1974 under the name of The Married Woman's Property Act, a title that clearly identified the fact that it adopted the socially progressive notion that a woman was entitled to share in her husband's assets. The discriminatory title was later changed to The Married Persons Property Act, recognizing that the new law also applied in favour of husbands.

This legislation was Saskatchwwan's response to the Supreme Court of Canada's decisions in *Murdoch v. Murdoch* and *Rathwell v. Rathwell* which highlighted an inequity in the law of that time. Unless a wife could show a financial contribution to the family assets, or at least a clear intention on the part of the husband and wife that she was to share in them, those assets belonged to the husband if he had the ownership, which was usually the case.

From 1974 to 1980, The Married Persons Property Act gave the Saskatchewan courts the discretionary authority to adjust unfair situations. The Matrimonial Property Act, introduced by the NDP government in 1979, brought a fundamental change, the full import of which might have escaped Colin Thatcher and the rest of the Conservative opposition. The new Act directed that the courts must distribute all matrimonial property of the husband and wife equally between them and removed the discretion formerly exercised unless certain stipulated exceptions applied.

As Attorney General Roy Romanow explained in the Legislature on April 19, 1979, under the 1974 Act, ". . .a judge was given the authority to divide the property of spouses in any way he thought appropriate." But under this new Bill, ". . .the court must distribute all property of the spouses . . . equally between the spouses unless it would be unfair to do so."

J. Gary Lane, now Saskatchewan Minister of Justice but then speaking on behalf of the Conservative opposition, said: ". . .we will be supporting this Bill. The Conservative Party endorses in Saskatchewan the concept of judicial discretion in a situation such as this. . . . But I just don't see — and I gather some of the judiciary is of the same view — much of a change with this Act.''

But there was a change and Mr. Romanow had clearly stated: ''Will there be judicial discretion? Mr. Speaker, the scheme is subject to a certain measure of judicial discretion. However, it operates from the assumption that all matrimonial property, except for most prior acquired property and the awards of damages, shall be shared equally.''

That there was little or no discretion left to the courts under the new Act was made clear by the Supreme Court of Canada in *Farr v. Farr*, a 1984 decision. The new requirement was an equal division between husband and wife, regardless of contribution. The Legislature had made The Matrimonial Property Act very clear. The Supreme Court approved the words of Saskatchewan Judge Dickson, who, dealing with another division of farm assets, had said, ''. . .it makes no difference if a farm wife spent time in the fields or not. Her care of the children and her management of the household is acknowledged by the Legislature . . . to be equal in value to her husband's tending of the crops and management of the farm.''

This new legal concept, coming into effect at a time when Saskatchewan farmland prices were just reaching the zenith of a wildly inflationary spiral, was to work with devastating effect upon many Saskatchewan farms and ranches. Land prices had far surpassed anything that could be justified according to their productivity. To pay a wife in dollars half the market value of these lands was beyond the capacity of Saskatchewan's ''land-rich but cash-poor'' farmers and ranchers. The forced sale and break up of the agricultural unit to settle these claims was often the only alternative.

This, then, was the new law in Saskatchewan which, when JoAnn Thatcher filed for division in January 1980, began to grind inexorably towards the assets of Colin Thatcher, politician, rancher and husband. That these assets were mostly the product of the energy, acumen and frugality of two preceding generations of Thatchers would be of no concern to the court called upon to divide them, because The Matrimonial Property Act provided no protection for such assets.

Following the first custody trial, J.R. Rushford, not being a litigation specialist, retired from the Thatcher case and JoAnn retained Gerald L. Gerrand, QC, of Regina, where she was then living. It was both a fortunate and an unfortunate choice. Gerrand was an excellent lawyer with a well-deserved reputation in the litigation field, highly regarded by his professional colleagues, and a year later would be president of the Law Society of Saskatchewan. He was, however, the very antithesis of Tony Merchant, who was already on the case for Colin. Gerrand and Merchant had a strong dislike for each other and the strained relations between the two lawyers made any settlement of the differences between their clients unlikely. The courts would have to settle the dispute between Colin and JoAnn.

The courts were kept very busy by Gerrand and Merchant. The custody battle in the Appeal Courts, the matrimonial property action which was coming on for trial, and the divorce action, with JoAnn's claim for interim support during the litigation, all boiled along apace. Everything was hotly contested, and Merchant appealed every order or decision Gerrand obtained. The blizzard of paper and process was such that Gerrand's court runner, the man who was delivering all the documents, quit under the pressure.

The war was not confined to the Saskatchewan courtrooms. As it escalated, JoAnn encountered serious personal harassment. Her weekend visits to the children at Redland Avenue were interfered with; her purse was rifled and her house keys stolen; the station wagon she had been driving was, without notice, taken by Colin the day the first custody hearing ended, leaving her, without funds, to find alternative transportation. She later complained of sinister telephone calls and slashed tires. Those she enlisted to her cause became Colin's adversaries and he reached for every lever to use against them.

To determine the value of Colin's lands for the purpose of the matrimonial property action, Gerrand and JoAnn retained Art Hosie, a highly regarded Regina realtor and professional appraiser. Gerrand was forced to get an order permitting Hosie to inspect the lands. Hosie's wife, Paula, was employed as a secretary with the Conservative caucus in the Legislative Buildings in Regina. Colin pressured the Conservatives' new leader, Grant Devine, to discharge Paula, threatening to leave the caucus, and Devine succumbed. Paula was let go. Gerrand took out a subpoena for Grant Devine, but the soon-to-be premier escaped the embarrassment of having to describe the incident before the courts.

In the life of a practising politician there is seldom a point where it is convenient to take time out for a divorce, but being sidelined in the fall of 1979 was particularly galling to Colin Thatcher.

JoAnn's action pre-empted any thoughts Colin possessed of entering the competition that made Grant Devine leader of the Conservative party. Richard Collver had succumbed to his party's growing disaffection for him and had announced his resignation on May 29. The leadership convention was called for November and would take place in Saskatoon.

Colin had cautiously tested the leadership waters in the Liberal party three years earlier when he had been a fledgling MLA of one year's experience and was still regarded by Liberals as ''Ross's son.'' Now he had two successful elections under his belt and, somewhat like a prophet from a far land, was in a different party where he maintained his own image. Although to some he was still suspect as a fallen-away Liberal, Colin Thatcher in 1979 would have been a strong contender for the leadership of the Saskatchewan Conservatives.

But he was rendered ineligible by his divorce. Privately, Colin confessed his bitterness at what he regarded as a lost opportunity. He also remembered that one of the inducements Dick Collver had offered when Colin left the Liberals was the promise of the leadership when Collver gave it up. Now it was not to be.

As with the Liberal leadership contest between Ted Malone and Tony Merchant three years earlier, Colin Thatcher was not enamoured with any of the three candidates for the Conservative leadership, least of all with the front runner Grant Devine. Although he led Regina South MLA Paul Rousseau to believe he had his support, there was no endorsement and Colin maintained his usual position of neutrality from which he could criticize whoever succeeded.

Criticize he did. Six months after the Saskatoon leadership convention Colin was quoted publicly as saying he liked Grant Devine less then than when he had been elected leader.

Not long after the convention, Grant Devine, who had no constituency, approached Colin with the suggestion that he step aside and make Thunder Creek available. The proposal seemed reasonable to Devine, who had been raised in Colin's riding where he still had an interest in the family farm. Colin did not see it in the same light, however, and angrily rejected the idea. Colin was not at all contrite when, after the Estevan Conservative MLA gave up his seat, in the by-election Devine was rejected by the voters in a constituency where he had no ties whatsoever.

It was no surprise that Colin, who had been Conservative House leader under Dick Collver, did not continue in that position under Grant Devine.

As the spring of 1980 turned into summer, JoAnn began to achieve some success in the courts, but a new battle front opened up outside the court rooms. The Court of Appeal confirmed the MacPherson judgment giving custody of Regan and Stephanie to JoAnn but, while Merchant unsuccessfully attempted to take the matter to the Supreme Court of Canada, Colin refused to give up the children. Gerrand was back in court seeking enforcement of the custody order, even reaching for habeas corpus, in addition to contempt of court, as he tried to force Colin to recognize the court's authority. Merchant was busy trying to stay implementation of the custody order.

The house on Redland Avenue became the scene of a bitter personal battle as JoAnn found arrayed against her not only Colin but also Sandra Hammond, baby-sitter now turned housekeeper, and even her fifteen-year-old son Greg. A court order had given JoAnn weekend use of the house and visiting rights with the children but that arrangement had turned out to be very unsatisfactory, as JoAnn met resistance and interference on every visit. Another order gave JoAnn full possession of the home and Colin stormed over to Simcoe Street where he bought another house and, curiously, for a time became a neighbour of Ron and Jane Graham.

Physical violence now became an element as the Thatcher family continued to deteriorate. One afternoon Greg physically prevented JoAnn from leaving the Redland Avenue home with Stephanie, seizing the child from his mother, cursing JoAnn and injuring her as he shoved the protesting woman about the family home.

JoAnn gave up attempting to live at Redland and, with the help of some friends, was removing her possessions when Colin came upon the scene. He ordered JoAnn's assistants from the house and, when at JoAnn's request they declined, he removed his wristwatch and with raised fist approached the only other male in the group. Charges of assault and threatening were laid and came to trial in the fall.

In early May, as JoAnn finally secured custody of Regan and Stephanie, it immediately became apparent that her eleven-year-old son had undergone a transformation during the winter he had spent with his father. He would not stay with his mother, and a number of bizarre incidents occurred as the boy disappeared almost every time he had an opportunity. That he was being encouraged to run away by his father, JoAnn had little doubt. She found in Regan's pocket a list of telephone numbers to call when needed, in Colin's handwriting and headed by the number of Tony Merchant. When JoAnn and her two children were staying with friends at the resort area of Regina Beach, Colin was seen in the vicinity. JoAnn later testified that Stephanie had told her of overhearing Colin encouraging Regan to run away from his mother.

As the property action was coming on for trial in the summer of 1980, Merchant was able to secure a rehearing of the question of Regan's custody, and the Thatchers came again before Mr. Justice MacPherson.

The trial of the divorce and matrimonial property actions began in mid-June before Mr. Justice Edward Hughes and carried on into July. Judgment was reserved and not handed down until October.

Mr. Justice MacPherson picked up following Mr. Justice Hughes and heard the unusual and accusing stories of the runaway Regan. This time the trial was complete with a child psychologist and a psychiatrist. Even Regan had a lawyer. After the November custody trial, Greg had retained R.L. Barclay, QC, to represent him before the Court of Appeal and the Supreme Court in an attempt to have the court hear his opinions on the question of Regan's testimony. This time Mr. Justice MacPherson heard Greg. "Appalling," he called it as the boy testified against his mother.

On August 11, Mr. Justice MacPherson handed down his judgment. Regan, he said for the second time, would stay with his mother. The judge's initial negative impressions of Colin Thatcher, developed at the first custody trial the previous November, had now progressed to the point where he found Colin to be more than an unsuitable father. His decision was unusually extreme and scathing as he described Colin as "Articulate, domineering and intimidating. Determined to win custody of the son, Regan, by any means at all." Colin's "methods and purposes have been to destroy his wife in the minds of their children. In so doing, he had come a long way toward destroying the children themselves." If the court granted custody of Regan to his father, "the result would be such that Mr. Thatcher has won by cheating."

Custody of Regan was granted to JoAnn, and Colin and Greg were prohibited from communicating with him.

But Regan was never to return to his mother. As JoAnn and her father, Harlan Geiger, then visiting from Iowa, approached the Redland Avenue home with the court orders in their hands, Regan ran from the house and leapt over the back fence. He was not seen again in Saskatchewan until the following May. Colin, with the assistance of his mother Peggy, spirited the boy out of the province and down to Palm Springs.

Regan was registered in the private Palm Valley School as Regan Erickson. The surname belonged to one of Colin's resident lady friends, named Cindy, who posed as Regan's mother. Regan resided with his grandmother and her companion Bev Banbury. They lived in a nicer residence than Colin's, with a pool and whirlpool, which Peggy had purchased just that February for $140,000 (U.S.). Regan was unhappy, had no outside interests, and gained weight.

In Saskatchewan, Gerry Gerrand drew on every available legal manoeuvre in an attempt to enforce the custody order. In another motion before Mr. Justice MacPherson he referred to an obscure English precedent which suggested that the public could be called upon for assistance in such a case. The judge seized upon the suggestion and promptly called the media representatives to his court and asked them to publicize Regan's disappearance. It was an unheard-of proceeding in Saskatchewan.

Colin responded with a press conference of his own. He complained that Mr. Justice MacPherson's action had all but forced the media to carry coverage of his private affairs, something they had previously avoided. He described in some detail JoAnn's affair and the evidence of the many witnesses apparently ignored by the court. He thought Regan should be allowed to testify in his own custody trial, saying that the decision showed that children had no "inherent rights" and no "input over their destinies." In Colin's prepared statement he said, "I truly regret my sons have lost respect and affection for their mother."

Gerrand forced Colin into an examination for discovery to try to determine the whereabouts of Regan. Colin refused to answer the pertinent questions and Gerrand took action against him for contempt of court. That matter came before Mr. Justice Edward Noble, who had no difficulty finding Colin guilty of contempt. Before the penalty could be assessed, Merchant appealed that finding, too. It would not be until the spring of 1981 that the Court of Appeal confirmed that Colin was in contempt and returned the file to Mr. Justice Noble to fix punishment.

On October 20, 1980, Mr. Justice Hughes, in his last judgment before leaving the Saskatchewan Court of Queen's Bench to take up a position as a constitutional law advisor of the Government of British Columbia, ordered that Colin pay JoAnn $820,000 as her share of the matrimonial property. He rejected Colin's contention that his late father had imposed a "secret trust" in 1969 when executing the codicil to his will, leaving all his lands to Colin, and found the total value of the matrimonial property to be just over two million dollars. He recognized liabilities of $365,000 and applied a fifty-fifty division to the net assets. The $820,000 was to be paid to JoAnn by February 1,

1981, after which Colin's lands were to be sold to satisfy the judgment.

Colin regarded the judgment as just another stage in the irritatingly necessary legal process rather than as a final resolution of the property dispute. It was a setback, to be sure, but the decision was eminently appealable and the Court of Appeal and the Supreme Court would give him ample time to work out other strategies. A prompt notice of appeal stayed the judgment.

Thatcher and Merchant had been unsuccessful in the numerous court actions and, although Colin did not consider the decisions to be particularly binding or effective, he had become more resentful of JoAnn and hardened in his attitude towards her. In the fall of 1980, Colin approached Garry Anderson, a sometime Caron resident, with an offer of $50,000 for the killing of JoAnn. When Anderson turned down the proposition, Colin asked him to keep it in mind for someone who might be interested.

As JoAnn's action approached trial during the first half of 1980, Colin had embarked on a strange series of financial manoeuvres. Whether or not they were designed to partially evade the impact of the lawsuit, they substantially increased his indebtedness and contributed greatly to serious financial woes to come.

In the spring of 1980, Colin purchased two parcels of land for his sons — 320 acres each for Greg and Regan. This time Colin paid peak-of-the-market prices: a total of $425,000. Colin borrowed the entire sum, mortgaging his other lands as security.

At the property action trial Thatcher and Merchant argued that they should be entitled to deduct the loan from the valuation of Colin's holdings and ignore the acquired land, which he did not own. It did not work, and the trial judge ignored both the asset and the liability.

Colin also dabbled in property development. Early in 1980 he became interested in a condominium development proposed by his Palm Springs friend and golfing partner, Bob Gustav. In May he entered a joint venture headed by Gustav, agreeing to put up $418,500 for a 28 per cent interest in the development. Within a month he had contributed $130,000, an investment which did not surface during the property action trial.

Colin had more than business to occupy him in Palm Springs. In October 1980 he went on a blind date, arranged by Bob Gustav. Two decades earlier he had met his wife JoAnn this way in Iowa. This time he met thirty-year-old Lynne Ann Dally, sales director in the venerable Sheraton Oasis Hotel in downtown Palm Springs, owned by Hank Dally, her father.

Gustav ran into Lynne in the hotel lobby one day, and asked if she would like to meet a "wheat farmer from Moose Jaw."

"Don't do me any favours, Bob," was Lynne's reaction.

"Well, he's kind of an interesting man," Gustav replied.

They dined out with Bob and his wife Lettie, but Lynne recalls, "I was not impressed with Colin at all the first time." However, when he invited her out the next evening Lynne accepted, and, in spite of the fact that she had been seeing someone else, a relationship did develop.

Lynne had been born and raised in the Los Angeles suburb of Glendale, where she studied ballet and graduated from high school in 1967. In the fall of 1968 her father retired from the practice of law and bought the Sheraton Oasis. Lynne had been doing some modelling and acting, and says she was even offered a contract by Universal Studios. "I had many, many good breaks."

Instead, she moved to Palm Springs in 1969, to embrace the lifestyle she and her generation had protested. "I was never a good hippie anyway," she rationalized. "I always had new jeans."

While studying liberal arts at the College of the Desert for a year, she worked part-time in the family hotel. Her older brother Michael was also employed there. Later she worked full-time, and even lived in the hotel. Her job was fast paced and challenging, most suited to a self-described over-achiever who was at the same time unambitious.

Lynne considers herself to be self-educated, and certainly appears more learned than her formal schooling would suggest. She is well read, articulate and extremely bright, and it shows.

Lynne knew all the right people in The Desert. "It wasn't that I would date someone because they had money, it just seemed that those were the circles I found myself in." Yet she would also claim there were men who just could not afford her. Lynne saw wealthier and more sophisticated men than Colin, but never one as political. Politics appealed to her, and it was not long before she had a firsthand taste.

In November of that same fall, 1980, Colin invited her to the opening of the Legislature in Regina. Since California's population and economy are comparable to the whole of Canada's, Lynne viewed Colin as a big fish in a little pond, but liked what she saw during her ten-day visit. Later, when Colin suggested that Lynne be his constituency campaign manager, he was only half-joking.

That Christmas, and subsequent Christmases as well as her birthdays, Colin bought Lynne expensive clothes. In 1982 he even bought her a mink coat, though she would hardly need it in southern California. Not once did she receive a gift from him that could not be worn. Colin, Lynne quickly learned, wanted her to look the part. He loved putting on the dog, and later in the relationship Lynne would wonder if she had not just been an expensive prop all along. Was she merely someone to fill the passenger seat in his Palm Springs Mercedes 450 SL and his Moose Jaw yellow Corvette?

"I think he assumed I was essentially shallow," reflects Lynne. If Colin did see Lynne as a bright, perky, cute piece of California fluff, he also regarded her as another entrée to Palm Springs society.

Among those Lynne introduced Colin to was Mel Habor, owner of the famed Ingleside Inn and its exclusive restaurant, Melvyn's. He also owned Cecil's Disco Club, Palm Springs' most "in" night spot. Lynne and Colin were regulars at those two establishments when Colin was in town, and he would drop $150 (U.S.) on dinner for two.

"Colin wanted to go out every night. That was his whole thing when he was down here." Lynne asked him to take the girls he saw on the side elsewhere, so Habor would not see him out with others. Either out of spite, or because he liked being personally greeted by the restaurant owner, he would still move in the circle Lynne opened up for him, whether she was with him or not.

In public Colin was a big spender, a conspicuous consumer. Privately, with the exception of certain expensive tastes, he was extremely tight fisted. However, Lynne discovered that to be the least of his inconsistent extremes of behaviour. His unpredictable and dramatic mood swings were the most perplexing. She was the product of even-tempered family and outside relationships, and could not understand his violent rages or what would trigger them off. She even tried vainly to get him to have his blood sugar checked, thinking the problem might be medical.

Colin was as close as Lynne had ever seen to a split personality. When she was not looking out for her physical welfare, she would try to cajole him out of his bad moods, or refuse to see him. Colin had a little black book he would fall back on during these interludes, often with Lynne's encouragement. But eventually she would forgive him, and they would be back on their rocky road.

That road seemed to be leading somewhere, and in spite of the warning signals, Lynne was willing to follow it. She says they really did enjoy each other's company and she got used to the way he was, even though no one else in Palm Springs seemed to like him. Colin even admits, Lynne says, that she brought a lot of good things out in him, and helped him take a little more delight in life.

They called each other several times daily when separated. Colin provided Lynne with the number of his government long-distance credit card for that purpose, eliminating any incentive to use the more economical written word. Not once was a letter or postcard exchanged between the two long-distance lovers.

Eventually she even quit her job for him. Colin wanted her to be free to travel. When Lynne pointed out that she had to live somehow, he gave her about $1,000 (U.S.) a month when she had rent to pay, and less later when she moved into his condo.

Thatcher's recollection is a little different. He concedes that there was a period when she quit to "make herself more available" to him, but that she was still on full salary. He says his support came when the hotel was having financial problems, presumably implying that she was thus let go, and that he then helped her out from the fall of 1981 until the relationship ended in 1983.

Regardless of how the arrangement came about, the fact that Colin was willing to take some financial responsibility for Lynne seemed to indicate a more serious bond than he would later admit to.

JoAnn was a central figure in Colin and Lynne's relationship, much as both women would have certainly preferred otherwise. The decree nisi and custody orders had been handed down in July and August 1980, two or three months before their first date. On their second date Colin started harping about JoAnn, and Lynne was never to hear the end of his obsession. He was deaf to Lynne's reminders that his ex-wife was not her favourite topic and her analogies about his likely disinterest in her past liaisons. Indeed, over time the things Colin had to say about JoAnn would become more disturbing, not less.

In early November 1980, Colin Thatcher was acquitted of the charge of assault and threatening laid against him the previous May in the furniture moving incident. The Provincial Court judge hearing the evidence concluded that it had been a very minor affair and declined to register a criminal conviction.

Now that he was in the clear, Colin promptly and publicly claimed that he had been persecuted by the NDP government, who would "stop at nothing to embarrass a political enemy." He expressed "complete contempt, complete scorn for the Department of the Attorney General."

The Department of the Attorney General was in a quandary. Although no physical blow had actually been struck, an assault had likely taken place. The judgment acquitting Colin was very appealable, and the prosecutor was anxious to proceed with an appeal. It was, however, as the judge had found, a minor matter. The Crown had had its day in court and an appeal would not normally be taken in such a case involving any other citizen. To take the case to appeal would smack of persecution, and the Director of Public Prosecutions decided to leave the matter alone.

The political career that figured so largely in the Attorney General's decision was, at best, in uneven shape. With so much else on his mind, Colin understandably had little time for the Legislature in 1980 but, on one attendance, was again thrown out of the House, this time for casting an aspersion on the Speaker. Called to withdraw and apologize for stating that the Speaker had injected himself into the debate, Colin seemed unable genuinely to comply. "Mr. Speaker, if it will make you happy. . ." began one unsuccessful attempt. Colin tried again: "I'm quite prepared to withdraw any aspersions against the Chair. I'm not aware of having made any, but if you view them as aspersions which I don't, I will withdraw them in an unqualified. . . ." With that NDP Speaker John Brockelbank named the Thunder Creek MLA who had to leave the House.

Outside the chamber Colin was sincerely puzzled. He thought he had been almost abject in his apology, he told his fellow Conservative MLAs, and could not understand why he had failed in satisfying the Speaker. Colin, apparently, had the same difficulty with apologies as had his father.

Nevertheless, Thatcher was one of the stars of the Conservative opposition in the Saskatchewan Legislature during their drive, gaining momentum through 1981, to unseat the Blakeney NDP government. To his role he brought a prima donna attitude. He incurred the hearty dislike of his fellow caucus members as he ignored their morning sessions to plan House strategy, strode in late, and grabbed for himself the lead question issue of the day. A solo player, he paid little attention to the established party line and, on one issue, even broke ranks to side with former leader Collver, now sitting as a Western Union member.

Mr. Justice Noble's finding that Colin Thatcher was in contempt of court had been confirmed by the Court of Appeal, and Colin was still refusing to answer questions about Regan's whereabouts. On April 28, 1981, the matter came again before Mr. Justice Noble, this time to determine the appropriate punishment. The object of penalty for contempt of court, the judge said, is primarily to enforce the orders of the court. "The extent of the Court's sanction must take into account the seriousness of the contempt, the circumstances of the contempt, and the public interest which is manifested by the necessity that the public respect and uphold the lawful order of its courts." Pointing out that Thatcher was a member of the Legislative Assembly, Mr. Justice Noble said: "It seems incongruous that a lawmaker is prepared to hold an Order of the Court of Queen's Bench in contempt. . . . The public looks to its leaders for guidance by example and action."

"Mr. Thatcher," the judge continued, "has an advantage many citizens could not claim. So, when he commits a contempt of a court order, it holds the law and the Court up to ridicule because many members of the public expect people who have attained his stature in society to obey the law."

The Saskatchewan Legislature was then in session and Mr. Justice Noble felt that Section 28 of The Legislative Assembly Act applied. The section states that "No member may, during the session of the Legislature, be liable to arrest, detention or molestation for any debt or any cause of a civil nature."

Were it not for that section, Mr. Justice Noble said, "I would have sent Mr. Thatcher to a period of incarceration for his contempt." In the circumstances the judge had to settle for a fine, which he set at $6,000.

Had he known more about Colin Thatcher's attitude towards the contempt finding, Mr. Justice Noble might have fixed the fine somewhat higher. Just a month earlier, in March, Colin was walking in an abandoned farmyard north of Caron with a recent acquaintance, a man named Charlie Wilde. "I don't care how many fucking contempt of court charges are laid," Colin told Charlie, "I am not going to return the boy."

In the spring of 1981 the Thunder Creek MLA brought his custody battle before the Saskatchewan Legislature. Speaking in the budget debate, he said: "I'm sure every member in this Assembly, and probably every person in Saskatchewan, is aware that my family is a living example of the fact that children have absolutely no rights in this province. I'm sure my case has shown you very clearly that children have no rights before the law or before the courts."

Colin introduced a private member's bill which proposed to give effect to the preference of children in custody disputes as to which parent they chose to live with. The missing Regan's stated desire to live with his father had been denied by the court the previous year. Although viewed sympathetically by Attorney General Roy Romanow, the bill did not become legislation.

Colin spoke to the matter in the House on Friday, May 15, 1981, two days before a gunman shot and seriously wounded JoAnn Wilson.

73

II

A Strange Feeling

"It's just always deny, deny, deny."
— Colin Thatcher to Garry Anderson,
May 1, 1984

CHAPTER 6

The Patio Shooting

Colin and JoAnn's marriage was formally ended with the issue of a decree absolute of divorce on December 22, 1980. On January 3, 1981, at Brampton, Rev. John Sullivan married JoAnn and forty-six-year-old Anthony Wilson.

They had been seeing each other for ten months, having met when JoAnn, then working for Willson Office Specialty, did some interior decorating at the offices of Interprovincial Pipe and Steel Company (IPSCO) where Tony was a vice-president. He had been divorced two years earlier from his first wife, Ruth, whom he had married in 1955. Two sons had been born to that marriage, William in 1958, and Alexander in 1961.

Wilson was born in England and studied accounting at the London School of Economics. He worked as a computer systems analyst for Esso Petroleum before coming to Canada in 1963, where he worked for Northern Electric in Montreal, and later for a consulting firm in Toronto. In 1968 he continued west to Regina, to be executive assistant to the president of IPSCO. In 1969 he bought a house at 2876 Albert Street, just across the street from Saskatchewan's Legislative Buildings, and continued to reside there after his divorce. It later became JoAnn's home.

"Gracious home in prime street location" is the description of the Wilson home in a 1984 real estate listing. Of square, two-storey construction, it faces the Legislative Buildings to the east across Albert Street. The house sits on the north-west corner of Albert and 20th Avenue, which, on crossing Albert, becomes Legislative Drive and runs past the front steps of the Legislature.

The kitchen is on the west, or back, of the house and is joined to an elevated wooden deck by two sliding glass patio doors. A lane runs south to north behind the lot from 20th Avenue, the one block to Regina Avenue. The two-car garage sits on the south-west corner of the lot next to the lane and opens onto 20th Avenue.

The backyard of the 75-foot lot is enclosed by a solid six foot high board fence. In May 1981, an opening in this fence at the north-west corner gave easy access to or from the lane which also services the homes fronting on Angus Street, the next street west from Albert. Across the lane from the opening in the fence is 2865 Angus Street.

An amazing number of the participants in the civil and criminal actions involving Colin Thatcher live in this neighbourhood. Just a block south of 20th Avenue, at the intersection of Angus and McCallum, is Tony Merchant, Colin's lawyer. Three blocks south of the Wilson residence lives Gerry Gerrand, JoAnn's lawyer, and a block and a half north-west on Regina Avenue was Shane Kirby, an RCMP firearms and ballistics expert, who would be called out of bed to visit the Wilson home.

May 17, 1981, was a warm spring Sunday, and JoAnn and Tony Wilson spent it happily working in their garden. The barbecue season had begun and at 2900 Albert Street, just across 20th Avenue from the Wilson house, Debra Sandomirsky was hosting a cookout for a large group of her young friends.

Among the Sandomirsky guests were twenty-four-year-old Terry Stewart and twenty-two-year-old Pam Gerrand, daughter of Gerry, who was still enmeshed with JoAnn in the complex maze of legal tangles that her divorce, custody and property actions had become.

About 9:15 p.m. Terry drove Pam to her parents' home to pick up a barbecue for the party at Sandomirsky's. After dropping off Pam and the barbecue, just before ten o'clock he parked on the east side of Angus Street, just north of 20th Avenue, in front of 2865 Angus Street. Similarly parked in front of him, pointing north on Angus Street, was another car, to which he at the time paid no attention. Terry went back to the Sandomirsky party, leaving Pam's purse in his car.

At the Wilson's JoAnn and Tony continued gardening until dusk, not sitting down to dinner until nine o'clock. JoAnn's

78

seven-year-old daughter Stephanie had a playmate of the same age, Matthew Harris, visiting that evening and he was sleeping over. At 9:30 the children were put to bed. Tony Wilson went upstairs to take a bath; JoAnn was going to tidy up the kitchen before she, too, went upstairs.

In the Wilson backyard, the driver of the car parked on Angus Street, in front of Terry Stewart's, crouched in the shadows inside the north fence. He carried a loaded, heavy calibre rifle.

Pam Gerrand had left her watch in her purse in Terry's car. Terry walked Pam from Sandomirsky's back to his car to retrieve the watch.

JoAnn entered the kitchen, stood at the sink with her back to the patio doors and attacked the waiting dishes.

The man with the rifle crept to the edge of the raised patio deck and leaned forward with his elbows on the deck, much as one would position oneself for shooting across the hood of a car. This brought his rifle muzzle almost within six inches of the north section of the patio doors. He sighted the rifle upwards, at JoAnn's back.

Tony Wilson's patio doors were of good quality. They were made of specially tempered, case-hardened, shatterproof glass of the sort found in the side and rear windows of automobiles. Instead of slicing into dangerous shards on impact, this glass would instantly fragment into small sections, not unlike a fine jigsaw puzzle.

On Angus Street, Terry Stewart opened the passenger door of his 1974 Impala and Pam Gerrand reached in, took her purse and began to rummage through it looking for her watch.

The gunman at the Wilson patio doors centred his sights on the middle of JoAnn's back and fired through the glass. The picture he had of JoAnn at the kitchen sink instantly disappeared, as the entire glass door fragmented and became opaque. He had not counted on a second shot anyway, but the sudden disappearance of his target ensured there would be none. The gunman fled, not risking the exposure that would be required to look through the untouched south section of the patio doors and thus not knowing the results of his attack.

He ran through the opening in the back fence, across the lane and over the open yard at 2865 Albert Street.

Terry and Pam had heard the bang. Terry thought at first it was a back fire from a car. Pam thought her barbecue might have exploded and looked over towards Sandomirsky's, then bent back to her purse.

The gunman ran out onto Angus Street, crossed the sidewalk twenty feet in front of Terry and Pam, scurried around the back of his car carrying the rifle in his left hand, and jumped behind the wheel. His car started and accelerated quickly north on Angus Street. It did not turn its lights on.

"Get the licence number," Terry said to Pam, who had not seen the rifle. But the car was at the Regina Avenue intersection, where the brake lights came on briefly as it slowed for traffic. It turned left and was gone.

The bullet the gunman had fired at JoAnn pierced the patio doors two feet nine inches above the deck on its upward journey towards her back. When it left the rifle muzzle it was moving at about 3,000 feet per second and revolving or spinning at about 100,000 revolutions per minute, giving it a gyroscopic effect which would help keep it on its aimed course. It was carrying 2,500 foot pounds of energy. The bullet was constructed of lead with a copper covering or jacket.

The patio door the bullet passed through consisted of three panes of heavy glass. The bullet easily pierced these obstacles but was torn apart as it did so. The copper jacket ripped off the lead core and split into three pieces.

A projectile fired at an angle through heavy glass will tend to deflect in accentuation of its angle of attack. The bullet, reduced to its lead core as it passed through the patio door and crossed the kitchen towards JoAnn, had been fired from below and to her left. It thus deflected further upwards and further to the right than its original point of aim.

The lead core struck JoAnn about one and a half inches below the top of her right shoulder. It was still carrying enough energy that it knocked her six feet sideways into the hallway off the kitchen. Two of the jacket fragments struck the cabinets near her. The third fragment caromed off a door casing and fell to the floor.

It was just ten o'clock, or perhaps a moment or two after.

JoAnn screamed for Tony. As he raced into the kitchen his first thought was that the dishwasher had exploded, but the bullet hole in the patio door corrected that impression.

JoAnn did not lose consciousness. Taken by ambulance to General Hospital Emergency, she described hearing an explosion and feeling a sharp pain in her shoulder which she thought was glass sticking in her, until Tony pointed out the bullet hole in the glass door. She had seen no one, but immediately suggested that the shot could have been fired by her ex-husband, Colin Thatcher.

By Tuesday morning, when JoAnn was well enough to give the police a written statement, and after she had had time to give the matter a lot of thought, she was more positive about Colin being the culprit. "There is no one else that would do this," she stated.

It had occurred to Regina police, also, that Colin might be responsible. By 10:30 p.m. they had requested that the Moose Jaw City Police and RCMP set up road blocks, and this was promptly done. Nothing was netted by this manoeuvre.

Colin Thatcher had been at home in Moose Jaw all evening, working on the pool and yard at his Redland Avenue residence. That is what he willingly told the Regina police the next afternoon in the presence of his lawyer, Tony Merchant. His son Greg, then sixteen, had been out but said that Colin was home when he came in at 10:30.

Colin and Greg said they knew nothing of the shooting of JoAnn until Tony Merchant phoned with the news at about 11:15 p.m.

Merchant would testify at Colin's trial three and a half years later that he had been so sure that the police would be interested in Colin that, after hearing of the shooting only "ten or twelve minutes" after it happened, he had immediately phoned the Thatcher residence. He stated that Greg answered, but the lawyer insisted on speaking with Colin who was vacuuming his pool. Merchant then raced over to Moose Jaw to be with his client when the police arrived.

The next day, however, when all three were interviewed by Sergeants Marvin Malnyk and Bernie Jeannotte, Colin and Greg did not recollect Merchant speaking to anyone but Greg on the telephone, and they put the call at 11:15 p.m., with the lawyer arriving about forty-five minutes later.

In fact, Moose Jaw police watching the Thatcher residence saw Tony Merchant arrive at 12:45 a.m., two and three quarter hours after the shooting. The first of several discrepancies having to do with time, telephone calls to the Thatcher home and travel between Regina and Moose Jaw, had arisen.

As to who might have done the shooting the night before, Colin could only say, "I don't know who would do this to JoAnn." When Bernie Jeannotte mentioned a polygraph examination, Colin, on the advice of his lawyer, declined.

Earlier on that Monday following the shooting, the Conservative MLAs had gathered in the Legislative Buildings for a scheduled caucus meeting. Characteristically, the Thunder Creek MLA was late in arriving and the others had been discussing the incident which had occurred the night before across the street.

When Colin Thatcher entered the meeting, a loud silence filled the room as no remark, even "Good morning," seemed appropriate.

Colin broke the ice nicely as he slumped into his seat. "Well, if I hired a hitman, I guess I don't have to pay him," he told his stunned colleagues.

Tony Wilson wasn't ready for what Colin Thatcher had to say.

"Maybe it wasn't botched," Thatcher began.

"What do you mean?"

"Maybe it was a pretty accurate shot by someone who knew what he was doing. Someone trained for Viet Nam and now an expert at only one thing. If we can't get this thing settled reasonably, maybe there will be another time and maybe it'll be different. Maybe it'll be you too."

Tony couldn't believe his ears. He was sitting in his own living room discussing murder and hired assassins with Colin Thatcher over a glass of Scotch.

It was only a week after the shooting and JoAnn was still in the hospital. Colin had phoned Wilson at his office in the early afternoon and asked for a meeting. Tony had suggested his home after work and that was where they were now sitting, only a few feet away from where JoAnn had been shot. Colin had explained that he was sick of lawyers and courtrooms and publicity. He was concerned for Regan, whose custody was again before the courts. It would be best for everyone if Regan was allowed to stay in Moose Jaw, he said.

Colin wanted to settle his financial dispute with JoAnn. He was prepared to be generous, he said, but wanted a generous time for payment, perhaps ten to twenty years.

"I won't be bled," Colin said. Immediate payment of the $820,000 judgment was unthinkable and he would "do anything to avoid being bled."

"What does 'anything' mean?" Wilson had asked, and then Colin had explained, giving the other to believe that he had arranged for the shooting of JoAnn.

"Maybe two can play that game." Wilson decided to be tough too. "Maybe I could hire someone and we could have our own little private war."

Then Wilson returned to his senses and turned the conversation back to the matter of the outstanding judgment. JoAnn was in a strong position to maintain the judgment in the Court of Appeal he said. No so, replied Colin; recently appointed Chief Justice E.D. Bayda was more sympathetic to him than former Chief Justice E.M. Culliton.

As an immediate cash settlement JoAnn might be prepared to accept $675,000, Wilson suggested. Colin angrily leaped to his feet and began to leave.

"If that is JoAnn's position, you and JoAnn had better take steps to protect yourselves," he said as he stalked out of Wilson's home.

That it had really happened, that Tony Wilson had not imagined the bizarre event, was confirmed a few hours later when Colin Thatcher phoned back. He said he would be prepared to pay $1,000,000 to JoAnn with the payments spread over twenty years. It was a generous offer, Colin claimed, if properly examined. He would be very careful, Colin assured Wilson, never again to make the kind of statements that had been made in the earlier conversation. Tony Wilson jotted down this recollection of the strange talk and gave it to Gerry Gerrand.

Two weeks later Tony Wilson and the recovering JoAnn went

83

off to British Columbia to spend a month in rest, relaxation and reflection. JoAnn decided to throw in the towel on her fight for custody of Regan. Her son had spent little more than a week with JoAnn in the more than a year and a half since the courts had first decided that she should have custody. When she returned to Regina in early July, she instructed Gerrand to abandon the litigation over the custody of her now twelve-year-old second son. The lawyer did so, and JoAnn called a press conference to announce the abandonment. JoAnn told Saskatchewan that she had been personally terrorized for months, that her car tires had been slashed, sugar had been put in her gas tank, and she had been subjected to sinister telephone calls.

After the press conference, Gerry Gerrand and his wife left Regina for a short summer holiday. An hour down the road their car radio told them that Tony Merchant and Colin Thatcher had announced that they had "won the battle" for custody of Regan. "They won all right," the angry lawyer told his wife as he nearly drove into the ditch. "They won, but not in court they didn't."

Gerrand was not the only one who felt that Colin Thatcher's activities outside the courtroom had been in disregard of, and perhaps an attempt to influence, what went on in court. On July 21, 1981, F.W. Johnson, then Chief Justice of Saskatchewan's Court of Queen's Bench, wrote Attorney General Roy Romanow: "There are indications that W. Colin Thatcher deliberately flouted the order of this Court with respect to custody of the child, Regan Thatcher, and that he was actively involved in the removal of Regan from the jurisdiction of this Court so that the custody order in favour of the mother would be defeated."

Thatcher's actions "Likely constituted contempt of the Court of Queen's Bench of Saskatchewan, and [would] serve to undermine this Court's authority," Chief Justice Johnson went on. He suggested that appropriate steps be taken "to maintain the integrity of the courts and the administration of justice." The Chief Justice was asking the Attorney General to initiate contempt of court proceedings against the Thunder Creek MLA.

While this was under consideration by the department's lawyers, Colin Thatcher stepped forward and revealed more clearly his attitude for Saskatchewan's judicial system. Commenting to the media upon his "victory" in securing custody of Regan, the MLA said, "Regan was a victim of some animosity between a member of the judiciary and his [Regan's] grandfather," suggesting that Mr. Justice MacPherson had been less than judicial in determining the two custody trials. Thatcher went on to say, confirming the view he had expressed to Tony Wilson, that the case had been "quickly resolved once there was a change in the Chief Justice of the Saskatchewan Court of Appeal from E.M. Culliton to E.D. Bayda."

The Crown law officers were properly horrified. This, as opposed to the civil contempt of disobeying a court order as complained of by Chief Justice Johnson, was probably criminal contempt. Thatcher's remarks suggested that the personalities of the judges who had heard his cases had influenced the results. Mr. Justice MacPherson was also upset and seriously considered bringing his own defamation action against Thatcher but was dissuaded by his fellow judges. The statements would be criminal contempt of court if they were found to impair or interfere with the fair administration of justice, or to bring the court or judge into contempt or lower his authority. The Attorney General's Department was of the opinion that the statements did constitute criminal contempt of court. An investigation was conducted and instructions issued to launch a prosecution. In mid-November, just as the contempt motion was about to be filed in court, Attorney General Roy Romanow suddenly intervened. He directed that the proceedings be held until final approval came from him.

The approval never came. More than two months later, in late January 1982, Tony Merchant learned of the prosecution pending against his client. He wrote Mr. Romanow suggesting that, because of the delay, the prosecution would now look like political persecution. It was not bad advice from one who had experience in such matters. Five years earlier, Merchant himself, then an MLA, had nearly been charged with contempt with respect to one of Mr. Justice MacPherson's custody orders, and the same Attorney General had hesitated about initiating proceedings against a member of the Legislative Assembly.

Colin Thatcher, too, escaped prosecution through procrastination. In March 1982, with a provincial election only a month

85

away, and no proceedings yet commenced, the Department of the Attorney General closed its files.

The police investigation of the May 17 shooting of JoAnn Wilson soon sputtered out. No one who had been in the neighbourhood that night, other than Pam Gerrand and Terry Stewart, had seen anything. Interviewed under hypnosis, both witnesses improved their recall but not sufficiently to provide a description of either the gunman or his car. The licence number Terry had asked Pam to note would not come forward in their minds. The most prominent feature of the car they could remember was the tail lights they had seen when the red lights came on as the car slowed before its turn west on Regina Avenue. Their description of the car seemed to fit a Ford Capri. Jeannotte and Malnyk borrowed a 1981 Capri, bittersweet in colour, and placed it on Angus Street in darkness. Stewart and Gerrand agreed that it was a close fit. There were 161 Capris in Saskatchewan. All were checked but with no results.

In spite of the huge hint that Colin Thatcher had left with Tony Wilson a week after the shooting, police investigators working around Colin's home, ranch and associates came away with nothing. Sandra Hammond, the bucolic nineteen-year-old baby-sitter turned housekeeper, was found to be very unco-operative. The police were advised by Sandra's family doctor that she suffered from a serious nervous condition and should not be subjected to interviews. By mid-summer all leads had been exhausted and there was nothing left to go on. The Regina police were left with nothing but their suspicions.

Had they been able to interview Colin's stateside companions, the police might have had better luck. Lynne Dally had become used to Colin's disdain for his ex-wife. What concerned her increasingly was the nature of his obsession. The divorce was settled and the property action was still in the courts, but for Colin the money and the principle that JoAnn could not do this to him, were the paramount issues. He had a solution, one he had been trying to arrange since 1979, well before Lynne entered the picture. She never knew Colin any other way.

Even if every damning thing he said about JoAnn was true (for a long time it never occurred to Lynne that it might not be), surely murder was going too far. Yet, while Lynne maintains that she tried to dissuade Colin from his determined course, she did nothing to inhibit him and cooperated when called on. She may have acted out of fear, a sense of unreality, or an instilled belief that she had something to gain, but certainly not because she doubted Colin's seriousness.

Unlike some who only knew of Colin's professed evil intentions and might have doubted his willingness to carry them out, Lynne was privy to his ongoing arrangements. In 1980 he told her about meetings held on his property with potential hit men, and the failure of that approach. Early in 1981 he told her that someone was obtaining a car and rifle on his behalf.

Colin spoke freely to her of the May 17 shooting, using Ron Graham's condo, to which he had a key, rather than within earshot of the bugging devices he was sure had been placed in his own condo. He told Lynne with glee that the police were brighter and quicker than he had anticipated, and described how he had outsmarted them and their roadblocks by going through the country in his small orange getaway car. Somewhere out there he had ditched the rifle and the red wig he had worn as a disguise. He speculated that the shoulder wounding was a result of his failure to compensate for shooting through glass.

He would later testify that on the evening of the shooting Lynne asked over the telephone if JoAnn was dead, and responded, ''Oh, shit!'' to the negative answer. Lynne does not remember, but says that might have been her reply.

In the same month as the wounding of JoAnn, Colin Thatcher acquired another girlfriend, a young lady, seventeen years his junior, who was immediately very curious about the shooting.

Colin told her that he had hired an American assassin to kill his ex-wife. A few hours before the scheduled attack, he said, he had changed his mind and, with luck, had been able to contact the assassin and alter the instructions to wounding and a good scare. The next time would be different, Colin claimed.

The assassin, Colin told his young travelling companion, was a master of disguise who would look old one day and young the next, so that Colin himself did not know his true features.

Whether or not he was bluffing Tony Wilson or bragging to his lady friends, Colin clearly thought that the wounding of JoAnn gave him an advantage in working out a settlement of the

87

property dispute. He told Lynne Dally: "They're scared now. I can negotiate with them much better."

As the appeal from the $820,000 judgment dragged on, JoAnn and Tony Wilson were not averse to the initiation of negotiations towards settlement. Except for a very brief and fruitless discussion during the trial, the two lawyers, Gerrand and Merchant, had never explored the possibility of a compromise between their clients. Neither lawyer was aware that, prior to the trial, a friend of Colin's, former Conservative leader Dick Collver, had been working on a settlement, and had thought that he had achieved one, only to have it rejected by Colin.

Over the course of several weeks, beginning in July 1981, Tony Wilson and Colin Thatcher carried on reasonable, amicable talks towards settling the property and custody dispute. They actually got a consensus down on paper, but it failed, each side blaming the other for backing away from the deal. They turned it back over to the lawyers.

When Gerrand pointed out that communication between him and Merchant was not possible, Tony Wilson retained his friend W.M. (Bill) Elliott, QC, of the prestigious Regina law firm MacPherson, Leslie and Tyerman. Over the winter of 1981-82, Bill Elliott worked between Gerrand and Merchant, and in February a deal was struck. Colin and JoAnn would settle at $500,000.

The agreement signed by them on February 19, 1982, provided that Colin would pay JoAnn $150,000 immediately, $87,500 on February 1, 1983, the same amount on February 1, 1984, 1985 and 1986, and a final payment on February 1, 1987 of $99,250. Colin was also to pay interest at 10 per cent.

In the event of Colin's death, the agreement provided for a moratorium or suspension of the payments for five years, presumably to enable his complex estate to be straightened out.

Curiously, however, the agreement provided for a similar one-year suspension of payments should JoAnn die.

Colin borrowed $150,000 from the Moose Jaw Credit Union to make the first payment to JoAnn. In between signing that mortgage in mid-January and the settlement agreement in February, Colin was in Palm Springs. While he was there, he bought a gun, a Ruger .357 magnum.

CHAPTER 7

Politics, Palm Springs and Revenge

However unreliable he might be in the Legislature, the Saskatchewan Conservatives found Colin Thatcher's political judgment to be a valuable asset as they developed the platform that was so successful in the 1982 election. Thatcher's instinctive and intuitive assessment "added immeasurably to the weight of correct decision making on the campaign committee," says one Conservative strategist.

In the early 1960s Ross Thatcher's Liberals were able to harness the anti-NDP vote in Saskatchewan, partly because they were free from any association with the Conservative administration in Ottawa which fell in 1963, only a year before the defeat of Woodrow Lloyd. Twenty years later the situation was reversed and the Saskatchewan Liberals, hobbled by the unpopularity of Pierre Trudeau and the Ottawa Liberals, were unable to maintain their position as the alternative to the NDP. It was the turn of the Saskatchewan Conservatives, who, unhampered by any such unpopular association, capitalized upon the growing disenchantment with the NDP government of Allan Blakeney. The replacement of Dick Collver with Grant Devine removed the last reservation the Saskatchewan voters had about changing the government.

In the general election of April 26, 1982, the Conservatives swept Saskatchewan with the greatest electoral victory in the province's history. They won fifty-five of sixty-four seats with 54 per cent of the popular vote.

Premier Grant Devine selected the easily re-elected Thunder

Creek MLA to serve in the new cabinet, and on May 8, 1982, W. Colin Thatcher was sworn in as Saskatchewan's Minister of Mineral Resources. Four months later the name of his portfolio was changed to Saskatchewan Energy and Mines.

On the day he took office, one of the first actions taken by the new minister was to appoint Tony Merchant as solicitor to the Saskatchewan Mining and Development Corporation (SMDC), one of the Crown corporations for which Thatcher had been assigned responsibility. When it became known, the appointment of the Liberal lawyer infuriated the Conservatives. Colin blandly gave assurance that Merchant's retainer would be promptly cancelled but, in fact, he had no such intention and did nothing.

Colin took over his department with flair and confidence, exciting the admiration of his cabinet colleagues as he quickly surrounded himself with people loyal to the new minister. Some staff members were replaced without notice, but ruthlessness was considered to be the order of the day.

No one complained when Colin engaged another Liberal, James Whiteside, a close friend and onetime executive assistant to Premier Ross Thatcher, to perform an appraisal of SaskOil, the government's entry in the oil and gas industry. The executive offices at SaskOil got the message quickly and switched the Crown corporation's objectives from long-term exploration, research and development to short-term profits, in keeping with the new government's philosophy.

Thatcher was a demanding employer who refused to be drawn into administrative detail. In cabinet, Colin was respected for his ability to quickly grasp the core of issues which came before the group. In a government made up of members who had never before served in office, Saskatchewan's Energy Minister received a high rating.

With his personal affairs Colin Thatcher's touch was less sure. His financial commitments had extended far beyond the ability of his cash flow to service them. Yet Colin pressed on as if nothing was amiss.

At the time of the property action trial in the summer of 1980, Colin's indebtedness to financial institutions, including the $425,000 borrowed to purchase land for Greg and Regan, exceeded one million dollars. In February 1982, he had

90

borrowed another $150,000 to make the first payment to JoAnn. He still owed her $350,000.

Colin's joint venture with Bob Gustav was in trouble. He had defaulted on the remaining $288,500 of his agreed contribution, but had induced his partners to keep the development going by promises to pay and had signed promissory notes as evidence of his intention to make good. The notes were not paid.

As late as March 5, 1982, the joint venture was still struggling and Colin agreed to come up with $52,000 within a week to keep it alive. When that undertaking, too, was not met, the joint venture collapsed. A month later, Bob Gustav and the other partners sued Colin Thatcher for their losses.

A month after the commencement of the Palm Springs litigation, Colin and Lynne Dally, planning marriage, began thinking of a more up-to-date home to replace the elderly residence on Redland Avenue. He was attracted to a recently built dwelling on an acreage not far out of Moose Jaw and agreed to buy it. The owner arranged for a formal agreement to be drawn, but, although Colin was in the yard frequently making plans to take possession, he never quite got around to signing the documents, and the transaction failed. The purchase price was to have been $335,000.

Two months later, in August 1982, the Moose Jaw Credit Union lost patience with its borrower Colin Thatcher and made the first overtures towards foreclosing its mortgage loans.

By this time, the Conservatives' fury over Colin's appointment of Tony Merchant as solicitor to SMDC had reached the office of Premier Grant Devine. Colin again promised that the appointment would be terminated but Merchant carried on.

Colin enjoyed the prestige and power of his position. He soon discovered the perks of office — such as trips paid for by corporations — and began to travel extensively. He made several trips to California, to discuss "sensitive matters" with officials of Getty Oil, he said. In November, accompanied by Lynne Dally of Palm Springs, he travelled to Europe.

Lynne Dally had been included in other activities pursued by Colin Thatcher. In California a state driver's licence is required for the purchase of firearms and Colin had advised Lynne that he

91

was obtaining a licence for that sole purpose. From February to June of 1982, she was aware that he kept the handgun he had bought in a local shop in his condominium and that he used empty Perrier and Scotch bottles for target practice in the desert. When Colin asked Lynne to check about obtaining a silencer for his gun, she even made one inquiry for him.

Early in June 1982, Colin applied for and was issued a Firearms Acquisition Certificate by the Moose Jaw Police Department. That document would be required for the purchase of any firearm, whether handgun, rifle or shotgun, but there is no record of Thatcher buying any gun in Canada.

Later that month, in Palm Springs, Lynne saw the gun, wrapped in a *Los Angeles Times* and tightly stuffed inside a "Cindy Shower" toy box, being packed in Colin's suitcase for his return to Canada.

Why had she never warned JoAnn or the police, much less stuck with Thatcher? Theirs was a stormy relationship, full of ups and downs. "It was close and many times it was not," reflected Lynne. There were many break-ups, and both of Lynne's summer-long visits to Saskatchewan were cut short because of disagreements.

In Palm Springs one can have trouble relating to reality at the best of times — it is hard to sit in paradise and identify with the problems of a cold, cruel world. Sometimes during conversation, Lynne comes across as being in a distant world of her own. JoAnn was someone Lynne had never met, who was killed in another country, and was reputedly a bad person anyway. It is conceivable that the reality that something terribly wrong was happening did not fully register with Lynne until it was too late. People, after all, can be callous about things they are far removed from. In Lynne's case, however, reality finally did surface.

It had actually started to on her second visit to Saskatchewan, in the summer of 1981, when she saw a scared JoAnn on television during her news conference regarding the custody of Regan. Her shoulder was still in a cast, and laying eyes on her for the first time, Lynne suddenly realized JoAnn was a real person. But some time between then and the next incident her complacency returned.

Early on in their relationship, Lynne and Colin had twice taken

92

her parents out for dinner. Her father found Colin a bragging bore with whom he did not feel comfortable, and asked his daughter not to include them again in spite of his initial interest in meeting this accomplished Canadian.

Lynne held her father in high regard and valued his opinions, whether or not they coincided with hers. He was prominent and well thought of in The Desert business community, the type who was elected to positions he had not even run for. She talked of him often.

She once told Colin about the legal advice he used to give adulterous clients who did not want to lose their families — "deny, deny, deny." Colin loved the line, and started to recite it himself. Little did he know that the phrase would become a widely notorious feature of his vocabulary when he in turn used it in advice to one Garry Anderson in a different context.

Semantics aside, Colin's denials and lies were just one more flaw Lynne learned to live with. When he said he was forty-two years old, but his driver's licence and his sons said he was forty-four, he insisted they were wrong. Every time he added Grecian Formula 44, used to keep the grey out of hair, to the household shopping list, he would deny it was for his own use, saying it should be around for company. He would even deny to Lynne's face having ever hit her, or any woman for that matter.

Colin even created a new image for himself in Palm Springs, magnifying his wealth and connections. His worth became twenty, thirty or forty million. He became a crony of Canada's prime minister and a nephew of England's. He alluded to a Learjet he did not have.

"He was a pathological liar to the point that he believed what he said," observed Lynne.

One apparent lie was to cause Lynne more embarrassment than amusement. Colin often told her that he wanted to get married, but Lynne didn't take him seriously. In the spring of 1982, however, a barrage of roses and other flattering attentions convinced Lynne that he was sincere. With Colin's consent, she announced the news to her family and friends, burned her bridges, and left for Canada.

Lynne did not want a formal engagement and ring. Both agreed it would be inappropriate for two people over thirty. The wedding was to be in Moose Jaw. There would be a new house — Lynne could design it — but Colin had already chosen the plot on his rural land. Both the Redland Avenue house and another Colin owned on Simcoe Avenue would be sold.

Colin was low key but, after all, it would be his second time. Like any prospective first-time bride, Lynne talked about their intentions to everyone, including Colin's mother, children, employees and colleagues. Slowly she realized the only one she could not discuss it with was her future husband. True, the houses were up for sale and they had discussed their new home — but that was it.

"He kept lying, and I'm only stupid to a point. One evening I confronted him. I said we've got to talk about this, and he became violent, verbally and physically."

Colin's later explanation in court did not sound like the same incident. He claimed the boys and Lynne had disagreed over what music to play, and that because of the tension she was causing, he asked her to return to Palm Springs. On the subject of marriage, he would only say that Lynne had a misconception from the outset.

They do concur on the second stage of the incident, if not the reason: Lynne attempted suicide. But half an hour after taking an overdose of Colin's 292's, Lynne realized he was not worth killing herself for, so she went upstairs to get help. Colin had gone straight to bed after the showdown, and Lynne found him deep in an undisturbed sleep.

The incident ended with a discreet visit to the Moose Jaw Union Hospital in the company of Colin and Greg. Lynne was given ipicac, an oral medication which induces vomiting, and shortly afterwards returned to the house. She got the impression that Colin's first concern was for his reputation, not her well-being, but he did treat her with more consideration for a while.

Incredibly, the relationship dragged on.

Colin was twelve years older than Lynne, but in many ways he was less worldly. She was more cultured, and had no luck interesting him in literature or the arts. Colin depended on her savoir faire, even down to telling him which wine to order. She had done the drug scene in her youth, but Colin tried it now.

94

Lynne had also taught Colin much about sex. In their capacity to consume large quantities of alcohol — usually expensive Scotch — they were even.

Neither, however, was well-travelled. In October and November of 1982 Energy Minister Thatcher visited Europe, accompanied by Lynne. It was the first time either had been out of Canada and the United States.

They flew first class, stayed in posh hotels, ate at the best restaurants, and were chauffeured everywhere. Colin was oblivious to his new surroundings, and uncomfortable when faced with unfamiliar situations. Lynne, her dream come true, was wide-eyed and eager. "I don't pretend to be a sophisticated traveller." She exhibited none of Colin's nonchalance.

In London they took a suite at the elegant Savoy, on the Strand overlooking the Thames River. Lynne slept off her jetlag while Colin made his rounds. Returning to collect her for supper, he advised her that she had missed meeting his Aunt Maggie, Great Britain's Prime Minister Thatcher. Later Colin came clean — Aunt Maggie had been out of town. The rest of the truth, that the two Thatchers were unrelated, never came from his lips.

There was one thing Lynne had to have to show for her European travels, a classic Burberry trench coat. Douglas, the chauffeur, deposited them at the internationally famous store, and Lynne picked out a pricy, top-of-the-line style. "I'll wear it my whole life," she rationalized to Colin. "For that price, your grandchildren had better be wearing it," Colin wittily chided as he produced his credit card.

Returning from the last London supper in a smart basic black dress and pearls, Lynne was feeling content. This was the life she would like to become accustomed to. Then suddenly she was being knocked around the room.

Apparently, she had been brought along for one reason only, and it was not to have headaches. She passively conformed to Colin's expectations, and, after essentially being raped, quietly arranged a second room for the night.

In the morning she called Colin to ask for her plane ticket and was turned down. After some futile negotiation with the airline, she approached Colin again, reconciled, and proceeded to Paris with him. Lynne had wanted to see Paris all her life. Nobody was going to rob her of that opportunity now. Among the gifts she picked up there was a navy police smock for Stephanie.

Things improved as the two-and-a-half-week trip progressed. After Paris they made several stops in West Germany, and then Colin had their return rerouted through Paris, as a special favour for Lynne. He was not so bad after all. They spent a romantic evening in their hotel room at the Intercontinental, in the most romantic of all cities, then returned together to Moose Jaw.

It was Lynne's fourth visit to Saskatchewan. In fateful 1984 there would be a fifth and sixth. Colin would be paying for those too — dearly.

Early in 1982, with the litigation behind her, JoAnn paid up her legal bills and started a new life. She and Tony Wilson had formed a business, Radius 2 Interiors, which enabled her to work in the field she loved best, interior design and decorating. She was ambitious and determined and soon developed a respectable clientele among Regina's business and professional community, concentrating on office layout and furnishing.

In the fall of 1982, JoAnn was asked to design a suite of executive offices in downtown Regina for the new chairman of SaskOil, one of Saskatchewan's Crown corporations. It was an attractive offer, exactly the sort of work JoAnn was actively pursuing. Unfortunately, the offer came from the new chairman himself, W. Colin Thatcher, and good sense forced JoAnn to decline the commission.

JoAnn's unusual strengths had stood her in good stead as she struggled to rebuild her life. She had come through a very burdensome time, was still under heavy siege, and was not only coping but showing every sign of enjoying life. A Regina psychiatrist who had assessed Regan and who testified at the second custody trial in the summer of 1980 also spoke of JoAnn. His description was of a "very strong woman, mature in most ways, a good mother, a homemaker, [who] carried a tremendous amount of responsibility through her years of marriage, well educated, superior intelligence, and with a great deal of warmth towards her children." JoAnn, the psychiatrist said, "had undergone an incredible amount of stresses over the past year and a half and had come through it rather remarkably well."

Her own depth and resilience had surprised JoAnn, who had not previously tested her character to such an extent and who had not anticipated the hardship that had befallen her. Testifying at the same trial, she told the court, "If I had not been a determined person, I would not have survived this year."

Attractive and always pleasant, with the toughness not showing, JoAnn was seen bustling about downtown Regina on behalf of Radius 2 Interiors.

While JoAnn was more than ready to leave the past behind, Colin was not. At a bull session of Conservative MLAs, not long before, the members had been discussing some of the policies of their government, over drinks. One member suggested jocularly to the Thunder Creek MLA that he could use the new farm loan program to pay off the heavy settlement to JoAnn. "That will be the day when a bullet costs a dollar," replied Thatcher.

At about the same time as the offer to JoAnn in October 1982, Colin Thatcher secured a nondescript car from Garry Anderson, an acquaintance from the Caron district. Anderson had provided a similar service to Colin in May 1981. Colin kept the car for several days during which time it was impounded by Wascana Centre Authority police for overparking in the grounds of the Legislature. Colin reclaimed it and returned it to Anderson.

That same month of October, on a commercial airline flight into Regina, Saskatchewan's Energy Minister Thatcher, who had imbibed too well, confided to a Moose Jaw acquaintance that he expected to have daughter Stephanie back with him in January. Her nanny would be leaving, Colin explained, and JoAnn was too busy with her new firm to look after the little girl.

Ten days before Christmas 1982, Colin, who was in Palm Springs, telephoned JoAnn and asked if Stephanie might join him in California for the Christmas holidays. Because JoAnn and Tony had holiday plans of their own with Stephanie over Christmas, Colin's proposal was refused.

Colin spent three weeks in Palm Springs over Christmas and the New Year. He enjoyed the holiday, perhaps more than usual. Mixing business with pleasure, he made a trip to Los Angeles to discuss heavy oil with officials of a major oil corporation. The corporation was pleased to send its executive jet to Palm Springs to pick up Saskatchewan's Energy Minister for the meeting.

Energy Minister Thatcher returned to his office on January 10. Almost immediately he arranged to have a new Central Vehicle Agency car temporarily assigned to him. He was issued a blue Oldsmobile.

Premier Grant Devine had reached some resolutions over New Year's and had a serious matter to discuss with his Energy Minister upon the latter's return. The mild-mannered premier had decided he could no longer accept Colin's insubordination with respect to the continued employment of Tony Merchant by SMDC. There were one or two other similar examples of Colin's ignoring the wishes of Conservatives and even fellow ministers in patronage appointments. The premier was being urged by other members of his cabinet to divorce the government from the maverick Thatcher. Colin's earlier public criticism of Devine and his refusal to give up Thunder Creek had not created a well of good favour that could now be drawn upon. The two discussed the matter over a couple of days, but the premier did not permit the outcome to be in doubt. Colin would not be permitted to continue in the cabinet. To Devine's surprise, Colin was most concerned about the loss of his government car, credit cards and ministerial expense account, and the premier kindly assured him that these perquisites could be settled up at a later date.

On Friday afternoon, January 14, 1983, it was all over. Colin Thatcher, Saskatchewan's Energy Minister, would resign, citing the usual family and financial reasons. Colin returned to his office, advised his staff of his firing, poured a few drinks, and then broke down in tears at the loss of his job.

Since the split with JoAnn, Colin had been juggling the political, business and personal sides of his life at an ever increasing pace. The week of January 17, 1983, all three plot lines reached a climax.

On Monday, January 17, the news of Colin's resignation from cabinet became public, with an announcement to the press. Premier Devine personally wrote Tony Merchant to advise him of the termination of his appointment as solicitor to the Saskatchewan Mining and Development Corporation. This time the termination was effective.

W.M. Elliott telephoned to remind Colin that, under the

98

settlement agreement, a payment of $87,500 was due to JoAnn at the end of the month.

Later in the week, the Moose Jaw Credit Union gained court approval to foreclose on Colin Thatcher's farmland. Colin's creditor was still a long way from realizing upon its security, but this story, too, made a splash in the press.

Also on Monday, January 17, Tony Wilson phoned JoAnn at the offices of Radius 2 Interiors to tell her of the ouster of Colin from Premier Devine's cabinet. As JoAnn hung up the phone after hearing the news, an associate heard her say, "Now I'm nervous."

"Why?" asked the associate.

"Colin is out of the cabinet. Now he has nothing to lose. When he was a cabinet minister he couldn't afford the bad publicity, but now he is free to go after Stephanie any way he wants."

Later that Monday, in the late afternoon, a blue car was parked on 20th Avenue in Regina, just west of the home of JoAnn and Tony Wilson. In the car sat a bearded man.

The car and the man were there again on Wednesday, and again on Thursday.

The next day was Friday, January 21, 1983.

CHAPTER 8

January 21, 1983

Marja Leena Lahtinen left the Wilson home on Albert Street before eight o'clock that Friday morning. The twenty-one-year-old Finnish girl had come to Canada a year and a half earlier to work for JoAnn and Tony Wilson as a housekeeper. She was also assisting them with the business, Radius 2 Interiors, and it was to those offices Marja went early that Friday morning, leaving JoAnn, Tony and Stephanie still at home.

There was a touch of flu in the Wilson household. Stephanie was not well and would be staying home from school that day. Tony was suffering too. He tried going to his office, but came home early that afternoon. Marja returned later in the morning to care for Stephanie.

JoAnn had a busy day. She had been commissioned to do the interior design for a small building to house the offices of a law firm and spent the morning in consultation with the firm's senior partner, the architect and the engineer. She had a luncheon date at a popular downtown Regina restaurant and an afternoon full of appointments. During lunch, and again early in the afternoon, she telephoned Marja to check on Stephanie's condition.

Colin Thatcher, too, had a busy day. Out at Caron in the morning he kept an appointment made the afternoon before and met briefly with a one-time local resident. The two agreed to meet again in Moose Jaw early in the afternoon of that day.

Colin's men had delivered some wheat to the Cargill grain elevator in Moose Jaw, and Colin dropped in to pick up his cash purchase tickets. The tickets were not ready, but that was "no problem," as Colin cheerfully agreed to drop back for them later. The Cargill manager noted that the often surly Colin was in an unusually good mood that morning.

Back out at Caron, Colin dropped in for coffee at the Caronport Gulf service station. As he entered, the man he had met with earlier was just leaving. The two passed each other without speaking.

Shortly before noon Colin was back at Cargill and this time the grain tickets were ready for him. His good humour was by now so evident that the Cargill employees could not help but remark on his unusual disposition that day.

At one o'clock Colin again met the man from Caron, this time on Henleaze Avenue in Moose Jaw, four blocks west of Colin's home. Colin was walking and borrowed the car brought by his acquaintance, dropping him off at the Moose Jaw bus depot. Shortly afterwards Colin parked another car, the blue Central Vehicle Agency Oldsmobile, on Redland Avenue a couple of doors away from his home.

About four o'clock in the afternoon Tony Wilson gave up at the office, and took his flu home to bed.

JoAnn's afternoon crowded in upon her. She had over-booked herself, and her 4:30 meeting with a client ran overtime, causing her to miss a 5:15 appointment with a consulting engineer. At ten to six she left her meeting, climbed into her Audi 5000 and headed for home. She drove the fourteen blocks quickly, came down Albert Street from the north, swung west on 20th Avenue to the two-car garage behind her home, opened the door with her electronic signal and drove in beside and to the right of Tony's Oldsmobile station wagon. The garage remained dark. The interior lights were not working.

As JoAnn stepped from her Audi, her fur jacket was seized from the rear, forcing the metal clasp, closed tightly against the cold, against the left side of her throat. A rain of blows from a metal instrument began to fall upon her uncovered head.

Stunned and shocked, JoAnn began to fight for her life. There was no escape to the front of the garage, where the cars were parked tightly against the wall, and the 5 foot, 4 inch, 130 pound woman tried to force her way to the back and the open street. In the confined space between the two cars, she could not go around her assailant but had to force him back with her.

101

Still the blows continued. JoAnn fell to her knees and put her leather gloved hands over her head in protection. Her hands and fingers were smashed and her left forearm broken. JoAnn continued to struggle and actually got out from between the cars. Her attacker, perhaps now concerned that she might yet escape, fired a heavy revolver into her right ear. JoAnn fell dead, partially under the rear bumper of her Audi. Scuff marks and blood stains showed that JoAnn's desperate defence had ranged the entire length of the two cars in the garage.

Craig Dotson, a thirty-eight-year-old researcher with the NDP opposition caucus, had just left his office in the Legislative Buildings across Albert Street. He had seen JoAnn pull into her garage and, as he continued his walk westward, he began to hear cries. At first he was unconcerned, thinking he was hearing children at play. As the cries continued Dotson began to imagine a child in distress. Turning, he retraced his steps along the south sidewalk across 20th Avenue from the Wilson garage, looking for the source of the sounds. As he returned, the screams increased in intensity until, punctuated by a loud crack, they suddenly stopped. The noise did not cause Dotson to think of a gunshot.

Dotson, who had not quite reached the lane running across 20th Avenue beside the Wilson garage, saw a man emerge from the garage, walking not running, and turn north up the lane, ducking his right hand inside the left side of his three-quarter-length coat. To Dotson, who had not yet connected the departing figure to the sounds he was investigating, it was as if the other was concealing something in his right hand.

A few feet further and Dotson had crossed the lane and came directly opposite the Wilson garage. When he spotted JoAnn's body, the full realization of what had happened hit him. He ran back to the lane and looked northward after the man he had seen. No one was there.

Dotson approached the garage and JoAnn's body. He saw the pool of blood surrounding her head on the concrete floor and knew she was dead. He panicked a little and, not wanting to go first to the Wilson door, ran across 20th Avenue to the Sandomirsky home where a barbecue had been in progress the night JoAnn had first been shot. Tonight there was no one home to answer the frantic knocking. Dotson ran back across the street to the rear door of the Wilson home and alerted Marja who was in the kitchen making supper. Marja had seen JoAnn's headlights pull into the garage and also had heard the "bang." But the sound was so diminished that she thought it was her microwave oven and had gone over to check its contents.

Marja heard the excited Craig Dotson explain that Mrs. Wilson had been shot and accompanied him out to the garage. Upon seeing JoAnn the girl broke into sobs and ran back into the house to arouse Tony Wilson. Tony, clad only in a bathrobe, came down from his bed and once more Craig Dotson led the way to JoAnn's body. Wilson kneeled by JoAnn for a moment then returned to the house and called the police reporting the shooting of his wife.

The bereaved husband returned to the garage and knelt again by JoAnn. Noting the bare feet and legs in the $-9°C$ January weather, Dotson removed his parka and draped it around Wilson's shoulders. Wilson felt for JoAnn's pulse, then returned to the house and phoned the police again. This time he advised them that JoAnn had not only been shot, she was dead.

In the third week of January 1983, Superintendent Jim Kane made the decision to close his police career and handed in his notice. It was to be effective in June.

His wife, Lois Kane, felt that some celebration and softening of the pain was in order and suggested that they take their grandchildren and spend the weekend in a motel with an indoor pool, a common winter diversion in Saskatchewan. On Friday afternoon, January 21, they drove over to Moose Jaw's Heritage Inn, where the walls in the lounge are hung with replicas of newspaper stories chronicling the deaths of prominent political leaders. Included with Winston Churchill and John Diefenbaker is Moose Jaw's most famous son, W. Ross Thatcher. There was nothing much brewing at the office and Kane, wanting a quiet weekend, did not leave a number where he could be reached.

When the call reporting the murder of JoAnn Wilson came in to the Regina police station at 6:05 p.m., a time that was to become of crucial importance, the Superintendent in charge of Criminal Investigation was relaxing with his family not half a mile north of 1116 Redland Avenue, Colin Thatcher's residence.

Had Kane left his number, he would have been advised immediately. Undoubtedly, as he says, he would have gone straight to the Thatcher home and asked to speak to Colin. And the question of Colin Thatcher's whereabouts in the thirty minutes following the murder would have been settled at the start.

But Kane relaxed in isolated ignorance of the killing until the 11:00 p.m. news ruined his quiet weekend. He returned to duty the next day and relieved Inspector Ed Swayze, who had taken charge of the initial investigation.

The question of Thatcher's whereabouts might have been settled in another way. At 6:40 p.m. Moose Jaw police were asked to put the Redland Avenue house under surveillance. This was done, but not until 7:10 p.m., more than an hour after the murder, and then from a point which did not give a clear view of the front door and none at all of the back. Verification of Colin Thatcher's presence in or absence from his home by anyone not in that home during the critical moments following the murder was now impossible.

Again, not until it was too late did anyone think of the simple expedient of telephoning the residence and asking to speak to Mr. Colin Thatcher.

In this way the door was left open for the alibi defence Colin Thatcher presented at his trial. He was at home with his family all the time, he said. Eating Hamburger Helper, in fact.

Constables Joe Fraser and Steve O'Leary were first at the murder scene, arriving just after 6:05 p.m. They were followed closely by others, including Sergeant Lou Husli and Constable Tom Schuck.

Husli and Schuck spotted a credit card invoice, lying on the snow just four feet from the south-east corner of the garage. It was dated 18 January, 1983, three days earlier, had been made out at the J & M Shell Service Station at Caron, Saskatchewan, and bore the signature of Colin Thatcher. The invoice was dry and had obviously not been exposed to the elements very long.

O'Leary was approached by Duane Adams, Saskatchewan's Deputy Minister of Social Services, who lived a block west of the Wilson home, at 2878 Angus Street. He reported seeing an "older model" dark blue car with a single male occupant that had been parked near his home on the last few days. Adams and his housekeeper, Joan Hasz, had been suspicious of the car and man. Hasz had made a note of part of the licence number.

O'Leary turned the information over to Sergeant George Fonger who, with Sergeant Garry Proctor, was interviewing Joan Hasz by 7:30 p.m.

Hasz, a small, nervous fifty-six-year-old who admitted to having a curious nature, told of the car being parked on 20th Avenue across from the Adams home on several days preceding the murder, always in the later afternoon. On Wednesday, January 19, she became suspicious and began to take more note of the car and the man slouched behind the steering wheel. On Thursday, as she was leaving for the day at 5:00 p.m., she got a good look while cleaning the snow from her car parked behind the other. The strange car's licence plate was smeared with mud, but she was able to pick out the last three digits — 292 — and repeated them to herself all the way home where she wrote them down and hid the writing in a teacup.

The man in the car, Hasz said, wore a long, oval, trim, black beard and a toque. She was not sure about glasses or his age, but guessed him to be in his thirties. He wore a dark jacket. To Joan Hasz, the most upsetting feature about the man was his hands. He seemed to be wearing skin tight, silver-blue gloves, similar to surgical gloves.

The police made prompt arrangements and in a couple of hours Duane Adams and Mrs. Hasz were with Dr. Herman Dillenberg and being questioned further under hypnosis. Their recollections were not materially improved by this.

Twelve-year-old Andrew Stewart had been delivering the *Leader Post* in the 2800 block of Angus Street at 5:45 p.m. that afternoon. He had seen a man get out of a car parked on the east side of Angus and walk east on 20th Avenue towards the Wilson home. When Andrew was in the 2900 block of Angus he heard screaming and a bang which might have been a gunshot. The paper boy continued on his route.

Andrew had seen enough of the man to feel he could identify

him. His description was of a six-footer with a black beard and moustache, younger than thirty years, wearing a dark jacket and a small, round hat.

Andrew could describe the car, too. He remembered it as a two-door older model with big bumpers, brown or green in colour and with a triangular side window at the back.

Craig Dotson sat down with Constable Donna Hodgins-Locke, one of five Regina members who had training in the use of the composite kit, and between them they produced a composite drawing of the man Dotson had noticed at the Wilson garage. Dotson was very uncomfortable about contributing to the composite that evening. Locking Craig Dotson to a reasonably detailed recollection of a figure he had given only a passing glance, later appeared to have been a grievous mistake. Certainly, because the description was clearly not that of the man who would be charged with the offence, it would create a conflict in the Crown testimony at the trial.

To a man, the investigators of the Wilson murder had little or no faith in composites. Sergeant Wally Beaton can recall only once in his career where a composite drawing of a suspect turned out to be useful. Another key member of the investigation team, Staff Sergeant Al Lyons, feels that, because they are so often inaccurate, they frequently steer an investigation in a wrong direction.

But preparing composite drawings of suspects is basic police work and no one in the Regina Police Department the night of JoAnn Wilson's murder was intentionally leaving any of the basics undone.

Sergeant Bing Forbes and Chico of the Regina police canine unit were at the Wilson garage half an hour after the murder. Chico confirmed that the suspect had gone north up the lane but lost the scent a few houses up, just behind 2865 Angus Street.

A careful search of the Wilson neighbourhood, backyards, lanes, even roof tops, turned up nothing. But interviews with the neighbours disclosed an amazing number of people who had noticed the ''older model'' car parked on 20th Avenue watching the Wilson house. Others came forward as word of JoAnn's murder spread throughout the city.

The consistency of the descriptions of the car seen during the week of the murder as "older" caused a fixation in the minds of the investigators. Saskatchewan Government Insurance computers were asked to run down an automobile meeting the description and bearing a licence whose last three digits were 292. By the time the return came back that the car had to be a 1980 blue Oldsmobile 88, registered to the Central Vehicle Agency of the Saskatchewan government, it was obvious that this was so. Police had spotted the car, licence number KDW 292, parked on Redland Avenue in front of Colin Thatcher's home, where it had been all the while. He had taken the car from the CVA on January 10, and it was still signed out to him.

By midnight on the night of the murder Inspector Ed Swayze, who had been early at the murder scene, was satisfied that all initial leads were being run down and that all the routine checks were under way. The registers in all hotels in Regina and within sixty miles were being looked at. Bus, train and plane terminals had been checked and the airline manifests for the last two weeks were coming out of the computers. Car rental agencies, gun and ammunition stores, dry cleaners (bloody clothing), costume shops (beard and wig), would all be checked. An area of several blocks surrounding the Wilson home had been searched and the process of interviewing the residents for the first of three times had begun.

Although Jim Kane would relieve him in the morning, it was Swayze who, in the long run, headed the investigation team. Swayze had been a 24-hour-a-day cop ever since he joined the Regina force in 1960 at the age of twenty. He had lived all his life in Regina and had an intimate knowledge of its citizenry. Some of his schoolmates at Scott Collegiate had taken career paths that brought them into conflict with Policeman Swayze. For bringing down one such, an ambitious young criminal named Harold Junior, Swayze received one of his several commendations. From Junior he also received the nickname "Sam." When a reshuffle allotted Swayze badge number 100, the appellation "Sam 100" was a natural, and it stuck. Although the nickname was suggestive of the fictional detective Sam Spade, the chunky, round-faced and mustachioed Swayze is more reminiscent of Charlie Chan.

107

Swayze prides himself upon being a street cop. He joined the Regina force at a time when rookies were automatically assigned to foot patrol and Swayze spent five years walking a beat before he was assigned to the Criminal Investigation Division. There he was at home, and spent twelve years as a plain-clothes detective before being promoted into the NCO ranks. Even then he was never far from the CID and when he was commissioned as inspector in 1981, he was assigned to his favourite department. Swayze's ambition and outspoken style were not universally admired among the more than 400 members of the Regina force.

Swayze had taken a number of classes at the University of Regina, concentrating in criminal psychology. Among his several advanced police training seminars had been one in forensic pathology at the Ontario Centre of Forensic Sciences. There he had studied the investigation of the death of Christine Demeter which resulted in the trial and conviction for murder of her husband, Peter. The Demeter case was to prove strikingly similar to the investigation of the death of JoAnn Wilson.

Ed Swayze was president of the Saskatchewan Federation of Peace Officers and had been relaxing over an after-work drink with two out-of-town police friends when the call came telling him of the murder of JoAnn. By ugly coincidence, the Regina investigator had been describing the first shooting when he was interrupted.

Some hours later, Swayze identified one final thing that could be done before closing down for the night. After a discussion with Corporal Jim Card of the RCMP, Swayze requested that the Mounties' surveillance team, Special "O," be activated and directed to the Thatcher home on Redland Avenue. By 3:30 in the morning of January 22 "O" was in position. It would record some strange behaviour on the part of Colin Thatcher the next day.

Doug Britton, a senior Crown attorney, had been present at the murder scene in the very early evening and had been available since. Well after midnight he and Swayze conferred and assessed the situation. Neither man had any doubt that Colin Thatcher was responsible for the death of JoAnn, but neither believed that he might have done it personally. It was not logical that such an intelligent and prominent man with so much to lose would accept the terrible risks taken by the killer.

At least two Regina residents — Gerry Gerrand and Mr. Justice M.A. MacPherson — did not agree. Both believed (with good reason in at least Gerrand's case, as it later turned out) that they had incurred the bitter enmity of Colin Thatcher. If he was the killer, and if he had succumbed to his hatred, he might well be on a rampage to settle all scores. They could be next.

Neither man is timid but discretion appeared to be more sensible than valour. Both departed their homes for the night, Gerrand to a downtown hotel and MacPherson to the home of his brother, D.K. MacPherson, QC, of MacPherson, Leslie and Tyerman, the firm founded by their father.

While Swayze and Britton thought that it was far-fetched to regard Thatcher as the actual killer, their argument did not fit the report from the coroner, Dr. Stewart McMillan, describing the injuries suffered by the victim. It was just as illogical that a hired assassin would administer the savage beating JoAnn had received. This was a crime of passion, or insanity, or both.

One thing, however, was extremely clear to Ed Swayze that night. At a horrible price — JoAnn's life — Regina police, still smarting over the failure to solve the first shooting, had been given a second chance. There was no doubt in his mind that whoever had been behind the attempt in May 1981 had struck again. This time failure was unthinkable.

CHAPTER 9

First Leads

On the evening of January 21, Serge Kujawa, QC, Associate Deputy Minister of Justice, received a phone call from Richard Gosse, the deputy minister. Gosse told Kujawa what had happened to JoAnn Wilson. The two discussed the event and its possible implications. The deputy minister suggested that Kujawa make himself available to advise the Regina police during the investigation. Kujawa agreed and passed the word to Inspector Ed Swayze, an old friend, to feel free to call at any time.

Kujawa was accustomed to being assigned to highly publicized homicide cases. Although he was no longer an active prosecutor, during his ten years as Director of Public Prosecutions he had been employed throughout the province as the Department of the Attorney General's trouble-shooter on murder cases that were sensitive or likely to attract criticism.

There was an element of incongruity in giving a case involving the Thatcher wealth and privilege to a Polish-born Russian immigrant who had never tasted either. The youngest of four children, Kujawa had come to Canada in 1928 at the age of four when his father settled on a quarter section bush farm in the St. Walburg district of northwest Saskatchewan. Arriving just in time to experience the "Dirty Thirties," the Kujawas eked out an existence by living off the land. The courteous lawyer will still quickly decline an invitation to dine on wild game.

Kujawa could easily employ Abraham Lincoln's "short and simple annals of the poor" description for his own boyhood. School was a four-mile walk away and homework was done over the family's one kerosene lantern. He went on to normal school

110

and, as an eighteen-year-old teacher, faced forty-six pupils ranging through the first eight grades in a one-room rural schoolhouse.

After little more than a year the Second World War freed Kujawa from teaching, and the army promptly selected the country-wise youth for training as a non-commissioned officer. Discharged just before his twenty-first birthday with a taste for travel and adventure, Kujawa spent some years working from Saskatchewan to British Columbia in jobs varying from lumberjack to aerial-photo salesman to panning for gold. But he never stayed away long from the family farm where a "circle saw" took two fingers from his left hand, adding to his likeness as a member of the Russian nobility in a vodka advertisement.

At the age of thirty, Kujawa entered university and graduated from law school in 1957. Four years later he joined the Saskatchewan Attorney General's Department as a prosecutor and soon developed a reputation as one of the province's fairest and most astute Crown counsel. For several years he handled all the department's criminal cases in the Court of Appeal and the Supreme Court, building up an enviable store of experience and knowledge.

Disguising 200 pounds on a slim six-foot frame, Kujawa is justly proud of his outstanding physical condition and strength. He only recently gave up horizontal handstands from flagpoles and, although he claims to have retired from competition, can still, when provoked, tear the Regina telephone directory in two. He was to be provoked before he was clear of the Thatcher case.

Only the good or foolish will play much poker with Serge Kujawa, whose skill and judgment are no mean assets when transferred to a courtroom.

The Regina police were to call upon Serge Kujawa very early in the JoAnn Wilson investigation. They had another case on their hands the day following the murder.

On Friday evening, as the news of JoAnn's death circulated through Moose Jaw and Thunder Creek riding, a number of Colin Thatcher's political friends and associates gathered at his Redland Avenue residence. Coincidentally, one of the guests was an off-duty member of the Regina Police Department. The political consequences of Colin's "resignation" from the cabinet

111

and JoAnn's death were discussed. When one guest suggested that Colin would undoubtedly be a suspect in the shooting, the cool Thatcher, Scotch in hand, replied, "I came through the last one and it didn't really hurt me politically."

Although the last of his company had remained until after 2:00 a.m., Colin was out of the house shortly after eight o'clock on Saturday morning. He spent fifteen minutes driving around his neighbourhood, apparently checking on the presence of police watchers. The police would later learn that he was also interested in a certain car parked four blocks west of his home. Thatcher then made a trip out to the ranch, stopped for coffee at the Caronport Gulf service station, and returned home.

Shortly after 11:00 a.m. Colin, accompanied in his station wagon by Greg and Sandra Hammond, drove out to the highway and headed east towards Regina. At Belle Plaine, approximately midway between Moose Jaw and Regina, the station wagon suddenly made a U-turn, drove back west and then north on a gravel road. A few miles later another U-turn was made. Colin, for whatever reason, obviously wanted to make sure he was not followed. He was successful and carried on to Regina without the surveillance team.

Colin's group was on a mission to pick up Stephanie. Stopping at the Wilson home in Regina, they were rebuffed and learned that the girl was playing at a friend's house. "We'll talk to Merchant about this," Colin said and drove to his lawyer's home.

On January 1, 1983, only three weeks earlier, some important amendments to the Criminal Code had come into effect. The law had changed substantially and child snatching of the sort Colin had performed at Brampton in September 1979 was now prohibited. Tony Merchant was not aware of the change.

Stephanie was playing at the nearby home of her friend Kristen Kohli. Merchant's wife, Pana, went over to confirm that Colin's daughter was indeed there.

Just before 1:00 p.m. Thatcher's group, accompanied by Merchant, went into the Kohli home and, after a scuffle and ignoring the protests of Kristen's parents, took Stephanie away with them. Mission accomplished, Thatcher and his party returned to Moose Jaw.

112

The police were shocked at the audacity of the manoeuvre. Uncertain what to do, they telephoned Kujawa. "Arrest them," was his decisive advice. Arrest whom? "Arrest Colin Thatcher and Tony Merchant," continued Kujawa who, remembering Regan, had a vision of a light aircraft spiriting one more Thatcher child into the United States and out of the jurisdiction.

Half an hour after the taking of Stephanie, Sergeant Jim Street was in Tony Merchant's home advising the lawyer that he was under arrest for abduction. By 2:15 p.m. the cell doors in the Regina police station had closed behind Colin Thatcher's lawyer.

Kujawa went down to the station where he was greeted by Merchant's angry partners. Lawsuits for false arrest and imprisonment were threatened, and Kujawa remembers being assured that he "would be walking in his stocking feet." No actions were commenced.

The usual documents were completed and Merchant was released upon his undertaking to appear to the criminal charges of abduction and mischief. Thatcher was similarly charged.

Later in the afternoon, four Regina police sergeants led by Wally Beaton arrested Colin Thatcher at 1116 Redland Avenue. It was not a difficult arrest as Colin readily agreed to return to Regina with the officers.

Stephanie was returned to the home of Tony Wilson. Gerry Gerrand had secured another court order confirming that the girl would stay with her step-father, but another battle over permanent custody was about to begin.

Arriving at the Regina police station about 7:00 p.m., where Tony Merchant was waiting, Colin was questioned by Beaton as to his whereabouts at the time of the murder the evening before. Colin said he had been at home most of the afternoon, had gone out to the ranch about four o'clock, returning about 5:30 or 6:00 p.m., where he had remained all evening except for jogging between 7:30 and 7:45 p.m.

Shown the credit card invoice found at the Wilson garage, Colin promptly admitted that it was his and that it bore his signature. He had no explanation as to why it had been where it had been found.

Colin told Beaton that he had received threatening telephone calls in California and at the ranch and that he had later identified the voice as belonging to Tony Wilson's son, Willie. Colin said that he had been so upset by the threatening phone calls that he had inquired about hiring off-duty policemen for his own security.

On Sunday afternoon Beaton and Sergeant Gene Stusek again visited Colin at Redland Avenue. This time Beaton discussed with Colin the idea of a polygraph examination. Colin neither refused nor agreed; he said he would discuss the proposal with Tony Merchant.

Almost at the same time that Sunday afternoon Ed Swayze telephoned Tony Merchant and appealed to him for a polygraph examination of his client to eliminate him from the investigation. Merchant took the request under consideration but phoned back shortly to say that Colin was not prepared to take the polygraph because of the abduction charges. Swayze explained to no avail that Merchant could approve the questions to be put and that they would in no way reflect upon the abduction charges.

The police attached no special significance to these refusals of a lie-detector test. Almost no one who checks first with a lawyer ever goes near one of the machines.

That same Sunday afternoon, Gerry Gerrand opened his files on *Thatcher v. Thatcher* to Serge Kujawa, Doug Britton, and Sergeants Jim Street and Bob Murton. Jim Street had been at Gerrand's house the night of the murder and, although he did not disclose it, had been impressed with the emotion the lawyer had shown at the death of his client who had become a friend. The hard-bitten Street regarded one murder as much the same as another, but the incident had caused him to put the JoAnn Wilson case in a somewhat different category.

Gerrand's files contained two documents that he particularly wanted to bring to the attention of the police. The first was the $500,000 settlement agreement that had been negotiated between Colin and JoAnn a year earlier and which, in the event of her death, provided the strange one-year moratorium on the $87,500 payment otherwise due at the end of January. The second was Tony Wilson's written account of his weird conversation with Colin shortly after the first shooting.

Gerrand also reminded the investigators of the public

114

statement JoAnn had made in July 1981, in which she described the attempt on her life, slashed tires and other unpleasant incidents that had plagued her. Street later took a warrant out to CKCK-TV and seized copies of the film tapes of the press conference.

Gerrand told the investigators that he was completely convinced that Colin Thatcher was responsible, either directly or indirectly, for JoAnn's death. The lawyer felt that his own life was in jeopardy, and that others were also. The Crown and the police were in agreement with Gerrand on all aspects, but could only offer understanding.

So ended the weekend following the Friday night murder: the investigators had strong suspicions, and that was about all. But the team that would pursue Colin Thatcher over a long, meandering trail was already in place. There was Jim Kane, overseeing the investigation, and Ed Swayze, heading it. Down the ladder from them, the core team included Al Lyons, Wally Beaton, Jim Street and Bob Murton. All of them were colleagues in the Regina police homicide unit.

Wally Beaton was one of the senior members of the unit. Older than his peers because he was thirty before he began his police career, Beaton was one of the most effective "street cops" on the unit. A bulky six-footer, his affability enabled him to maintain a good network of connections in the sub-strata of Regina society. Almost half of his nearly twenty-five years on the force had been spent in major crime investigation and he had more than fifty murder cases behind him when Sergeant Bob Murton called him away from his supper table to attend the murder scene at the Wilson home.

Already there was the head of the major crime unit, Staff Sergeant Al Lyons, a veteran of forty murder cases who had taken charge of coordinating the investigation. Lyons, whose hawklike features belie his droll sense of humour, was a meticulous cop. He would spend the equivalent of more than a hundred man-days on the Wilson murder case. It would be the last case for both him and Wally Beaton.

Fifteen years earlier, Lyons had been kidnapped by a parolee

115

out of Toronto and driven at gunpoint into Montana, through roadblocks and a border crossing he would have occasion to visit again during the investigation just beginning.

The kidnapping had been spotted thanks to Jim Street's alertness. To his friends on the force the slight and wiry Street is an anachronism, a frontiersman born out of his time. To the twenty-year dogged and aggressive cop, "the street" is where he belongs; uniform and desks are for others. A congenial and sly investigator, Street has rare courage which would be called upon before the Wilson murder investigation was closed.

Another major crime investigator, chunky, easy-going and cheerful Bob Murton (soon nicknamed "Barney Rubble" by the press) became dedicated to the Wilson murder investigation. Good at maintaining his contacts, Murton would succeed in prying loose some very useful information.

The team that coalesced shortly after the Friday night murder would rely on many more officers from various forces, in particular Gene Stusek and Marv Malnyk of the major crime unit.

Early Monday morning, Wally Beaton, who believes that the best information in criminal investigations comes unsolicited, received an anonymous phone call from Moose Jaw. The caller told Beaton about a man who once lived near the Thatcher ranch, who had a history of violent acts, had done time for some, and who might be capable of the kind of violence under investigation. The man's name, the caller told Beaton, was Garry Anderson.

That same morning Al Lyons discovered that Wascana Centre police, who patrol the area surrounding the Legislative Buildings, had seized a 1978 Chevrolet for overparking on October 16, 1982. The car had been claimed by an angry Colin Thatcher, supposedly on behalf of a friend of his sons. The only remarkable thing about the car was the fact that, although the car itself was clean, the licence plates were smeared with mud, making it difficult to read them.

The Chevy was registered to Village Rental Centre Ltd. of Saskatoon, a Rent-a-Wreck agency. It had been rented from October 6 to 19 by one Bruce Anderson of Lethbridge. Some fast

116

checking was done with Lethbridge and Moose Jaw police and RCMP in La Ronge in Northern Saskatchewan. This produced the information that the renter was, in fact, Garry Anderson of Moose Jaw, who was then working in La Ronge, but who had been back in the Moose Jaw area for the past week.

Moose Jaw police were aware that Anderson was back in town. The bearded Anderson was not unlike the composite drawing Craig Dotson and Donna Hodgins-Locke had put together, and, whenever the Moose Jaw men spotted him, they observed carefully and reported quickly to Regina. On Tuesday night, Moose Jaw Constables Dunn and Reiger adroitly cornered Anderson in a restaurant and forced some seemingly casual conversation. When the subject was changed to the JoAnn Wilson murder, the two peace officers noted a sudden reddening of Anderson's complexion, although he did not slip a word in his conversation.

On the day of the murder Corporal Ken Hagerty of the Moose Jaw force had seen both Anderson and Thatcher at the Caronport Gulf station. As Anderson was leaving, Colin arrived and took Anderson's chair. It was an interesting connection.

The Regina police quickly learned a great deal about Garry Anderson. Thirty-seven years old, 6 feet 3 inches, 230 pounds, he had been raised on a dirt farm in the poor soil region southwest of Caron, where his mother still lived. He had a high school diploma, a year's general study at Aldersgate Bible College in Moose Jaw, and two years of business administration at the Saskatchewan Technical Institute, also in Moose Jaw.

Anderson had not developed much of a career and had tried a number of jobs before discovering collections, which he seemed to enjoy. He was a hunter and an outdoorsman, and the northern community of La Ronge suited him perfectly.

He had a complex personality with a flash temper and a problem with alcohol, all of which had combined in a failed marriage and a criminal record with some time served for offences such as assault and pointing a firearm. But Anderson had brought his difficulties with alcohol under control and had been a member of Alcoholics Anonymous for three years.

By Wednesday the Regina investigators knew that Anderson would be heading back north by bus and that they wanted to talk

117

to him. Wally Beaton and Gene Stusek dropped in on Anderson as he was having lunch in the Regina bus depot. He agreed to be interviewed at the police station and they waited while he finished his meal.

At the station Anderson told Beaton and Stusek that he had been in the Moose Jaw-Regina area since the nineteenth, staying with his mother on the farm at Caron, visiting about and having some dental work done.

For the previous Friday Anderson described activities in Moose Jaw during the afternoon and evening that, if substantiated, would make him unavailable to do murder in Regina at six o'clock. Beaton and Stusek promptly checked the alibi. It was confirmed. Anderson had been in Moose Jaw from 5:00 p.m. until after 6:00 p.m.

Anderson told Beaton and Stusek that he had left the Chevrolet on the grounds of the Legislature the previous October. He did not explain how it was that Colin Thatcher had got it back for him after it had been seized, but he did know Thatcher and admitted speaking to him on Friday morning at the Caronport Gulf station.

As Beaton said goodbye to Garry Anderson on his way back to La Ronge, his instincts told him that he would be talking to this man again. But he had no idea that he was watching almost the entire case against Colin Thatcher walk away.

On Monday, the day the investigators first heard of Anderson, the Regina Board of Police Commissioners authorized a $50,000 reward for ''information leading to. . .etc.'' The award was announced the following day, January 25. Behind this was the first lack of consensus in the Regina Police Department about how to handle the investigation. All of the investigators, from Superintendent Jim Kane, through Inspector Ed Swayze, Staff Sergeant Al Lyons to Sergeants Wally Beaton, Jim Street, Bob Murton and others, were opposed to the posting of a reward, perhaps at all, but certainly at such an early stage. The ''street cops'' felt putting up the reward so soon would not only improperly colour the investigation as stymied, but also hamper their efforts by provoking even more time-consuming tips when they were already coping with a plentiful supply.

Chief Vern New thought otherwise. ''If the reward brings

forth information . . . it will probably save the police department money, because it will speed up the investigation process.''

Mayor Larry Schneider stated the reward was being offered because of the complexity of the case and the difficulties police were having ''in coming up with a motive and suspects.''

By the time the reward went up, the police had interviewed a shocking number of witnesses who had seen the strange ''292'' car watching the Wilson household in the days prior to the murder. The investigators were amazed that so many had been suspicious of the car and its bearded occupant, but no one reported the matter to the police. After all, murder had been attempted on that street only eighteen months before. Joan Hasz told the investigators that on the Wednesday before the killing she had been about to telephone the police, but was deterred by her employer. Adams, a deputy minister in the Saskatchewan government, was concerned about the rumours of further firings of senior public servants being plotted by the new Conservative administration and thought that he might be the one under observation. Paranoia was rampant in Saskatchewan's civil service following the change of government the previous spring.

Paper boy Andrew Stewart was the only witness to see the suspect's car parked on Angus Street the night of JoAnn's death. His description was consistent with a 1976-77 Chrysler Cordoba and this was the car he picked out on Sunday afternoon when driven through Regina streets by Sergeant Dale Fleury.

Accordingly, the team was looking for not only the ''292'' car but also Andrew's Cordoba, until Erin Campbell, a Mary Kay cosmetics agent, came to Fleury. Campbell explained that she had been driving a Cordoba in the 2900 block of Angus Street just before 6:00 p.m. on January 21. Fleury got Andrew out of school during recess and he agreed that the Campbell car was the same type he had seen, but pointed out some differences.

Swayze and Lyons were satisfied that Andrew's Cordoba was Campbell's, even though the cars had been a block apart on Angus Street, and they lost interest in Chryslers. They did not think a public statement was necessary, however, and allowed the press to continue reporting police interest in Cordobas. This was the first of several elements of disinformation in the case allowed to be carried on by the media.

119

On Wednesday, January 26, Colin Thatcher drove the blue Olds, licence number KDW 292, to Regina, followed by Sandra Hammond. He parked the car in the grounds of the Legislature, left it and drove back to Moose Jaw with Sandra.

By Thursday, January 27, the CVA had its car back and Regina police had picked it up from CVA and were showing it to their witnesses. Duane Adams identified it without hesitation as the one he had seen the week before. Joan Hasz was not positive, so police parked the Olds on 20th Avenue in the spot she had seen the "292" car.

When Joan Hasz looked out the usual window of the Adams house at the car, she cried, "Oh my God, there it is," and broke down.

Other witnesses, including Margaret Johannson, an employee in the Legislative Buildings, confirmed the identity of the "292" car.

There was now no question but that the CVA car KDW 292, signed out to Colin Thatcher, had been the one on 20th Avenue before JoAnn's death. But was the bearded man behind the wheel a disguised Colin Thatcher? And if it was, was the bearded man Andrew Stewart had seen on Angus Street and Craig Dotson had seen coming out of the Wilson garage the same Colin Thatcher in disguise? Or was there another person involved?

CHAPTER 10

A Long Haul

When Kane and Swayze sat down to assess the evidence from the scene of the crime and attempt to reconstruct what had taken place, they were left with some unanswered questions, questions that would remain unanswered long after the case was closed.

Where had JoAnn's killer been when she drove into the garage? If he had been in the garage itself before she opened the door, he must have been on the far side of the Oldsmobile station wagon to avoid being picked up in her headlights. He could easily have entered the garage through the small door after Tony had parked the station wagon a couple of hours earlier, but the length of the wagon filled the garage from end to end when the large door was closed. To get to the other side of the car, the killer would have had to cross over its hood or the rear bumper, and there was no trace of any such movement.

No one in the Wilson house fit the bill. Only Tony, Marja and Stephanie had been at home. Wilson's two sons had their own residences.

Anyone waiting in the Wilson backyard would have been spotted by Marja through the patio doors off the kitchen. That left the lane or the street; Swayze opted for the former and Kane for the latter. Swayze thought the corner of the garage just up the lane was an obvious spot. From there it was just a few steps to come around behind JoAnn as she stepped from the car. The police dog had shown no interest in that spot, however. Kane thought it more likely that the killer had waited out on the corner of Albert Street, acting like a pedestrian until JoAnn turned the corner and he could follow her down 20th Avenue to the garage. But Craig Dotson should have noticed such a movement as he walked down 20th Avenue on the south sidewalk.

Both investigators decided that there was nothing significant in the fact that the garage interior lights were not working. When they had checked them they found no sign of sabotage; both bulbs appeared to be naturally burned out and Tony Wilson thought they had been in that condition for two weeks.

The beating JoAnn had received, and the instrument it had been performed with, raised a greater question. Aside from the fatal gunshot wound, the pathologist, Dr. J.M. Vetters, had identified head wounds that might have been fatal in themselves. He estimated that these wounds had been caused by at least twenty blows and, in addition, blows had been taken by the hands, arm and face. It was the pathologist's opinion that these wounds had been caused by a "cutting instrument of some weight," perhaps with a curved blade because of the short length of the cuts. Kane and Swayze had difficulties with that. The crime lab ballistics examination of the bullet fragments had concluded that the projectile was a .38 Special fired from either a .38 Special or a .357 Magnum. That was quite a lot of gun. Why was any other weapon needed?

The killer had held JoAnn by her coat collar for a time during the beating, making it difficult for him to handle two weapons. Perhaps the gun had been drawn and used only as a last resort, and was what Dotson had thought he had seen the killer tuck under his coat. What, then, had happened to the other weapon?

Something like a cleaver had been suggested as the second weapon. That did not seem possible. As severe as JoAnn's wounds were, Swayze had seen cleaver wounds and they were far more vicious. JoAnn could not have withstood that many blows from a cleaver.

Kane simplified it. There had been only one weapon, he suggested. The killer had pistol-whipped JoAnn before shooting her. The sharpness of some of the scalp cuts, however, did not support that theory.

On Wednesday, January 26, the Moose Jaw *Times Herald* ran a two-line banner headline across its front page: "CREDIT UNION FORECLOSES ON THATCHER'S FARMLAND."

Underneath the headline, and beside the story of the legal action, was the photograph of a funeral. The caption read: "JoAnn Wilson Buried at Regina Cemetery."

Stephanie was the only member of JoAnn's previous family who attended the burial on the afternoon of the twenty-fifth. Her parents, Harlan and Betty Geiger, her sister, Nancy, and her sister-in-law, Connie, were all in Regina for the funeral and were interviewed that morning by Sergeants Marv Malnyk and Bernie Jeannotte, who had done much of the investigating into the May 1981 shooting of JoAnn.

No one could tell anything that bore directly on the investigation. But Mr. and Mrs. Geiger were able to explain the stories the police had been hearing since the first shooting of JoAnn about Colin's supposed connection to the Mafia. Colin had identified his best man at his wedding to JoAnn, a fellow student at Iowa State, as being the son of a Mafia member.

With the Geigers' help the best man was identified as Joseph Savieno, a district sales manager for Inland Steel in Chicago. No connection with any underworld or illegal activity existed other than in the fertile imagination of Colin Thatcher.

On Thursday, January 27, Colin went back down to Palm Springs, where the Palm Springs police watched him being picked up at the airport by Lynne Dally. He returned to Regina on the following Wednesday, when Special "O" saw him met at the airport by Tony Merchant, with whom he would be appearing in court on the abduction charges the next day.

Ed Swayze was certain that Merchant knew things that would be useful to his investigation. He began to think that the blonde girl in Palm Springs might also.

Wally Beaton had formed the same opinion about Sandra Hammond, who was now practically the Thatcher household major domo, even acting as Colin's constituency secretary.

Beaton learned that Sandra had had a long-time boyfriend, Blaine Mathieson, who was now attending university in Saskatoon. Beaton and Stusek went up and had a chat with Blaine who was pleasant, admitting he had been almost a part of the Thatcher household for some time and had even spent the 1979-80 Christmas holidays with Colin, Sandra and the children in Palm Springs. But he did not seem to know anything useful to the investigation and Beaton and Stusek left, feeling they would be talking to the young man again.

Ed Swayze got the first break through a tip he received. Information is the glue that binds otherwise unrelated facts in an investigation and brings the picture into focus. Every good street cop has a wide range of sources of information, people who come to him with interesting facts or to whom he can go with certain questions and maybe get answers. Ed Swayze had a tremendous number of such sources. He was to use a lot of them, in high and in low places, during the Wilson murder investigation.

On February 1, one of Ed Swayze's connections called with a piece of information that became important enough to earn a recommendation two years later for a portion of the reward.

Ed Swayze had known Gloria Debolt since the 1960s. She had become a derelict of the culture of that time, had recovered, but had been drawn back. She was one of the most accomplished shoplifters in Canada, and had acquired a criminal record for that and other activities. A large woman in her early thirties, Gloria enjoyed her rapport with the policeman whose advice and understanding had often been helpful.

Gloria told Swayze that she had heard that one Cody Crutcher had been paid $5,000 to perform the first shooting of JoAnn Wilson and that she had heard this from Crutcher himself. This last was important to Swayze who had heard bits of the story before but only as a general rumour which was not enough for him to approach Crutcher.

Swayze knew Cody Crutcher had had lots of experience with the police and was not likely to start blurting admissions merely upon being confronted with a story making the rounds. Crutcher was then doing time in Drumheller, Alberta, for being involved in the torching of a surplus Regina apartment building, but Swayze knew that that was about the limit of Cody's nerve. Contract murder was not in Cody Crutcher's line.

What Swayze did not consider at the time, however, was Cody Crutcher's doing a scam, ripping off someone who was willing to pay for murder. That was very much in Cody's line.

A quick check with penal institutions established that Crutcher would have been available in May 1981. He would have to be talked to.

Swayze knew he would have to circle up on Crutcher to protect Gloria, his informant. He would have to get the story from others as well before approaching Cody and this was his play when he and Beaton were over in Drumheller two weeks later. Other inmates had also heard the admission from Crutcher, and Swayze was able to make his approach.

Perhaps, the care was unnecessary. About this time Gloria came to an unpleasant end, choking on her own vomit while under the influence of narcotics.

Cody Crutcher would not say much anyway. But he did tell of a murder contract made in the Fireside Lounge of Regina's Sheraton Hotel. Crutcher would give neither the names nor the occupations of the participants but said there were three, including "a middle man and a top man."

On February 7, Staff Inspector James Majury of the Metropolitan Toronto Police, an accomplished artist in his own right, came to Regina. Ed Swayze and others consider him the finest creator of identification portraits in Canada.

Majury sat down with the Regina witnesses and prepared three new composite drawings. The first was produced under the direction of Craig Dotson and Andrew Stewart, the only two to see the suspect on the night of the killing. The second was prepared with Duane Adams and Joan Hasz and was their version of the man they had seen in the "292" car before the murder. The third was done with RCMP Corporals Milt Wilhelms and Don Forth who had spotted a similar looking man driving the same car near JoAnn's office two days before the killing.

All three drawings were of a bearded man. The Dotson/Stewart beard was fairly long and mostly untrimmed, while the other two were short and neatly trimmed.

Superintendent Jim Kane looked at the drawings with interest. He took a photograph of Colin Thatcher from the *Leader Post* and asked Majury to put the short beard on it. They thought the resemblance was uncanny.

Kane gave his invention to Al Lyons and told him to take it

around to his witnesses. Lyons was shocked. He sputtered in objection, but Kane was only kidding, grimly kidding.

Without much faith Kane updated his reward circular with the new composite and gave it very wide distribution to police forces and penal institutions across Canada and the northern United States. Reports of supposed sightings flooded back from as far away as a harbour patrol in Newfoundland to the campus police in Victoria. The effectiveness of composite drawings in criminal investigations was not to be proven in the Wilson murder case.

Three days after Majury's arrival, Staff Sergeant Tom Barrow of the Calgary Police Department came in to Regina and had hypnotic sessions with Cinnamon Smith, a twelve-year-old neighbour who had seen the "292" car on Monday before the killing, as well as with Joan Hasz and Andrew Stewart. Like Majury, Barrow is highly regarded in his field and, when working with hypnosis, has an edge because of his experience as a peace officer.

All three subjects improved their recall of both car and man while working with Barrow, but no significant breakthrough was achieved. Their recollections squared with the Majury composite drawings.

The day after JoAnn's funeral, seven red roses were delivered to Colin Thatcher at the Redland Avenue home accompanied by a card that read only "See you around." There was no identification of the sender.

Colin promptly called the police. He was unhappy. He had received a similar delivery of anonymous red roses in Palm Springs shortly after the first shooting of JoAnn, in May 1981. Colin had been out golfing and Lynne Dally had accepted the flowers for him. Soon after, Colin received a telephone call, also anonymous, in which the caller had told him, "We know where you are, we can reach you anytime, anywhere. It just doesn't matter, Thatcher, you can't hide."

The Palm Springs roses had come from a local florist but, when Lynne checked at Colin's request, there was no evidence of the sender.

There had been other telephone calls, too. Once, when Colin had stepped into the house at the Caron ranch, something he seldom did, the telephone rang and he answered. ''Just to let you know we're watching,'' said the caller.

If the roses and the calls were intended to ''spook'' Colin Thatcher, they were working. Colin was properly nervous.

Jim Kane had to run down the roses. It was far too likely that whoever was behind them knew something that the Regina police would like to know.

It did not turn out that way. The roses and calls had been organized out of Vancouver by some people who, drawing some quick conclusions about who was responsible for the attacks on JoAnn, thought it would be helpful to keep Colin on edge and jumpy. Former police personnel acquainted with Tony Wilson, they had decided, without his knowledge, to make a contribution to the investigation.

Cunning as it was, the manoeuvre was actually counterproductive as it temporarily diverted the Regina investigation from the main job. The mystery solved, Kane and his men concentrated on their other leads.

By now, mid-February 1983, the Regina police knew they were in for a long haul. They still had plenty of leads to follow, but the case now had the flavour that told them to prepare for an investigation of some duration. Most murder cases that do not break in the first month run to some length, and the Wilson case promised to be no exception.

Inspector Larry Callens offered the use of the RCMP computers to the investigation, and the offer was gratefully accepted. The growing files and reports were fed into the computer system enabling instant call-up and cross-checking of the morass of information. Access to the computers was limited to Superintendent Kane, Inspector Swayze, Staff Sergeant Lyons, and Sergeants Henry Fisher and Al Weselowsky of Regina's special investigation unit.

Meanwhile, the bearded man in the composite drawings and the bearded Garry Anderson kept connecting in Swayze's mind and others. A reasonable hypothesis seemed to be that Anderson, in spite of his alibi at the time of the killing, was involved as an accessory and that one of his functions was to watch JoAnn's movements. Telephone logs showed that Anderson had called from La Ronge to Thatcher's office in the Legislative Buildings on January 10, the same day Colin had taken out the CVA Olds KDW 292. On Monday, January 17, the day Thatcher's resignation was announced, Anderson had called twice.

The Regina police needed to know a lot more about Garry Anderson, and the RCMP put their La Ronge detachment on to him. Some discreet inquiries established that Anderson had been around Regina and Moose Jaw in October 1982 and January 1983, but attempts to interview Anderson himself failed. Anderson told the RCMP that he had consulted a lawyer, Lloyd Balicki of Prince Albert, and had been advised that he did not have to talk to the police. He intended to follow that advice. Anderson suggested the police deal with Mr. Balicki if they had any further questions.

Al Lyons was the first to comment a while later that a lot of potential witnesses in the investigation seemed to feel a need for legal advice.

The weapon is a vital piece of evidence in a murder investigation and Messrs. Kane, Swayze and Lyons wanted to find the gun that had killed JoAnn. The other weapon, if there had been another, was likely much more prosaic and less susceptible to further identification. A gun, particularly a handgun as here, is good, solid, incriminating and, with serial numbers and rifling marks, can be traced and connected to owners and victims. The absence of the gun was another reason the team felt they were not dealing with a professional killer who would probably have used a ''clean,'' untraceable gun and then left it at the scene.

Regina police, like other forces, carry on a brisk trade in guns. In plea bargaining on the street, cops frequently receive offers of information concerning pistols that are illegally kept or have been illegally used. If the price is not exhorbitant, the police usually accept these offers, if only to get the guns out of circulation. Hints on the Regina streets about the police interest in the Wilson murder gun brought no response.

JoAnn's killer would have had his options on getting rid of the gun somewhat reduced by the weather. Saskatchewan in January is a frozen wasteland and a gun would merely bounce wherever it was thrown, on land or water. But there are some methods of making a gun disappear that are good all year around.

In early February, on a day when Sandra Hammond seemed to be in a pleasant mood, affable Wally Beaton scored a hit. Although Sandra told him she was under instructions not to talk to police except in the presence of Tony Merchant, she saw nothing wrong in accepting Beaton's suggestion that she had recently purchased some acid, a gallon of hydrochloric acid, in fact. Colin used it to clean the swimming pool, she explained. "In January?" Beaton thought.

Strangely, Beaton could elicit only an enigmatic smile from the Moose Jaw druggist from whom, Sandra said, she had bought the acid. No confirmation of the sale and no denial.

The RCMP crime lab in Regina told Swayze and Beaton that a gallon of hydrochloric acid would dissolve a handgun in three to four days, perhaps seven days if the weapon was stainless steel.

At the end of February the team came across the first hard evidence that Colin Thatcher had had a gun. Chuck Guillaume, one of Colin's Conservative supporters from Moose Jaw, who had joined the new minister in government service in the spring of 1982, had a gun holster in his desk drawer. He had found it in a CVA car, a blue Ford stationwagon, that Colin had taken out the previous October. Colin had asked Chuck to return the car and, before doing so, Guillaume had checked it and discovered the holster under the front seat. It bore the imprint of the cylinder of a revolver on the interior leather.

When Guillaume had shown Colin what he had found in the minister's CVA car, Colin had airily said, "Oh, really," and neither admitted nor denied ownership.

Other employees in the office of Saskatchewan's Minister of Energy and Mines were aware of the holster Chuck Guillaume had found in the boss's CVA car, but no one found the incident to be so out of character for Colin Thatcher to be worthy of remark.

As the investigation moved into March, the investigation team was able to begin concentrating more on Colin Thatcher. They were interested in his activities on the day of the murder and the preceding days. They were also very interested in talking to some of the people he had been associated with over the years. This

129

called for the exercise of considerable judgment and discretion. Clearly, Colin brought out strong emotions in the people around him. Of these emotions, fear was, perhaps, predominant. Some of these people were fiercely loyal and would have to be handled with care. It would be important to know the warmth or condition of the association between Colin and the subject before the approach was made. The order in which Colin's associates were interviewed would also be critical. Speaking to the wrong person first might destroy the chances of getting any help from another.

The team had been aware of the blonde Lynne Dally in Palm Springs for a good while before they chanced approaching her, and then only after getting a good indication that her relationship with Thatcher had cooled.

Lynne Dally had managed to become blasé about Colin's vendetta against JoAnn. But now she knew he had gone too far and that she had stayed around too long. Even though their relationship was all but over, she had cooperated by being available to make and receive telephone calls, five of them on the day of the killing. When Colin arrived in Palm Springs on January 27, six days after the murder, she went to the airport for the 4:25 p.m. arrival of Sunaire Flight 231 from Los Angeles and picked him up for the last time.

Lynne's lack of a congratulatory attitude was evident.

"You really did it, didn't you?" she scornfully accused. "I can't believe you really . . . How did you feel?"

Lynne was floundering and terrified. She did not know how to react, and maybe Colin did not either. Who knows if there was any remorse in his soon-to-be-famous reply: "Well, it's a very strange feeling to blow your wife away."

The number of women who were more than just friends to Colin Thatcher astounded the investigators. Almost without exception they were young, attractive and blonde. JoAnn had been attractive and blonde.

Not surprisingly, almost all of the ladies in Colin's life continued to be protective of him, although a few contributed considerably to the developing psychological picture of the bachelor under investigation.

The Neufelds and the Wrights, Colin's employees on the

130

Caron farm and ranch, were obvious candidates for interviews with the team. Back in July 1981, while investigating the first shooting of JoAnn, Bernie Jeannotte had interviewed Deborah Neufeld. She claimed her husband Larry had told her of Colin's offering "to make him a millionaire" if he would "get rid of JoAnn." In March 1983, Larry Neufeld denied this or even having heard Colin wishing harm to JoAnn.

Barbara Wright, who lived at the ranch but worked as a nurse at the Moose Jaw Providence Hospital, was interviewed by Wally Beaton in early March. She had been working on January 21, she told him, arrived home at the ranch about 6:00 p.m., and did not see Colin at all that day. She went on to say that she seldom did see the ranch owner when he did visit, as she paid little attention to him.

Beaton was to listen with special interest to the testimony Barbara Wright gave at the trial more than a year and a half later. Her recollection had changed and Beaton was to regret he had not secured a written statement.

On April 13, Wally Beaton was down in Palm Springs, talking to Lynne Dally. Colin Thatcher was also in Palm Springs at that time and, in fact, had been out with Lynne the evening before Beaton walked into her father's hotel looking for her.

Beaton was accompanied by Mike Hall, a detective with the Palm Springs Police Department, a perceptive man who was to be very helpful to the Regina police on more than one occasion.

Talking to Beaton and Hall that April morning in her father's office, the attractive blonde was obviously trying to appear frank, while disclosing as little as possible. She told them of her relationship with Colin, but said nothing that would interest a murder investigator.

As Beaton and Hall left Lynne, the Palm Springs detective remarked on how much she obviously could say and thought they would hear from her again.

At about 6:30 p.m. that same day, Lynne phoned Hall and said she wanted to speak again with Beaton. Hall told her that they had been expecting her to call, that she had obviously not told the truth that morning.

Beaton and Hall went back over to the Sheraton. This time Lynne told them of Colin's bragging about paying $50,000 to

131

have JoAnn "put away," and then having to shoot her himself. Because he had miscalculated the effect on his shot of the glass he had fired through, he had only wounded her. Colin had described his getaway from that first shooting and how he had disposed of the rifle and wig he had used for disguise.

Colin had bought a gun in California, Lynne said, a pistol that he used to practise with in the desert. He had taken it back to Saskatchewan, packed in a doll shower box.

Lynne told Beaton and Hall that, when Colin had been in Palm Springs over Christmas and New Year's, he had arranged with her that she telephone him frequently each day during the week in which the shooting took place. She had done this, and on one such call on the day of the murder, the twenty-first, at 4:30 p.m. Palm Springs time — 6:30 p.m. in Saskatchewan — Colin told her that Tony Merchant had just called with the news that JoAnn had been shot and killed.

That phone call, its exact time, and Beaton's knowledge of it, were to figure very prominently at the trial and even in the arguments before the Saskatchewan Court of Appeal two years later.

Lynne Dally's father, Hank, had given his daughter the same advice about talking to police that Colin Thatcher was to give Garry Anderson. Lynne was anxious that her father not find out that she had not taken his advice, particularly since she was sure that she had now put her own life in jeopardy.

No, Lynne said in answer to Beaton's question, she did not think she would like to go to Canada to testify at a murder trial.

It was Wally Beaton's opinion that Lynne Dally would not make the best of witnesses anyway. He would later admit to having called that one wrong.

Back in Saskatchewan, Al Lyons discovered that another potential witness, Blaine Mathieson, had consulted a lawyer. Wondering about a case where the baby-sitter's boyfriend needed a lawyer, Lyons sent Bob Murton back to find out why.

At first Blaine was still reluctant to talk, but a few days later, in mid-May, he reconsidered, called Murton and came in.

It was quickly obvious why Blaine Mathieson had felt nervous enough to get legal advice. He had not been around the Thatcher household at the time of the murder, but he had been almost a member of the family in 1981 and he knew a great deal about the shooting of JoAnn in May of that year.

Blaine told Murton that, for the week prior to the shooting, Colin had possession of an orange-coloured Mustang which had been rented from Scott-Ford in Moose Jaw. He drove it only at night and while disguised with a hat and dark glasses. On the Thursday, three days before the shooting, Blaine looked into the Mustang parked in the Thatcher garage. On the floor in the back was a rifle. He had seen that rifle before in Colin's truck.

Sandra Hammond and Blaine Mathieson had been very close and Colin's girl Friday kept her boyfriend well informed about the anti-JoAnn activities at the Redland Avenue house. She told him about moving funds by cheque from Colin's accounts through her own and returning them to him in American currency. Blaine told of seeing Sandra, in the spring of 1981, put approximately $1,000 U.S. in a paper bag and place it in a fertilizer spreader in the alcove between the house and the garage.

Although their relationship had been over for some months by then, Sandra had phoned Blaine with the news of JoAnn's death the day after it happened. Blaine felt that they should have reported what they knew after the first shooting, said so, and asked Sandra if she, too, felt remorseful. Sandra denied knowing anything. Shortly afterwards Blaine consulted a lawyer and suggested Sandra do the same. She refused to discuss the matter.

When Blaine Mathieson finished talking to Bob Murton, he explained that he had not earlier volunteered the information he had about the first shooting of JoAnn out of fear of the power of Colin Thatcher.

Jim Kane wasted no time in checking out Mathieson's story about the rented Mustang. He went along with Murton to Scott-Ford, the Moose Jaw Budget Rent-a-Car agency, and found that Garry Anderson had rented an orange ("bittersweet") 1981 Mustang from May 13 to May 18, 1981. The initial rental had been from the thirteenth to fifteenth, but on the fifteenth Anderson had extended it three more days. The Mustang had been sold and was now in Lethbridge, Alberta.

Jim Kane was very meticulous. He spent days pouring over the mass of reports and statements that built the files on the Wilson murder into the most voluminous in the station. He was good at picking out things that could do with a little follow-up.

Kane spotted the reference in Lynne Dally's statement about Colin's packing the gun in a doll shower box for the trip to Saskatchewan. He asked Tony Wilson to check nonchalantly with Stephanie about this. Yes, Wilson reported back, Colin had given Stephanie a doll shower and it was in the house on Redland Avenue.

Kane thought the fact that they could now establish that the Mustang rented by Anderson had been used in the May 17, 1981 shooting of JoAnn Wilson, might cause the man in La Ronge to become more cooperative. Anderson had been following his lawyer's advice carefully. In May, Gene Stusek and Bob Murton had gone to La Ronge to talk to Garry Anderson. He had ordered them out of his apartment.

Early in June, Kane called Anderson, but got nowhere. Anderson hung up on him. Kane telephoned Lloyd Balicki, told him of his client's involvement with the Mustang car and asked for help. Balicki passed the information to his client but Anderson would not comment, saying he wanted to consider his situation.

On June 30, Superintendent Jim Kane turned his office over to his successor, Superintendent Dave (Dutchie) Giljam, and retired after thirty-four years of service. Giljam did not have the same penchant for file reading that Kane did. Dutchie spent a day reading the material on the Wilson murder investigation. The files were by now about two feet thick.

By summer, one loose strand arising from the murder had been resolved — satisfactorily from Colin Thatcher's point of view.

Shortly after the killing, Tony Merchant launched another application to secure custody of Stephanie for Colin. Tony Wilson and Gerry Gerrand decided to hit the issue dead on. They filed an affidavit in which, in effect, Wilson accused Colin of having murdered JoAnn.

In the affidavit Wilson recounted the conversations he had had with Colin after the May 1981 shooting and then described a telephone conversation with Colin about a week after the killing of JoAnn. Colin wanted to discuss visiting rights with Stephanie but Wilson told him "that there was no way I was going to

134

discuss any of these matters with the person who had arranged for the murder of my wife." Colin, Wilson said, "made no response to this assertion."

"Nonsense," Colin said in his affidavit in reply.

The press leaped on Wilson's accusation, privileged because it was made in court proceedings. Stories ran saying that Colin Thatcher was alleged to have "orchestrated" his wife's murder.

Some of Gerrand's senior colleagues at the bar thought that this was going a little too far and Gerrand agreed that he had perhaps become more emotionally involved in the case than a good lawyer should. He advised Tony Wilson to retain another solicitor and retired from the custody dispute.

The court determined that Stephanie would stay with Tony Wilson at least until the end of the school year. By agreement she went to Moose Jaw for the summer, and then Tony Wilson, too, gave up, withdrawing his claim to custody of the girl. All three of Colin's children were finally home.

"We won," stated Tony Merchant.

CHAPTER 11

The Accomplices

After Jim Kane's retirement as Superintendent of Regina's Criminal Investigation Division in June, the Wilson murder investigation began to get bogged down. The loss of the spark Kane had provided was not the reason. That began to show only later, in the fall. What happened was that the investigation team ran out of pay dirt. Their leads petered out.

They had found the Mustang car used in the May 1981 shooting of JoAnn, and in July they found a 1974 Mercury that was probably the car that had been driven by the murderer on January 21, 1983, but not much more hard evidence of consequence turned up for months. By fall the investigation showed signs of failure.

After locating the Mustang in Lethbridge, the police brought it back to Regina, refitted it with rear window louvres as it had been in the spring of 1981, and showed it to Terry Stewart and Pam Gerrand. Pam had "a gut feeling" that the car was the one she had seen on Angus Street the night of the shooting, but Terry was unsure. To him the car had a different coloured roof. Blaine Mathieson, who had been taken over to Ablerta to see the car, was almost certain it was the one he had seen in the Thatcher garage with the rifle in the back.

At the end of July, Bob Murton and Jim Street interviewed Betty Ann Nagy of La Ronge. Nagy had been living with Garry Anderson since 1980 at Lethbridge, Caron and La Ronge. The team had heard of a small tiff between the two and moved quickly, hoping Nagy was sufficiently upset to talk to them. She was. She told Murton and Street that Anderson had gone down to

Regina and Moose Jaw in January, in a 1974 tan/brown Ford product, but had returned without the car, travelling by bus.

The next day Murton and Street were at Caron. It did not take long to locate a 1974 Mercury Montcalm, unlicensed, parked on a farm where Garry Anderson had left it in January. It was promptly towed to Regina and turned over to the RCMP crime lab and the Regina Identification Section, who examined it carefully but came up empty.

The Mercury fitted much of the description Andrew Stewart had given of the car he had seen on Angus Street the night of the murder.

This was one more tie-in to Garry Anderson, and Ed Swayze decided to increase the pressure on the La Ronge holdout.

RCMP Sergeants Carl Monaghan and Doug Anderson had worked in narcotics for several years and had come to know Garry Anderson well as a denizen of the Moose Jaw jungle. A strange friendship had developed between the two narcs and the large but immature man who liked to emulate the police by playing at surveillance and driving cars similar to their pursuit vehicles.

Swayze enlisted Monaghan and Anderson who, with the approval of Inspector Callens, went up to La Ronge to see if they could prevail upon the suspected accomplice to come clean.

On an early September afternoon the two RCMP sergeants visited Garry Anderson at the office where he was working as a collector for the Government of Saskatchewan. They were received well by Anderson who immediately perceived the reason for their visit. Anderson was visibly shaken and quickly went into a tirade about the earlier police visits he had received. He yelled that his phones had been bugged, his office and home searched, and that he and his friends and relatives had been harassed. The big man was obviously paranoid, insisted he had nothing to say, and referred his visitors to his lawyer in Prince Albert.

Monaghan and Anderson persisted, succeeded in calming their subject and, pointing out that he was deeply involved, suggested it would be in his best interest to be cooperative.

All three men were careful not to use the words "Wilson" or "Thatcher" as references, but no one was in doubt as to what

137

was being discussed and Anderson made no denial of his involvement or knowledge.

He would reveal nothing, however, and, after three quarters of an hour of parrying, Anderson politely asked the two RCMP sergeants to leave his office. Upon securing permission to speak to Anderson's lawyer, Monaghan and Anderson left.

At noon the next day, the two pursued their quest with Lloyd Balicki in his Prince Albert office. Balicki, a former Crown prosecutor, was quick to appreciate the implications of the matter. He told the Mounties that his client had called after their visit with him. He explained that Anderson had told him of his situation "in vague terms only." He had no other instructions.

So long as Anderson remained silent, he had the investigation stymied.

Another possible political consideration had entered the investigation in July, and Swayze began to wonder if there was going to be any limit to the connection, coincidental or otherwise, between his case and the Saskatchewan Conservative government.

Sid Dutchak, senior partner in the law firm of Dutchak, Balicki and Popescul, had been elected a Conservative MLA in the Prince Albert-Duck Lake by-election in February. On July 15, 1983, Dutchak had been appointed Minister Without Portfolio in the Devine government. Garry Anderson's lawyer would now naturally be more sensitive to the politics of the investigation.

In the late summer, Sergeant William Harrison, a Regina member of the RCMP, with a number of contacts in the criminal community and known to his associates as "Mad Dog," picked up a story that one Charlie Wilde had recruited Cody Crutcher in a "rip-off" of someone attempting to arrange the death of JoAnn Wilson. Armed with this information, Swayze, accompanied by Al Lyons, paid another visit to Crutcher who, although still an inmate of Drumheller Institution, was temporarily in RCMP cells in Regina.

In this first week of September 1983, Cody Crutcher was a little more accommodating. He confirmed that Charlie Wilde had organized the meeting in the Sheraton Hotel that he had attended

138

and that the third man had been acting on behalf of Colin Thatcher. Money and killing had been discussed.

The team knew Charlie Wilde well, and promptly went looking for him. Strangely, he was nowhere to be found.

Not long after the two Mounties' trip to La Ronge, discord in Regina CID began to affect the investigating team. Progress was all but stopped, and the Wilson murder began to lose some of its priority status. Some of the men on the case felt that Superintendent Dave Giljam regarded it as someone else's problem since it had begun prior to his posting to CID. Morale suffered when Giljam attempted to assign some of the homicide investigators to a routine missing persons complaint. The final straw for Ed Swayze came during one of their up-date meetings, when Giljam said, "I don't think we're going to get him." To Swayze, this attitude would be self-fulfilling.

In September a reporter had overheard Swayze stating that the police knew Colin Thatcher had done the murder and that their only difficulty was proving it. Chief Vern New thought the remarks were improper and called Swayze on the mat.

Swayze would not recant. Not only had he been speaking the truth, he said in defence, but he wanted Colin Thatcher to know what the situation was. Swayze felt at the time that Thatcher would be more likely to make a mistake if he was aware of how much police attention was focused on him.

In October the disgusted CID inspector applied for a transfer. It was granted almost immediately and he moved over to Patrol. Inspector Bill Graham came in as Swayze's successor.

Although Swayze left CID, he did not leave the Wilson murder investigation. His transfer meant that he no longer had any responsibility for the case, but unofficially he maintained his interest and spent as much time on it as before. The rest of the team continued to look to Swayze as the chief investigator and surreptitiously followed him over to the Patrol offices for discussions and direction.

The fall of 1983 was a very dry period in the investigation, but none of the team lost heart. "Stale but not stagnant" is Al Lyons's description. The police carefully reviewed all their results to date, checking their possible leads, went back again and again to their witnesses for fresh thoughts, and kept all their lines open.

It was never discussed as a likelihood, but some of the investigators began to shudder privately at the fearful thought that they might never close the murder and would have to go with the May 1981 attempted murder. They knew that, even if that charge stuck, the sentence would be light in comparison and Colin Thatcher would never be brought to trial for the main offence.

Lloyd Balicki had promised Sergeants Monaghan and Anderson that he would at least discuss his client's situation with Inspector Swayze and, on October 13, Swayze, Monaghan and Lyons met with the Prince Albert lawyer while he was in Saskatoon on business. Swayze gave Balicki an outline of the case against Garry Anderson and suggested that a charge of conspiracy to commit murder could be made out against Anderson and two others. The alternative of Anderson's becoming a Crown witness was put forward.

Balicki understood, was receptive to Swayze's proposition, and agreed to put it to his client. He promised to get back to Swayze.

In November 1983, Serge Kujawa, as he often does, went down to Ottawa on department business. By coincidence, Chief Vern New was booked on the same flight and Air Canada gave them both some unscheduled time to kill in Toronto's mausoleum-like No. 2 terminal. Kujawa took the opportunity to make some very concerned comments about the negative effect the change of personnel in Regina CID was likely having upon the Wilson murder investigation. Superintendent Jim Kane had retired in June and now Inspector Ed Swayze had transferred. Maybe, the Assistant Deputy Minister suggested, the loss of continuity in the two senior investigators was more than the file could stand. And rumour had it that more moves were pending.

No formal representations respecting the lack of progress in the Wilson murder investigation were made by the provincial Department of Justice to the Regina Police Department. Public criticism was developing, however, and some pressure was being felt in the executive offices at the Regina police station. Whether

140

due to that pressure or Kujawa's unofficial and unsolicited hints, Chief New assigned Inspector Ed Swayze special responsibility for the Wilson case.

Swayze had no hesitation in accepting the assignment since he had never really been off the file anyway. He had always felt it was his case and was happy to have that recognized.

Then a wave of transfers hit the major crime unit and the Wilson murder team was decimated. Staff Sergeant Al Lyons was transferred out and so were Sergeants Jim Street and Marv Malnyk. Only Wally Beaton and Bob Murton remained. To this day, none of the men involved have found a logical explanation for what happened.

Swayze confronted Chief New. His comments verged on insubordination and likely would have been treated as such if the Wilson case had not been so sensitive. Six months later Swayze was to learn just how unacceptable he had become to the chief of police.

But the inspector got his team back. Al Lyons was restored on special assignment and Jim Street was also returned. Marv Malnyk was lost.

By mid-January 1984, the chaos was mostly cured and the Regina investigation team returned to the biggest case in the police department's history. Almost immediately they began to achieve startling results.

At the end of January 1984, Swayze telephoned Lloyd Balicki. He had waited patiently for some results out of their meeting in Saskatoon in October. What was Anderson going to do?

Balicki reported a problem. Anderson had called him to say that he had decided to cooperate with the police but had lost his job because of all the police interest in him. Anderson wanted his job back and, if the police could not arrange this, the accomplice would stay quiet and "let the chips fall where they may."

Swayze quickly confirmed that what Anderson said was true. The collector had been a contract employee of the Department of Northern Affairs, his contract had expired at the end of 1983, and it had not been renewed because a concern had developed in government circles in La Ronge that Anderson might prove to be an embarrassment because of his possible involvement in the

141

Wilson murder. Anderson's superiors gave him a high rating as a collector of hopeless accounts.

Ed Swayze was not deterred by this small problem. He reached again into his bag of contacts and explained his need to Eric Bernston, Deputy Premier in the Saskatchewan government and the minister in charge of the department, who was quite powerful enough to solve the problem. Anderson was rehired, but this time on an open contract that could be terminated at any time. Swayze came away from this little setback with an additional lever to use on the recalcitrant Anderson if it was needed.

Swayze telephoned Garry Anderson in La Ronge and told him he had his job back. The proposed witness was pleased and replied that, as soon as he was back on duty, they would have "to sit down and talk."

Two weeks later, on February 22, 1984, Inspector Ed Swayze, by invitation, was sitting in Lloyd Balicki's Prince Albert law office. So was Garry Bruce Anderson. The time had come.

It was one year, one month and one day following the murder of JoAnn Wilson. It had taken this long for the complicated conscience of Garry Anderson to work its way through all the considerations and conclude that salvation lay in cooperation with the police. From Wally Beaton's first approach at the Regina bus depot five days after the killing, through Monaghan and Anderson's visit in September, this unusual personality had, until this day, withstood pressure, blandishments and promise. No one who was involved in the process feels today that Garry Anderson could have been, by any means, hurried in reaching his decision. Now it was made and he was ready to talk.

There were some serious preliminaries, however, and Balicki laid out to Swayze four conditions which would have to be met if his client was to provide the police with a statement. They were:

(1) Immunity from prosecution on both the attempted murder of JoAnn Wilson and the murder;
(2) Change of identity and relocation for Anderson after serving as a witness;
(3) Payment of Balicki's legal fees;

(4) Acknowledgement of Anderson's application for the $50,000 reward which had been posted.

Swayze naturally wanted to know what Anderson's testimony would be. Balicki provided the answer. His client remained silent during the entire interview.

Balicki told Swayze that Anderson could testify on such matters as the rental of getaway cars, the surveillance of the victim, the acquisition of guns, fees paid for criminal services, and conversations with Colin Thatcher. It was an impressive, evidentiary list, but Balicki threw in a bonus. His client, he said, was prepared to wear a monitoring device and engage Thatcher in conversation.

Swayze did not have any doubt that Balicki and Anderson's conditions were reasonable, given the quality of the information and assistance that would be forthcoming, and he already had informal approval for this kind of an arrangement, but he needed much more authority before he could proceed. On the reward, which seemed to have been added to the list on the suggestion of the lawyer, Swayze told Balicki that would be decided by others, but he would be willing to support Anderson's application if the information was as represented.

As to the rest of the list, the policeman suggested a further meeting the next week and returned to Regina.

Two days later an impressive group gathered around the conference table in the Regina CID office. Serge Kujawa, QC, Associate Deputy Minister of Justice, Kenneth MacKay, QC, Director of Public Prosecutions, and Douglas Britton, Senior Crown Prosecutor, represented the Department of Justice. From the Regina Police Department were Superintendent Giljam, Inspectors Swayze and Graham, and Sergeants Beaton, Murton and Al Weselowsky of Special Investigation. Chief New had already given his approval to the Balicki proposal.

The Crown and the police examined the Garry Anderson proposition in careful detail. The conclusion was to go for it, and Ken MacKay agreed to carry that recommendation to Saskatchewan's Minister of Justice, Gary Lane.

Three days later Swayze had the minister's approval and set up

143

the further meeting with Garry Anderson and his lawyer. On the afternoon of February 29, Swayze, Ken MacKay, Wally Beaton and RCMP Inspector Larry Callens gathered in Balicki's office. They advised the lawyer that his client's conditions had been met. MacKay, as Director of Public Prosecutions, handed over his written assurance to Anderson that "You will not be charged in connection with the wounding and/or murder of JoAnn Wilson." He also agreed to the payment of Anderson's legal fees and to "arrange with the R.C.M. Police for the usual witness protection and change of identity."

In return Anderson was to ". . . make a statement and testify in Court as to the person or persons responsible . . . on the understanding: 1) Your testimony is direct evidence implicating the person or persons responsible for the wounding and murder, and 2) Your evidence is true."

Attending to these technicalities and working through the details of the relocation for Anderson proposed by Larry Callens took up the afternoon, and it was early evening before Swayze and Beaton could sit down with their witness and get his story.

It was a lot of story and it took a lot of telling. At 11:00 that night they quit and adjourned until early the next morning. Starting at 8:45 a.m. they broke for lunch at 12:30, returned after an hour, and carried on into the afternoon.

Anderson had known Colin Thatcher for about six years. They were neighbours in the Caron district, but not much more.

Thatcher had approached Anderson in the fall of 1980 with the proposal that he kill his then-wife, JoAnn. Anderson declined, but Thatcher continued the suggestion and asked him to "keep it in mind for someone who might be interested."

By late 1980, Anderson had approached one Charlie Wilde in Regina, a man he had met while serving his last jail sentence earlier that year. Wilde set a price of $50,000, payable in instalments, and set up the meeting with Cody Crutcher that Swayze had already heard about.

Anderson, who did not know that Wilde and Crutcher were merely running a scam for Thatcher's money, continued as a go-between for some weeks, delivering money to Wilde on two occasions. Once he had picked up this money from the same spot

144

in the Thatcher residence where Blaine Mathieson had seen Sandra Hammond place some American currency.

Anderson had introduced Wilde to Thatcher at a meeting on an abandoned farmstead of Thatcher's, north of Caronport in March 1981. Here Colin contracted with Wilde to have the killing of JoAnn done during her visit to her parents in Ames, Iowa, at Easter. Wilde and Thatcher agreed to meet further in Regina to work out the details of this arrangement.

Anderson had, when all these plans produced no killing, later in the spring of 1981, purchased a rifle for Thatcher, a .303 calibre Lee Enfield army rifle. Thatcher had lost faith in his contract killers and told Anderson he was determined to do the job himself. He drove Anderson to Regina, parked on Angus Street, and walked through the lane to the rear of the Wilson house at 2876 Albert Street. Colin showed his accomplice the opening in the Wilson rear fence and explained how JoAnn could be shot through the patio doors and the getaway made to the car on Angus Street over the yard at 2865 Angus.

Anderson's story fitted exactly with the manner in which the May 1981 shooting had been carried out. The Mustang car had been, as Swayze and Beaton knew, rented by Anderson at Thatcher's request. It had been spotted on a street four blocks west of the Redland Avenue home, where Colin picked it up. After the shooting, as prearranged, Anderson picked it up from the same spot and returned it. Before turning it in, Anderson had washed the car and he remembered that it had mud smeared over both licence plates.

After the May 1981 shooting of JoAnn, Thatcher kept in pretty steady contact with Anderson. When Colin explained that he had missed on the attempt, Anderson asked him: "How the hell could you miss at that range?"

Thatcher asked Anderson to get him a handgun, but then said he could get one down in California. Later he gave his accomplice a .357 revolver and holster, both in new condition, and asked to have the gun fitted with a silencer. Anderson got a design for a silencer and had a machinist make four or five models.

Anderson had kept the .357, but returned the holster to

145

Thatcher during a meeting at the abandoned farm. Colin was driving a station wagon that day. Was this the car in which Chuck Guillaume had found the holster?

In October 1982, Anderson had rented another car for Colin, this time the Chevy from Rent-a-Wreck in Saskatoon. The accomplice was to pick the car up in the grounds of the Legislature in Regina, but it was not there when he went to get it. He called Colin who met him in front of the Legislative Buildings with the car and the explanation that the Wascana Centre police had towed it away.

When he returned the car to Anderson, Colin had removed from it a tire iron and a bag containing a black wig. (Swayze thought of JoAnn's head wounds when he heard of the tire iron.)

On Thursday morning, January 20, 1983, Anderson had accidentally encountered Colin Thatcher near the Caron ranch. The two had talked. Colin told his accomplice that he had been "stalking" JoAnn for the past week, and that he was going to try to kill her that night. If he failed, he wanted to borrow Anderson's car the next day, Friday. Thatcher asked for the return of the .357.

Colin explained his modus operandi to Anderson. He had run road tests to determine the time needed to get from JoAnn's house back to his own in Moose Jaw. He could get into his house from the back without being observed, and his sons and Sandra Hammond would vouch for his presence at home.

The next morning, the day of the murder, Thatcher and Anderson met at the abandoned farm. Colin said that the night before he had been in the Wilson garage and "almost got her, but missed." The two parted, met briefly at the Gulf coffee shop (where Corporal Hagerty had by chance spotted them), and then met again by arrangement in Moose Jaw at 1:00 p.m.

Anderson picked up Thatcher as he was walking down one of the streets near his Redland Avenue home. Colin was wearing blue jeans, a black three-quarter-length parka, a toque or similar headgear and sunglasses. Colin took Anderson's car, the 1974 Mercury, which had a full gas tank, the .357 revolver and a bag of shells, and arranged that Anderson recover the car on the street west of Redland.

On Sunday, two days later, Anderson picked up his car on the

146

same street where he had found the Mustang in May 1981. The licence plates were smeared with mud. In the car was a black jacket, blue jeans, a tuft of black hair from a wig, some loose change, a credit card receipt, and the sunglasses, which were in a case like prescription glasses. On the floor in front was a dark stain. The gas tank was registering on empty. Anderson took the car out to his mother's farm at Caron, burned the contents in a trash barrel and, two days later, abandoned it on the farm where Murton and Street found it in July.

Garry Anderson had not spoken to Colin Thatcher since he had turned his car over to him on the day of the murder. His only pay had been $500 which he had taken from one of the fund transfers to Charlie Wilde.

When Inspector Ed Swayze returned to Regina on March 1, 1984 with Garry Anderson's statement in his pocket, his thoughts about the attitude he wished Colin Thatcher to have towards the investigation had reversed completely. He no longer wanted his suspect to be nervous and concerned. Now he wanted him to have a feeling of confidence, a belief that he was beyond the reach of the police.

Swayze knew his case was a long way from being complete, but now he had witnesses to protect. The deal with Anderson and Balicki had included an understanding that the witness would be allowed to continue in his work for a few more weeks, so he could clean up some bills. That would not be a problem because it would take a good month to implement the change of identity and relocation. Swayze now was anxious that nothing happen to the accomplice before he was safely tucked away.

Maintaining security on the progress of the investigation, and the way in which it was closing in on the Thunder Creek MLA, was going to be a critical problem from this point on. In fact, it very soon became a crisis.

Ed Swayze was not a politician, but he knew the dangers and he had a case that not only involved a prominent politician but that reached into high political levels almost everywhere he turned. So far, political considerations had not affected the investigation, and Swayze wanted to keep it that way.

In this view he knew he had the support of the Minister of

Justice, Gary Lane. As the province's senior law enforcement officer, Lane had the onerous responsibility of ensuring that the administration of justice went forward in this case, as in all others, without any suggestion of political interference, either in encouragement or in restriction of the investigation. Other than approving the assignment of Serge Kujawa to assist the police, Lane had maintained an excellent hands-off posture to the extent that was possible and was to continue that posture to the end of the case.

That meant that the minister could not discuss any aspect of the case with any of his cabinet colleagues, and Gary Lane did not. Thus, when Eric Bernston, Deputy Premier and Minister of Economic Development, spoke to Lane in a knowing way about Garry Anderson, the "northern witness," Lane was shocked. He immediately issued instructions that a total blackout be imposed on the investigation and that the case be brought to a conclusion as quickly as possible.

Ed Swayze was embarrassed. He had to explain that he was the source of Bernston's knowledge because of the assistance sought respecting Anderson's job. As far as a blackout on the investigation was concerned, security was already as tight as humanly possible. And the case could not be wrapped up yet. Too much remained to be done.

The Crown counsel involved in the case, MacKay and Kujawa, backed up Swayze and he was allowed to continue without regard to ministerial concerns.

Swayze was now in a position to turn his attention to Charlie Wilde and Cody Crutcher. With the Anderson statement he had enough to be firm with them. Their casual ripping off of Colin Thatcher had the perfect makings of a criminal conspiracy, a very serious charge likely to produce a sentence of several years.

Wilde was as well known to the Regina police as was Crutcher. Both men were in their thirties and had not developed much in the way of conventional careers. Both were of the "old school" of minor criminal activists and regarded the police as normal occupational hazards. When apprehended, as they often had been, they would accept their penalty philosophically and without rancor. Neither would "fink" on a fellow player. Both were excellent confidence men and the good actors that role requires. Both had been involved with narcotics and Charlie Wilde was an addict.

Because Crutcher was in jail, the investigators knew where he was. Partly because he was not in jail, the police had not been able to locate Wilde, although they had been looking for him since the previous September, when they had first learned of his involvement in the case. Bob Murton and Gene Stusek had been to Winnipeg looking for him and had traced him into Ontario where he disappeared. Wilde had been "whereabouts unknown" for months.

By great coincidence both Wilde and Crutcher became available just when they were most needed. Charlie had surfaced in Winnipeg and Inspector Bill Graham dusted off an old warrant and sent for him. Crutcher was even easier.

Crutcher was serving an eight-year sentence for his arson conviction, and had been moved from Drumheller to the Edmonton Maximum Security Unit. He was, however, in RCMP cells in Regina in early March 1984 to clean up a breaking and entry and theft matter. Swayze had him transferred over to the Regina Police Detention Centre.

On March 3, Swayze and Beaton explained the grim facts of life to Cody Crutcher and offered him a proposition similar to the one put to Garry Anderson. Cody thought he would like to discuss things with Charlie Wilde. His real concern was that cooperating with the police would not be well understood by his fellow inmates in Edmonton Max.

On March 6, Charlie Wilde was in the Regina Police Detention Centre looking at Ed Swayze and Wally Beaton. He looked at something else, too. Swayze silently handed Wilde four photographs: Colin Thatcher, Garry Anderson, Cody Crutcher and Charlie Wilde.

Wilde was badly shaken. Visibly upset, he asked to see a lawyer. Swayze explained that he was only interested in the murder, that he knew Charlie and Cody had been involved only to shake Thatcher down for money, but that alone would support a conspiracy conviction good for, perhaps, fourteen years.

Charlie wanted a lawyer and he chose Harold P. Pick, QC, general counsel to Saskatchewan Legal Aid. Pick, a highly experienced criminal lawyer who had prosecuted for many years before joining Legal Aid, was reluctant to respond. But Swayze and Pick had been friends for years and the inspector prevailed upon the lawyer to accede to Wilde's request.

Pick came over to the detention centre and listened with Wilde, as Swayze outlined what he could prove about Wilde's contracting with Garry Anderson and Colin Thatcher for the murder of JoAnn Wilson. Later, after conferring with Wilde, Pick asked for full disclosure of the Crown case.

The next day the Director of Public Prosecutions, Ken MacKay, was again dealing with a lawyer for evidence. In a meeting with Pick, Doug Britton, Swayze, Beaton and Murton, MacKay denied Pick's request for full disclosure but offered immunity for Wilde. In return he set three conditions: that Wilde not be involved in either shooting, that he cooperate fully with the police, and that he testify at any proceedings. MacKay's proposal still required the approval of the Minister of Justice.

Cody Crutcher then got his opportunity to talk things over with Charlie Wilde. Swayze arranged for the two recipients of Colin Thatcher's murder money to have dinner together in a Regina police interview room. At the end, each man agreed to cooperate if the other one did too.

By Thursday, March 8, the Minister of Justice had approved immunity, relocation and change of identity for Charlie Wilde in return for his cooperation and testimony. Similar arrangements were available to Cody Crutcher also, but his imprisonment reduced the attractiveness of the offer to him, although he was to be eligible for day parole in nine months. Crutcher decided to have Pick represent him also.

The next morning Swayze and Beaton met with Charlie Wilde and Harold Pick in Pick's office. Wilde told them of his participation with Colin Thatcher three years earlier and signed a lengthy statement.

That afternoon Beaton and Murton brought Cody Crutcher over to Pick's office from the RCMP cells and the process was repeated.

The team now had all three of the accomplices to Colin Thatcher's murder efforts in the bag. Their case was building quickly.

Cody Crutcher had played a small part in the sordid

conspiracy. Charlie Wilde had come to him looking "for a guy to play the role of hit man." Cody's share was to be $7,500 and he readily agreed. He dressed up in a three-piece suit with a contrasting shirt — "Wopish," he said — and met with Garry Anderson and Charlie in the Sheraton lounge where the deal was made. He used the name "Gold." Anderson gave them a photograph of JoAnn and a set of keys to her Thunderbird. Charlie split Colin's money with Cody later. "In total I got $7,500 for my ten or fifteen minute act," he told Beaton. The money bought a car and a holiday, and Cody passed out of the play. Charlie was to explain "Gold's" disappearance by telling Anderson that he had been killed in a shootout.

Charlie Wilde, who had organized and directed the scam, stayed around a little longer. When he had first been approached in late 1980 by Garry Anderson who was looking for a hit man, Charlie had passed. But when Garry came back a few days later, Charlie was ready and the Sheraton meeting took place.

Wilde recalled Garry Anderson giving specific instructions and information about the killing and when it was to be done. The sham killers were given the address of JoAnn's condominium on Gordon Road and her place of work, then Willson Office Specialties. The job could be done anywhere but not until Colin was "clear in Palm Springs," where he would spend Christmas and New Year's. The murder could be arranged in any way at all, so long as the daughter Stephanie was not harmed.

A month or so after New Year's 1981, Anderson was around to see Wilde, asking why the murder did not "go down." Charlie put him off by saying "Gold" would "still look after it."

Anderson then gave Wilde fresh information and instructions. He told Charlie that JoAnn was now married, that her name was Wilson, and he took the con artist around to the house at 2876 Albert Street where the intended victim now lived. Anderson then specified a time in February when Thatcher would again be in Palm Springs.

Again, nothing happened and in March Anderson was back talking to Wilde. He said that Thatcher wanted to see Charlie and that he was "hot" because "the job hadn't been done."

Wilde kept playing along. He met Anderson in Moose Jaw and

drove out with him to the abandoned farm at Caronport, where he was introduced to Colin Thatcher. Colin questioned Charlie about "Gold" and his whereabouts. He asked if he could have back the keys to JoAnn's car, as they would "tie him in."

Then Thatcher asked Wilde to do the murder himself and suggested a price of $50,000. Charlie at first declined, saying he did not have a gun; but then, considering the size of the offer, added maybe he could at that. Charlie was planning on leaving Regina and the opportunity to score on the obsessed Thatcher one more time was irresistible.

Colin told Charlie that JoAnn was going down to her parents in Ames, Iowa, for Easter and asked if Charlie would "go down and kill her there." Again, Wilde demurred, pleading no gun and no money. Colin promised to put up $3,500 or $4,000 for travel and a gun, and Charlie reeled in his fish. Colin said he would need a bit of time to put together the money so that no withdrawals would show. The two agreed to meet later near the Legislative Buildings in Regina.

(At the trial, three and a half years later, Dawn Trickett, Charlie Wilde's common-law wife of some years, made a crack about the mental calibre of Premier Devine's cabinet, if Colin Thatcher was an example. "The man couldn't tell a hit man from a junkie.")

Colin and Charlie did meet in the grounds of the Legislature. Colin gave Charlie specific instructions about the job: when JoAnn was leaving to go to Iowa; the address and location of her parents' home; their name. He gave Charlie $4,500 in small bills, $1,400 of it in American currency.

Then Charlie Wilde, too, stepped off stage. Shortly before midnight on April 19, 1981, the Brandon City Police accosted Charlie inside a pharmacy which had been closed for some hours. Charlie had just helped himself to some morphine.

"What are you doing here?" they demanded to know.

"Everybody's got to be somewhere," replied the already cheerful Charlie, hit man/junkie.

In Charlie's pockets were three Canadian one hundred dollar bills and thirty-eight American twenty dollar bills. The rest of Colin's money he had given to Dawn Trickett. He had not even bought a gun.

CHAPTER 12

Operation Wire

The safety of Charlie Wilde was now added to Swayze's list of problems. The witness was to be relocated and his identity disguised. But that would take a little time. Meanwhile Charlie was assisting the team in confirming his story and showing them the various locations he had been to with Garry Anderson and Colin Thatcher.

Swayze was concerned that the irrepressible Charlie did not fully appreciate the seriousness of the situation and the danger he might be in.

Charlie, complaining of another attack of chronic cash shortage, had jokingly suggested to the inspector that he might run another scam on Colin Thatcher, this time pretending to sell information about the police investigation. Swayze was not amused and lectured the confidence man severely.

Wally Beaton had a nicely fitted van with smoked windows that had attracted a lot of ribald humour. It was ideal as a travelling observation platform for Charlie as they drove around the Caron area, looking for the abandoned farm where he had first met with Colin Thatcher. At this time, the police did not know where the meeting place was and a long afternoon was spent on the road allowances before they found it. Once they came across it, Charlie was in no doubt with his identification. The team was to see a lot of that farmstead, just north of the Caronport Gulf station, in the next few weeks.

On March 13, the case which had been developed against Colin Thatcher was laid out before Serge Kujawa and Doug Britton. The team believed that they had now pulled together all the evidence they were going to get.

The only further source they could see was a former political associate and crony of Thatcher's, Dick Collver, deposed leader of the Saskatchewan Conservative Party, now living in Arizona. Their considered conclusion here was that, if Collver did know anything about Thatcher's involvement in the murder, he was not going to discuss it with the police. Later events were to prove that the view was correct at that time.

As the Crown counsel sorted and analyzed the available evidence, the police were confident that there would be enough to support a successful prosecution. Certainly, there was a lot of evidence. Murder, motive, method and means were all present, and so was the accomplice, Anderson, even if the evidence on the actual killing was only circumstantial.

After careful evaluation, Kujawa delivered his opinion. There was not enough. The experienced prosecutor did not think that a jury would convict Colin Thatcher on the evidence before him, and he did not think it was proper to charge a man with murder if a conviction was improbable.

He explained that the onus of proof on the Crown in a case involving an accused of the prominence and stature of Colin Thatcher was greater than ordinary. It was fine, he said, to speak of equality before the law and the impartiality of justice, but in practice and reality those fine concepts are less than perfectly applied. Any average jury would be slow to believe that this crime was committed by the son of a former premier, himself a former cabinet minister and still a sitting MLA, a man of wealth and position, with no criminal convictions to blemish his record. And, before a jury, a clean record would speak for an accused as much as a previous conviction spoke against him.

Not all of the evidence the police had acquired could be put before a jury on a murder charge, Kujawa explained. A great deal of it had to do with the first shooting and, unless a charge of attempted murder was included, would not be relevant or proper evidence on the main charge. And, he pointed out, they knew as well as he did, that, if a lesser charge was available to a jury, they would go for it every time.

Finally, Kujawa told Swayze and his men, it would not be fair or in the public interest to run a partial case against Colin Thatcher. The trial would attract unheard of publicity, many reputations and lives would be affected, and nothing would be resolved except that, he emphasized, an acquittal would mean that Colin Thatcher would be free for life; he could never be charged again with the murder of JoAnn Wilson, no matter how much evidence might surface in the future.

So there it was. There was no argument. The high regard police all over Saskatchewan had for Serge Kujawa, which was shared by the Regina investigators, precluded any attempt to influence his opinion.

"But where do we get any more evidence?" Swayze asked. "It's your case," Kujawa replied, "but I can think of only one place and that's the man himself."

Everyone present knew what that meant. They were all aware of Garry Anderson's offer to attempt an approach to Colin Thatcher while wearing electronic equipment. From long experience the police knew, however, that the odds against success in such a venture were astronomical. Just bringing about the contact was a delicate and difficult feat. Even if that was achieved, the chances of securing incriminating admissions from an obviously wily subject were very slim.

The possibilities were discussed in a hypothetical way. Charlie Wilde was considered as an alternative to Garry Anderson.

Where and when were problems in addition to how. Colin was spending a lot of this time of year in Palm Springs and was expected to go down for Easter and remain until the end of April.

Kujawa noted the disappointment on the faces of the policemen as they left his office with their case that he had judged incomplete.

Ed Swayze had booked to take his wife, Marion, to Hawaii for four weeks. There seemed to be no compelling reason not to go.

Before leaving, Swayze buttoned up the investigation as best he could. He secured approval to his appointment of Al Lyons as supervisor on the case and left specific instructions that no arrest of Colin Thatcher be made during his absence unless it became necessary and then only if it was so decided by Al Lyons and Wally Beaton, with the approval of Serge Kujawa. Lyons and Beaton were instructed to make such a move only if the lives of the witnesses became threatened by a leak.

A contingency plan had been prepared providing for the

155

immediate relocation and protection of Anderson and Wilde in the event that Colin Thatcher got wind of the progress being achieved by the police. Garry Anderson had told Swayze that Thatcher had bragged of an information source inside the police department during the investigation of the first shooting. Security was tightened even further. A phony report was allowed to stray from the prescribed channels as a test of personnel, but it was returned immediately and there was no leak.

Methods of quietly slipping loose some disinformation on the state of the investigation to create confidence in the mind of Colin Thatcher were considered. Chief New vetoed the suggestion that the Crimewatch program, which solicits public assistance in crime solving, be used for this purpose.

In March the inspector and his wife had little more than begun their rest and relaxation when the Hawaiian holiday turned into one of the most stressful times in Ed Swayze's life.

Shortly after Swayze left, an excited Bill Graham burst into the CID offices where Al Lyons and Wally Beaton were comparing reports.

"Doug McConachie knows the whole story," he blurted. "I was just talking to him on the phone. He knows we're going to charge Thatcher."

The two NCOs stared back at the inspector as the possibilities raced through their minds. There were many, and none were good.

McConachie was a reporter with the *Star-Phoenix* in Saskatoon. He had worked with the Regina *Leader Post* twenty years before and the police knew him as a good newsman.

"He's going to run the story," Graham continued. "What the hell do we do now?"

All three of them knew what to do. Graham phoned Swayze in Hawaii. On Swayze's advice Graham invited the reporter to come down to Regina for a personal chat. McConachie accepted, agreeing to hold his story until they met.

Graham had to agree that McConachie's story was basically correct. The reporter had done some digging and concluded that Colin Thatcher was about to be charged in connection with the murder of JoAnn Wilson. He did not know if the charge would be first degree murder or something lesser, but the difference

156

meant nothing to the CID inspector. He, Swayze, Lyons and Beaton were convinced that one whiff of such a story and Colin Thatcher was gone and so was their case.

Graham did not tell McConachie that, though. But he did tell him that the police had some very real concerns about the safety of some of the people involved.

"Is there any reason we can't run the story?" McConachie wanted to know.

"You can do whatever you want to do, but we have some real problems," Graham pleaded.

The reporter and the policeman finally settled on an understanding that the *Star-Phoenix* did not want to jeopardize anyone's safety and that it might be possible to let McConachie have a little advance notice if Colin Thatcher was going to be charged. Neither agreed to anything.

McConachie went back to his editors and recommended that they hold off on the story. They agreed.

Over on Maui, though, Inspector Ed Swayze felt no relief. Rendered impotent by distance, he worried that his case was about to blow up.

When Swayze returned in mid-April, he determined to risk an operation to record a conversation between Garry Anderson and Colin Thatcher. Although the situation with the press seemed stable, he knew it would be only a matter of time now before the story got out. After that his case would only get worse.

The team had not been able to come up with any new and promising avenues of investigation and merely watching and waiting now was out of the question. They would have to make things happen. Planning began immediately for the operation which came to be called "the Wire."

Colin Thatcher was in Palm Springs as expected and due back on April 30. That settled the question as to when to make the attempt. It could not be before Colin's return and there was no point in delay once he was back. In fact, the team saw an advantage in the situation. They were confident that the cattleman in Thatcher would take him straight to his ranch after his absence. Precise foreknowledge of Thatcher's movements would be essential to the planning of an accidental meeting with

157

Anderson. The team had extracted from the accomplice all the knowledge he had about Thatcher's habits and likely actions and reactions.

The idea of using Charlie Wilde had been quickly discarded. Only Anderson had an excuse to be in the Moose Jaw-Caron area and it was to be expected that Thatcher would be extremely suspicious and wary. Also, only Anderson had the degree of knowledge of Thatcher's actions the day of the murder to make an incriminating conversation plausible.

Garry Anderson was still willing to make the attempt but only under conditions that minimized the risk to his life that he saw in the venture. The accomplice knew that Thatcher had another gun in addition to the .357 he had handed over to him on the afternoon of the murder. That was believed to be the murder weapon and long since disposed of. He was quite satisfied that Colin would use that second gun on him if he was perceived to be a threat.

It was assumed that Thatcher kept the gun in his Moose Jaw home. That fact dictated that Anderson not make the approach there, but it would not be first choice anyway. The natural place for the meeting was in the country around Caron. That in turn meant that the meeting could not be set up by appointment if Thatcher returned to Redland Avenue after the first contact.

Thatcher was booked to fly back from Palm Springs on Monday, April 30, using the Frontier Airlines flight from Denver that usually reached Regina within an hour of its scheduled arrival time of 9:30 p.m. That would be late enough to finish that day, and the team placed their bet that Colin would drive alone to the Caron ranch the next morning. They decided to have Anderson encounter him en route.

Anderson had met with Thatcher so frequently after he had been enlisted into the murder planning that the two had developed an accepted procedure, although it had not been used in fifteen months. Little or no recognition was permitted where they might be seen, but a hand signal, palm edge forward and down, from one would soon bring the other to the usual meeting place, the abandoned farmstead at Caronport. The team chose this as the most likely site for their meeting to occur (see map, page 324).

The Caronport Gulf station was a likely place for Anderson to signal Thatcher, and two other locations, Thatcher's grain farm six miles north of Caron and the ranch at Caron, were possible meeting sites.

Electronic eavesdropping has been used in police work since the equipment became available. Criminal investigators are quick to adapt modern technology to their work, and the team all had experience in gathering information in this way. The operation proposed against Colin Thatcher had an additional requirement. What was sought was not so much information but, rather, evidence. The product here was headed for court and had to be secured in such a way that it would pass all the stringent tests it would meet in a courtroom.

The RCMP maintain a special unit, "I," which specializes in electronic surveillance. Without hesitation, Special "I" was made available to the Regina operation. Special "O," the surveillance unit, was also activated again. It would be needed to observe Thatcher, coordinate Anderson's movements so as to bring about the intercept, and witness the meeting.

The chosen site was inspected. To avoid the suspicion that strange activity raises in rural farming country, the visits to the abandoned farmstead were always made at dusk or later. Technique and equipment were selected.

Anderson would be equipped with two systems, a recorder and an FM radio transmitter that would broadcast the conversation to a receiver where the conversation would be again recorded as a back-up. Special "I" provided a Swiss-made Nagra miniature high quality recorder about three quarters of an inch thick. An FM receiver/recorder would be installed behind the seat in Anderson's half-ton truck. In the event Thatcher chose to talk inside an empty barn on the farm site, this also was fitted with a hidden FM receiver/recorder.

The security of Garry Anderson was of concern to the police as well as to him. The murder suspect was considered extremely dangerous and the team was about to proffer up to him in very tempting circumstances his accomplice, the only man who could directly implicate him in the murder activity. Anderson would wear a bullet-proof vest, but more protection was called for.

A Special Weapons and Tactics (SWAT) unit consisting of

159

three constables under the command of Corporal Ron Strassburger was activated. His orders were to conceal his men in the farmyard, cover the meeting, and protect Anderson. This meant, at the ultimate, that if Anderson's life was threatened, Thatcher was to be stopped, by shooting him if necessary. Also, if the surveillance was exposed, Thatcher was to be arrested on the spot and the SWAT unit, the only police to be at the scene, would have to accomplish this.

Every effort to continue the deception was to be made, however. The farmyard provided little cover for the SWAT unit and it was recognized that Thatcher might spot them. If that happened, Strassburger was instructed to tell Thatcher that they were there anticipating a large cocaine transaction to take place at the site, apologize, and, if the story sold, leave. No one thought that, if it came to that, the wary Colin would believe such an explanation of armed and camouflaged police on his farm, but all possibilities were being provided for.

The SWAT unit would be equipped with two FM receivers which would enable the wearers to listen to the conversation between Anderson and Thatcher and determine if danger was developing. Strassburger would have radio communication with Special "O."

Anderson was out of La Ronge and in the process of being relocated. A strange and ubiquitous man, he was in Moose Jaw one day, back in La Ronge the next, and in Regina the third. To the team it seemed that he travelled at least 400 miles every day, but he dropped in on them frequently enough to be kept abreast of the planning.

This was a big event in Garry Anderson's life and he was excited and fearful. For his part, Swayze had no illusions and knew that the accomplice, who had for so long resisted coming over to the police, might any day have a change of heart and refuse any further cooperation. The planning went forward as if all the necessary elements, including the main one, Anderson, were assured.

A command site from which the operation could be directed was needed. The team was looking at a highway motel near Moose Jaw when someone suggested Besant Park, the

160

campground closed for the season and just seven miles west of Caronport. It was perfect.

The manager of the campground was located and his approval to the use of its facilities secured. For cover the team explained that an undercover narcotics operation was in play. The story found its way back to the RCMP detachment in Moose Jaw who were not in on the scheme and had to be placated.

Staff Sergeant Nel Silzer, who had succeeded Al Lyons as head of the major crimes unit, took charge of equipping and provisioning the command base. Since the team had no reason to believe that the intercept would succeed or fail on the first day, they prepared to stay with their plan as long as necessary, two days, three days or even four days. All the units involved, Special "I," Special "O," SWAT, an arrest team, a search team to go in if an arrest occurred, other RCMP, and the supervising investigators would have to be accommodated during the entire event. In all, more than thirty police personnel were required to bring off the operation.

Silzer, an experienced outdoorsman and outfitter, was up to the task. Already on hand was a large communications trailer which had once travelled with Royal American Shows, a midway operator that had come to grief in Regina some years before. Two Winnebago mobile homes were procured, one a little ancient. Steaks, bacon, eggs and other staples were laid in. Bedding was arranged.

On Sunday, April 29, Silzer moved his caravan down the Trans-Canada Highway to Besant Park and set up camp. Telephone hook-ups were made to the communications trailer. Radios were set up and tested. The command base was ready.

To ensure the effectiveness of Special "O," air surveillance was ordered. Regina Constable Ken Gartner, a qualified pilot and flying instructor, was conscripted. Gartner secured a Piper Archer and flew two reconnaissance missions with team members and a photographer, taking aerial photos, familiarizing themselves with landmarks and testing radios. RCMP Constable Bob Britton of Special "O" would fly with Gartner and act as radio operator. Two radio systems would be used with a back-up for each. Britton was equipped with four radios.

161

On Monday, April 30, the personnel of "Operation Wire" filtered unobtrusively into Besant Park. The RCMP specialists arrived in their own motor home. When darkness came, the SWAT unit ran a drill at the abandoned farm, picked their places of concealment, and rehearsed their roles. Sergeant Bob LaPorte of Special "I" fitted Garry Anderson with the equipment he was to wear the next day to give him a feel for it. Anderson left to spend the night at his mother's nearby farm. In the late evening Colin Thatcher disembarked from Frontier Airlines in Regina and drove to his Moose Jaw home. Besant Park bedded down for the night.

One man at the Besant Park camp did not sleep that night. Inspector Ed Swayze remained alone in the communications trailer.

The SWAT unit was the first to move on Tuesday morning. Ron Strassburger and Constables Ron Seiferling, Jim McKee and Ray Golemba were up at 3:00 a.m. They dressed in the tiger-stripe camouflage Strassburger had chosen for them and borrowed from the RCMP, breakfasted, and left on their mission. They travelled to the selected site in Bob Murton's half-ton with the topper cover and, as the truck drove slowly by the farmyard, they rolled out over the tailgate like frogmen and slithered into their positions. Using groundsheets for some protection against the damp and frozen soil, they checked their weapons and settled in for the long, cold wait. It was five o'clock in the morning.

At the same hour, the Special "O" surveillance team under the command of RCMP Corporal Fred Waelz moved onto Redland Avenue and began their wait for the emergence of Colin Thatcher.

An hour later Garry Anderson arrived at the command site and was fitted again with the electronic equipment by Bob LaPorte, this time for real. His instructions in the use of the equipment were simple. The Nagra recorder had a capacity of more than three hours. It had no erasure capability. The accomplice was to turn the machine on well before the meeting began and let it run. Also before the meeting began, he was to begin speaking out loud, identifying his locations and activities, both to help him keep calm and to assist in later proving the integrity of the tape.

162

Over the Nagra microphone and the FM transmitter system, went the bullet-proof vest. The heavy, loose coveralls Anderson was wearing adequately concealed everything.

At ten minutes to seven Garry Anderson left Besant Park and drove to the Gulf service station at Caronport where he pulled into the parking lot and waited. Perhaps hoping to expiate his guilt, he had accepted a tremendous challenge. If this morning's ploy worked, and he thought it would, he expected to secure Colin Thatcher's plain and simple confession of murder.

Ken Gartner and Bob Britton in the Piper Archer flew the short hop from Regina to Moose Jaw municipal airport, six miles northeast of the city, where they sat on the ground waiting for word from Special "O" that Colin Thatcher was on the move.

At 8:12 a.m. the report came and the Archer took off. Britton was carrying a set of binoculars, 12-volt powered and gyroscope controlled, that could read a licence plate at five miles from 10,000 feet. He picked up Thatcher's truck on Main Street before it reached the overpass and began to turn down the ramp to the westbound lanes of the Trans-Canada. The sighting was confirmed with Fred Waelz on the ground who, with other "O" personnel, followed Thatcher westward down the highway.

Colin Thatcher had left his house, gone to his GMC three-quarter-ton in his driveway, returned briefly to the house, and then taken his usual route out of the city. In less than twenty minutes from leaving Redland Avenue he would reach the intersection at Caronport where the grid road runs three miles west from the highway to Caron and his ranch.

If Thatcher should stop at the Gulf station for coffee, Anderson would make his contact there. Two Special "O" operatives, a young, apparently married couple, were in the coffee shop to observe the contact if it took place.

It was too early for coffee, though, and Special "O" decided that their man would go straight to his ranch. Anderson was signalled. He pulled out of the Gulf parking lot, drove west on the grid road, turned around and waited for Thatcher to come towards him. He switched on the Nagra recorder.

At 8:35 a.m. Colin's truck reached the intersection and turned west on the grid road. Anderson started up and drove eastward towards Colin who met and passed him, ignoring the accomplice

163

and the signal given in the old way. Colin drove on to his ranch.

Anderson persisted. He drove back to the Gulf station, turned around, and, chattering like the pilot of a fighter-bomber approaching target, followed Thatcher back to the ranch.

"I'm proceeding down to Caron. Still heading down to Caron. Just crossing the railroad tracks. Just crossing the railroad tracks. Going to go in. Going to go in. At entrance. He's over at the fuel tanks. I'm going over."

Colin was filling his truck. "I needed gas," he said. "Head up by the nuisance ground road, okay?"

"I'll meet you at the abandoned farm," Anderson replied. "At the what?" "Abandoned farm," Anderson repeated.

"Yeah. Okay." Thatcher had agreed to the meeting.

"Contact made. Contact made. Contact made." Anderson, still chattering, drove to the rendezvous point.

"Going to meet at abandoned farm. I'm on my way there now. Going to meet at abandoned farm. He looked awful surprised to see me. He looked awful surprised to see me."

Gartner and Britton were at 1,700 feet, taking advantage of the low, scudding cloud that gave them some cover. They watched the two vehicles in the ranch yard and knew that contact had been made.

Anderson described his drive to the farmyard. "I've crossed highway. I've crossed highway. There's a farmer in the field on my right. I don't know if that will spook him. I don't know if that will spook him. I'm going to go in anyways. Turning into abandoned farm. I'm in the abandoned farm. I can pick up the sounds of that plane pretty good."

A low-winged airplane, as the Archer was, is not ideal for air-to-ground surveillance, and Gartner and Britton now learned this. Colin Thatcher disappeared beneath the wing as the Archer passed — and he did not reappear.

A few moments of near panic struck Operation Wire. Contact had been made, Thatcher had agreed to meet Anderson at the chosen site, and Anderson had gone there. But Colin's truck remained in the ranch yard and there was no sign of Colin.

At the command base Swayze decided that Thatcher was having trouble starting his truck, would meet with Anderson, but would be late. Afraid that the nervous Anderson might conclude

164

that he was being ignored again and leave the farmyard, Swayze radioed Britton to relay a message to the waiting accomplice telling him to stay put. Britton would have to pass the message to Ron Strassburger hidden in the grass, who would have to step out of concealment and speak directly to Anderson.

"Mr. T. is here."

The words came into Britton's radio just as he was about to relay the command that would have broken the SWAT unit's cover. Gartner and Britton were still watching the truck in the ranch yard for some sign of Colin Thatcher and did not see him drive into the farmyard four miles away in a grey Ford car. As he did so, Strassburger announced his presence and the emergency was over. A moment later and the SWAT leader would have had to test the believability of his story of a cocaine sale.

Just across from the Thatcher ranch headquarters on the edge of Caron is the building housing the offices of the Rural Municipality of Caron. Employed there was thirty-eight-year-old Sandra Sparkes, a friend of Colin Thatcher's. In the moment that Gartner and Britton had lost sight of Colin, he had stepped over to Sandra's office and borrowed her car, the grey Ford which he had driven into the farmyard to meet Anderson.

Colin told Anderson, and testified later, that he had indeed had trouble starting his truck, that he had boosted it at home that morning before leaving. But Special "O" who had watched him leave saw no such performance. Had the wary Colin changed vehicles just as a precaution? In any event, his manoeuvre nearly foiled the entire Operation Wire.

At the vacant farm the SWAT unit members watched, their rifles trained, as Garry Anderson and Colin Thatcher walked about the farmyard engrossed in conversation. At one point the two strolled so close to McKee and Golemba that the hidden constables could see the unshaven stubble on Colin's chin and hear the conversation without electronic assistance.

"Been having truck trouble," Colin said as he stepped from the strange car. "Let's get in this car and go for a ride."

"I'd prefer to stay around," replied Anderson, who certainly did. "How you been keeping?"

"Fine," said Colin. Then, "Have to be awfully cautious, one never knows."

165

The two exchanged pleasantries and some comment on the weather and then Colin asked, "Everything is . . . there's no problem, have you been hassled?" referring to the police.

"Once. About the Chev car and that was about it. How about you?"

"Just the once, the day after . . . no question there's been some attempts to put us together and we should not be seen together." Thatcher told the accomplice about some of the police inquiries.

Colin wanted to know where Anderson had been. Garry explained about his job "up north" and then brought the conversation back to the point of his mission. "Everything went okay though, eh?"

"Yeah, there's no connection back," replied Colin, and told Anderson that it now looked as if the police were interested in Ron Graham.

"I got rid of the stuff out of the car," Anderson stated.

"Good," said Colin.

Anderson tried to go for a direct reference to the killing. "You kind of give me a scare there with . . . I found the stuff laying in there and then I wondered what the hell . . . I didn't know where the hell you . . . what the hell you'd done with the gun?" He got an excited reaction.

"Don't even talk like that, don't . . . don't even . . . walk out this way a little, away from the car." Colin was being wary.

"There are no loose ends," Colin told Anderson, and then asked about a "loose end from a couple of years ago." Obviously referring to Charlie Wilde and Cody Crutcher, with whom he had been "discussing some business," he asked "is there any way there'd ever be a problem surface from them."

"I located one of them," Anderson told him.

"The one that I met, or the other one [Crutcher]?"

"The other one."

"Son of a bitch," Colin swore. "Is he about to cause any problems?" Anderson did not know.

Colin told Anderson of his concern that people in trouble with the police would fabricate stories implicating him to improve their bargaining position.

"Do you need some bread?" he suddenly asked.

166

1.	An Ontarian who came west in 1912 to homestead in the Caron area, Bill Thatcher was the first of three generations of Thatchers to demonstrate a knack for making money, even when the prairie economy was depressed.

2.	Ross Thatcher at the Thatcher Hereford Ranch in the early 1960s. Bill's eldest son became a politician as a young man, but he also expanded the family hardware business and began the ranching enterprise. Colin, Ross and Peggy Thatcher's only son, started working at the ranch in 1962.

3. Colin Thatcher marries JoAnn Kay Geiger, August 12, 1962. His father's comment at the wedding: "I sure hope Jo can handle him."

4. The Thatchers — Peggy, JoAnn, Ross and Colin — arrive at the victory celebration the night Ross became premier, April 22, 1964.

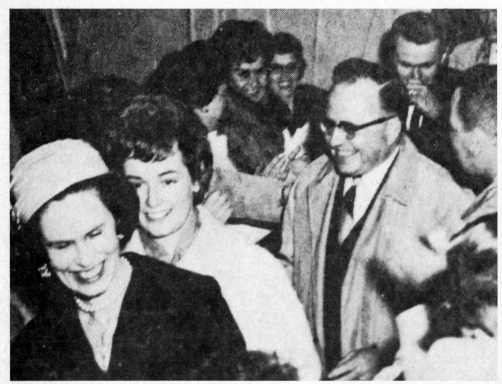

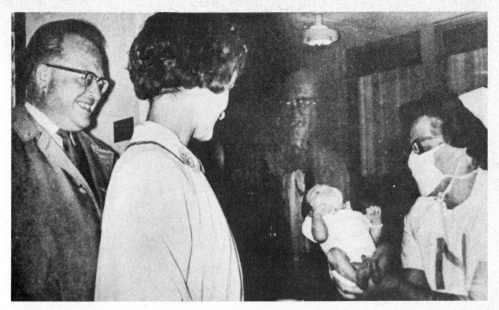

5.   JoAnn and Colin's first child, Greg, is admired by JoAnn and Ross, June 1965. Though often cold to his son, Ross was deeply fond of his daughter-in-law and grandsons.

6.   1116 Redland Avenue, Moose Jaw. Ross sold the family home to Colin and JoAnn at a bargain price after the election victory required a move to Regina. The younger Thatchers resided here throughout their marriage.

7. Ross Thatcher died suddenly a month after losing the 1971 election. Peggy and Colin Thatcher unveiled this memorial at the Saskatchewan Legislature in 1974.

8. Though friends suspected problems in her marriage, JoAnn was outwardly happy, and supportive of her husband's career.

9-10. *Above left:* Conservative leader Dick Collver announces in 1977 that Colin Thatcher, Liberal MLA for Thunder Creek since 1975, is crossing the floor. *Above right:* Colin speaks at his 1978 nomination meeting.

11. In 1977 the Thatchers purchased this condominium in Palm Springs, California. After their marriage began deteriorating, JoAnn made no use of it; but Palm Springs became Colin's second home.

12. Colin and Lynne Dally in Palm Springs. The two met in 1980. Their relationship lasted until 1983, with interruptions brought on by Colin's rages.

13. Greg on Christmas Day in Palm Springs. When the family split up, Greg chose to stay with his father. Colin would not give up custody of Greg's younger brother Regan. The third Thatcher child, Stephanie, remained with her mother over Colin's protests.

14-15. *Top:* Regan and Greg congratulate their father on being part of the Conservative landslide victory over the NDP on April 26, 1982. *Left:* Colin is sworn in as Minister of Mineral Resources (later Energy and Mines), May 8, 1982. The same day, he appointed his friend and lawyer Tony Merchant as solicitor of a Crown corporation.

16. Aerial view of the Wilson home on the corner lot at Albert Street (on the right) and 20th Avenue (across bottom). JoAnn was killed in the garage at the corner of the lane (left of centre) and 20th Avenue. Nineteen months earlier she was shot from the patio seen just above the garage.

18-21. Members of "the Team" on the Thatcher case. *Above:* Inspector Ed Swayze, known as "Sam 100" to colleagues. *At right:* From top, Staff Sergeant Al Lyons, Sergeant Jim Street, Superintendent Jim Kane.

17. *Opposite bottom:* The murder scene as the police found it. JoAnn had received multiple head wounds from a sharp metal instrument and finally was shot in the head.

22. Colin and his lawyer, Tony Merchant, at a February 1981 court appearance on charges of abducting Stephanie the day after the murder.

23. Composite drawing of the murder suspect by James Majury, of Metro Toronto Police. The resemblance to Garry Anderson complicated the investigation.

24. On May 1, 1984, Thatcher and Garry Anderson wandered around this vacant farm owned by Thatcher, conversing about the police investigation. Thatcher told Anderson: "I still don't trust the bastards for bugs," little realizing that his former accomplice was wired for sound by the police. The covert taping — codenamed "Operation Wire" — closed the case.

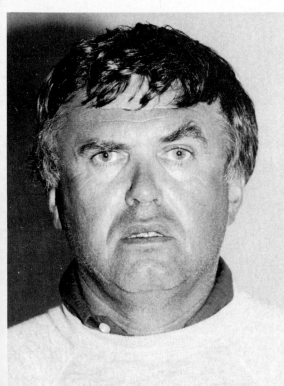

25-26. *Above:* Thatcher is arrested May 4, 1984. The plain-clothes police officers, from left, are Sergeant Jim Street (back to camera), Inspector Ed Swayze, Sergeant Wally Beaton and Sergeant Bob Murton. Swayze is reading Thatcher his legal rights. *Left:* Photo of Thatcher taken after his arrest.

27-28. *Above:* Pursued by reporters, defence lawyer Gerry Allbright arrives at the Saskatoon courthouse for the murder trial. Media from across the country competed for thirty-five spots in the courtroom. *Left:* Serge Kujawa, Saskatchewan's Associate Deputy Minister of Justice, was Crown prosecutor. With him is assistant prosecutor Al Johnston.

29. Colin Thatcher is transported in handcuffs from the Saskatoon Correctional Centre to the courthouse.

30. Tony Wilson (right), JoAnn's widower, leaves court. With him is Sergeant Bob Murton.

31. Garry Anderson was brought to the courthouse under heavy security, hidden under a blanket in the back of a police car.

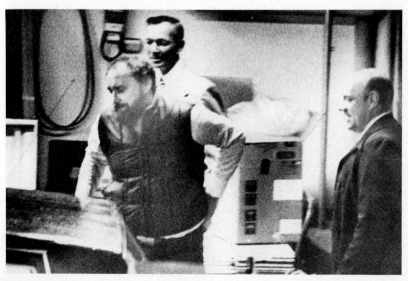

32. Lynne (Dally) Mendell arrives in court: "It doesn't ring true until it happens."

33. Sergeant Wally Beaton (centre) and Crown prosecutor Serge Kujawa chat with Crown witness Charlie Wilde,

34. The surprise witness — former Conservative leader Dick Collver (left), accompanied by lawyer Ron Barclay. Barclay advised Collver that he was not legally bound to tell police of Thatcher's talk of murderous intentions.

35-38. Members of the Thatcher family were present in the courtroom throughout the trial. From top left: Peggy, Regan, Greg and Stephanie, escorted by Thatcher housekeeper Sandra (Hammond) Silversides.

39. "I am innocent . . . but it wasn't in the cards." Thatcher is taken from the courthouse after being sentenced to life imprisonment for the first degree murder of JoAnn Wilson.

"Yeah, I can use some. I can use some for that car," Anderson agreed.

Colin was "really strapped," he said, but he would "round some up." He would leave it in a plastic bag on Friday, he promised. "I don't think we should even converse again for a good number of months," he said.

"I always have a great fear of those parabolic mikes that they have." Colin explained his wariness to the wired Anderson.

"That car that you used to have, has it disappeared?" Colin asked. "Which one?" Anderson wanted particulars.

"Whichever . . . the stuff that was left, you know."

"You mean the jacket and that? I got rid of that."

"The car too?"

"The car was cleaned and sold," Anderson lied.

"There is no question my phones are bugged. They probably always will be," Colin complained, and then asked again, "Did they hassle you at all?" He was clearly worried that Anderson might have told the police something.

Anderson assured Colin but wondered what he might do for a lawyer if it came to that. He wanted to bring Tony Merchant into the discussion.

"It ain't coming to that," Colin was confident. "It ain't coming to that 'cause they have no way of . . . there's only two places to put the connection together, and they got zero else. They've got zero else, and I mean you know what there is to put together and it ain't possible, and it ain't coming from me. I mean, just always remember that if you were ever to say that I said this or that, it's a crock of garbage. It's just always deny, deny, deny."

It was Hank Dally's advice borrowed from Lynne and now Colin was passing it on to Garry Anderson.

Colin went on. He had an alibi, he said. "I was just lucky that night. I was home with four people. Four people, pretty solid, and that's pretty hard."

Anderson was curious. "Under questioning . . . would they ever crack . . . your witnesses?"

"No. Never." Thatcher was positive.

"Never?" Anderson persisted.

"Never."

167

"No?" Anderson was pushing.

"Never. Never. Never. They tried. They worked on Sandra. . . . oh, they tried to . . . they tried to crack Sandra. . ."

"Oh, I had a hell of a time to clean the car out." Anderson got back down to business.

"Is that right?" Colin showed some sympathy.

"Yeah," Anderson continued, working in a deception, "I had a bitch of time getting the blood and stuff off."

"Yeah," Colin showed a different concern. "Is there no chance that it can ever surface? There is no chance it can surface?"

"No," Anderson assured him again.

Colin worried some more about Charlie Wilde. "The other guy, the one was here, is he still in Manitoba?"

"I'm assuming," said Anderson.

"You know, should go just visit that son of a bitch some day, but not right now." Charlie occupied an unpleasant place in Colin's mind.

Colin told Anderson that the police investigation was slowing down. From eighteen investigators initially, he said, they were now down to Wally Beaton, "a nice guy, but don't trust any of them."

As they walked around the farmyard, Colin pointed out a spot near the old barn where he would leave the money for Anderson on Friday.

"There are no loose ends," Colin again assured Anderson, "there's nothing for them to find, you know."

Anderson knew. "It's all been taken care of."

"All, sure. Heavens yes. Heavens yes. I still don't trust the bastards for bugs . . . when we talk, just assume the bastards are listening."

Anderson switched the conversation to politics and Colin bragged that his Conservative party was in a little trouble and that Premier Devine "likes to talk to an old pro again."

The accomplice with the electronic eavesdropper had been instructed to find out, if he could, what Colin's lawyer, Tony Merchant, might know about the murder.

"If I had to get a lawyer, could I get Merchant?" he asked.

"Oh, I think so."

"Is he familiar on. . .?"

"Nope," Colin was again positive.

"No?" Anderson again persisted.

"Zero. Knows zero. But it ain't coming to that."

Anderson was not so sure. "We went second . . . well, basically went one step further, you know, really."

Colin did not want his accomplice worried. "Well, it ain't coming to that because you're covered that night . . . are you covered good?"

"Well, I'm covered," was all Anderson would claim.

"Don't even tell me. But if you're covered good that night, there isn't anything. And they got no interest in you anyway. It's me."

Colin continued to calm any concerns Anderson might have. Lawyers, he said, would be "the least of your problems."

"But just remember, it's, you know, deny, deny, deny," he cautioned Anderson.

"If they ain't hassling you then there's nothing going on. I didn't know how heavily they'd leaned on you." Colin was still probing to see if Anderson had let anything slip. The accomplice turned the conversation back to the murder.

"I'm glad it went down," he said to Colin.

"Yeah." Colin agreed.

"I'm glad it's over."

"Yeah." Colin agreed again.

"How's your feelings with your old buddy Gerry Gerrand?" Anderson tried a new tack as the discussion drew to a close.

"A guy I could do. That guy I could do." Gerry Gerrand, too, was filed in an unpleasant niche of Colin's thoughts.

"Let's not push it. I think we should move on." Colin was leaving. "Next time I see you, just give me that same sign and there is no problem unless you do something stupid."

As Colin climbed back into the grey Ford, Anderson made a final attempt for a clear admission of murder.

"I'm glad you got her," he put to Thatcher.

"Okay," was Colin's acknowledgement. He was gone.

The recorder Anderson was carrying disclosed that his conversation with Colin Thatcher had lasted twenty-eight minutes.

169

It was just before 9:30 a.m. when Anderson and Thatcher separated and drove back out of the farmyard, Thatcher back to his ranch and Anderson back to the Gulf station. Anderson was far from exultant. Rather he was disconsolate. He had hoped and believed that he could induce Thatcher to describe his method of murder in stark detail. The wily rancher had confined the conversation to euphemisms and Anderson feared he had failed. More experienced men would determine that he had not. He phoned Swayze at the command base, was told to come in, and drove to Besant Park.

Sergeant LaPorte removed the equipment from Anderson and handed Ed Swayze a set of headphones. The chief investigator listened in silence to the conversation between the suspected murderer and the accomplice.

When he had heard it all, Swayze knew it was enough. He also knew there would be no more. Operation Wire was over. He ordered the base camp to be struck and headed for Regina and Serge Kujawa.

Swayze was right. The tape was enough. When it was played for Serge Kujawa, Ken MacKay and Doug Britton that afternoon, the question as to whether there was now enough evidence to prosecute was not even discussed. What was now of concern was how to proceed.

Kujawa pointed out that the investigation had been under way some fifteen months now. It would be a shame if any part of all that had been accomplished was jeopardized by precipitous action at this juncture. Further, there was more evidence to gain, perhaps quite a bit more, and it might be needed.

Thatcher had asked Anderson, "Do you need some bread?" and had promised to drop off some money for the accomplice on the coming Friday. He had pointed out a spot in the farmyard where he would leave it. A garbage bag had been mentioned.

It was easily decided that the planned money drop was too important a tie-in to ignore. Thatcher would be allowed to remain at large long enough to make the pay-off to his accomplice. The team set about planning the coverage of Friday's action.

On Wednesday afternoon Staff Sergeant Nel Silzer had just finished disposing of all the equipment and materials he had gathered up for the command base when he received orders to set

170

up Besant Park again. He recovered the Winnebagos and, with Sergeant Henry Fisher, returned to the campground and re-established the command base and its communications.

Special "O" was called out again and Gartner and Britton were directed back into the air. This time Gartner secured a high-wing plane, a Cessna Cutlass.

The team had to inspect the planned drop location on Thursday night to be able to disprove any contention that might be made that the money had not been deposited on Friday and could have been placed at any time by anyone. It had rained, raising the problem of how to get Jim Street, who had been assigned the job, into the farmyard and out without leaving telltale tracks. Gunny sacks was the solution, and at 11:00 p.m. Street, ungainly on wrapped feet, stumbled through the pitch-dark yard praying that he would not find the abandoned well. He verified that nothing had yet been put in place.

The investigation was approaching a successful climax and the police and prosecutors associated with it were affected by the building excitement. They could not resist setting up a pool — all proceeds to go to the one who made the nearest estimate on how much money the millionaire rancher would pay his accomplice for three and a half years of assistance and silence in a matter as serious as murder.

On Friday morning Special "O", on the ground and in the air, watched as Colin Thatcher left Redland Avenue at 7:30 a.m. and drove out to Caron. He visited some cattle in a pasture, spent a few minutes at the ranch, dropped three bags at the Caron dumping grounds, and stopped in at the Gulf station for coffee. At 10:00 a.m. he drove into the abandoned farmyard, stayed only a minute, and then drove home to Moose Jaw.

Forty-five minutes after Colin Thatcher left the farmyard Jim Street was back. At the spot Colin had indicated to Garry Anderson, behind the barn and under a plank, Street recovered a plastic garbage bag that had not been there on his inspection twelve hours earlier. In the bag was $550.

The pool participants screamed as Deputy Chief Tom Savage and Crown Prosecutor Doug Britton split the penny-ante proceeds. They had guessed that the pay-off would be $500. All the players had discounted their estimates severely because of

171

their knowledge of Colin's tight-fisted reputation, but $550 was, they felt, beyond reason.

Even Garry Anderson, who knew Colin better than any of them, was angered at Colin's valuation of his contribution.

"He's a cheap son-of-a-bitch," said the accomplice.

CHAPTER 13

Closing the Net

During the month of May 1964, and for some time after, the Thatcher residence at 1116 Redland Avenue was the object of intense curious observation by many Moose Jaw and area residents. As the home of Premier-elect W. Ross Thatcher, the first non-CCF/NDP premier in twenty years, it became a site of considerable local interest, not only to the curious but also to a sizeable number of job and favour seekers. The traffic on Redland Avenue swelled noticeably.

In the early morning of May 7, 1984, a very different group of visitors was interested in the Redland Avenue residence. Nearly a dozen Regina police were parked in a shopping mall parking lot only a few blocks to the east. They were armed with search warrants and were planning to attend at Redland Avenue as soon as they were told of the arrest of Colin Thatcher.

The arrest on a charge of murder of a person with the power and prominence of Colin Thatcher would have called for some caution in any case, but here there were good additional reasons for care and forethought, and a carefully conceived plan had been put in place. Colin Thatcher was believed to be dangerous and in possession of firearms. Also, there was every likelihood that important evidence would be located in his residence or at the ranch or on his farms. A thorough search had to be coordinated with the arrest.

Ed Swayze and his team were convinced that Colin Thatcher was not only capable of, but would be inclined towards, desperate action when cornered. They knew from Garry Anderson that Colin had stated that he did not intend to give up

173

quietly, if it ever came to that. Also, Colin had shown a callous disregard for legal process through an almost continuous series of civil and criminal actions stretching over the previous five years.

Also from Anderson, as well as from other sources, came the information that Colin had at least one pistol in addition to the .357 magnum Garry had returned to him, if it was still around. Again, in the recorded conversation with Anderson, it was evident that Colin did not easily give up a grudge.

Finally, a psychological profile which the Federal Bureau of Investigation had prepared on Colin for Ed Swayze confirmed all of the above. The FBI had developed this specialty to assist in predicting the behaviour of hostage takers, hi-jackers, etc. and the Regina Police Department had brought this modern tool to bear upon their planning. It told them what they already knew, but it helped them keep their concerns foremost in their minds.

Swayze was certain that Colin's firearms, particularly the pistol he was known to have, would be at Redland Avenue.

The basic requirements for bringing about the arrest of Colin Thatcher, thus, were obvious and quickly agreed upon. He would have to be taken when he was away from Redland Avenue, alone, in circumstances where he would be least likely to be armed, and in a situation where evasive action could be prevented.

Wally Beaton fondly thought of the ease with which Colin could be handled at the Regina airport. After clearing security they could be certain he would not be carrying a gun. All agreed that would be the ideal set-up, but it wasn't available. They had had to let Colin come in on the Frontier flight from Denver the night of April 30 because of the Garry Anderson arrangements, and he had no further immediate travel plans.

Timing was another problem. Colin had told Anderson that he would make the money drop on Friday morning. His reason was that he was due in court with Tony Merchant on Friday afternoon to hear Provincial Judge R.H. Allan's reserved decision whether or not he would commit them for trial on the abduction and mischief charges.

Friday afternoon, after the drop, was the earliest the arrest could be made. The courthouse would have been an excellent location for the arrest, too, but Swayze and Kujawa were

174

sensitive to the negative publicity and feelings such a move would create, regardless of whether Judge Allan's decision went for or against Thatcher. It might smack of persecution.

Saturday and Sunday were out because Colin's weekend behaviour was not reliable. The arrest would be a big operation and to mount it and then stand it down would involve the movement of a lot of people and would jeopardize security.

The team was reluctant to wait, well aware that a lot can happen over a weekend to throw off well-laid plans, but finally decided to go Monday morning.

The greatest predictability Colin had disclosed was in his morning trip to the ranch. Somewhere between home and the ranch on that journey on Monday morning an intercept would have to be arranged. The Regina cops really didn't think Colin carried a gun on those trips, although one in the truck was a possibility.

When Swayze pointed out the down ramp from the Main Street overpass to the Trans-Canada, which was on the route Colin took almost every time, the site's obvious advantages caused it to be immediately selected. There would be a minimum of traffic and no room for evasive action. It was close to perfect.

The ramp had another advantage. It was just outside Moose Jaw city limits and, accordingly, the Moose Jaw police would not have to be involved or even informed until after the event. This further limited those in the know and maintained security.

On Sunday afternoon, May 6, all fifteen members of the Regina force detailed to the arrest and search, together with the RCMP Special "O" and "I" representatives, gathered in the CID quarters of the Regina police station for briefing. Ed Swayze was his usual meticulous self in ensuring that each participant knew and understood exactly what was expected of him.

Early Monday morning Staff Sergeant Nel Silzer, for the third time in eight days, lumbered down No. 1 Highway to Moose Jaw in the ancient Winnebago. This time he was loaded with equipment for the search team — metal detectors, shovels, crowbars. By 6:00 a.m. he was parked just off Main Street in the Town & Country Mall making coffee. Six unmarked cars were with him.

From their vantage place in the mall, the arrest team could,

175

and did, see Colin Thatcher turn onto Main Street and head north to the overpass.

Colin Thatcher was well known to, and less than a favourite of, the members of the Moose Jaw RCMP detachment. His attitude towards law enforcement officials had been made very plain to them. When two members of the detachment were asked to participate in the arrest manoeuvre, they were quite willing to oblige, even though they were called out earlier than their normal shift.

The plan was to have Colin stopped on the ramp by a fully marked and equipped RCMP cruiser. He had been stopped by these cars several times, usually for ignoring the seat belt requirement, and was familiar with them.

At 7:52 a.m. word came to the mall from Special "O" that Colin Thatcher had left his house on Redland Avenue. As he turned north on Main Street the RCMP cruiser pulled in behind him and, when they turned down the ramp, put on its flashing lights. Colin immediately stopped and stepped quickly from his truck so it would not be apparent that he was once again not wearing his seat belt.

The four unmarked Regina cars that had been following the cruiser swiftly boxed in the Thatcher truck. It could go nowhere.

Sergeant Wally Beaton had driven his car with Inspector Ed Swayze directly to the rear of the truck. Swayze went straight to Thatcher and said:

> Wilbert Colin Thatcher, I have an information charging you with the first degree murder of JoAnn Wilson. You are under arrest. You need not say anything. You have nothing to fear from any threat and nothing to gain from any promise or favour. Anything you do say may be used as evidence. You have the right to legal counsel without delay. Do you understand your rights?

Colin Thatcher responded "Yes," as Sergeant Jim Street handcuffed his wrists together in front of him, although no one who was there is certain that he fully comprehended.

Almost any citizen, no matter what his experience, suffers tension and mild shock when stopped by the police. Colin's arrest that morning was dramatic in the extreme — instantly

176

surrounded by five cars and ten policemen, he was told of his charge for a murder of which he thought he was clear.

Street and Beaton promptly put Colin in the back seat of the nearest car and got in with him, Beaton on his left, Street on his right. Bob Murton took the wheel and drove down the ramp to the highway, did a U-turn at the first median cut and headed for Regina. The entire event had consumed only a flicker of time.

Colin Thatcher was in something close to shock. Ed Swayze had noticed, as he was performing the required ritual, that Colin's mouth was agape and dry and that his eyes were dull.

In the car Colin sat in stunned silence. Murton, Beaton and Street are all big, imposing men. They did not encourage conversation, either by appearance or behaviour. They were under instructions not to. Street was wearing a wire to catch anything Colin did say, and they wanted it to come straight from him and not be contaminated by any questions or provocation.

The ride continued in complete quiet until the car came almost to Belle Plaine, seventeen miles down the road. Colin then asked, in a low and halting tone, "What did you say that charge was?"

"Murder One," replied Beaton.

"I thought that was what you said," Colin said.

Colin then asked a question, the significance of which loomed during the trial five months later.

"Has Greg been arrested too?"

"No."

They were still driving through Colin's Thunder Creek constituency and the MLA, now accused of murder, recovered his aplomb sufficiently to comment on the state of the fields they were passing.

As soon as the search team back at the mall received word that Colin Thatcher's arrest had gone off successfully, they headed for 1116 Redland Avenue, arriving at 8:30 a.m. The Winnebago was parked directly in front of the house and used as a base.

Sergeant Gene Stusek had the search warrants. He had had them for a week now. If anything had gone wrong during the Besant operation precipitating an early arrest, his team would have moved then.

Stusek and Constable Sharon Fettes, the only female officer on

177

the team, and there because of Stephanie, went to the house while the rest waited. Stusek presented his warrant to Greg, the oldest one present.

Greg had left the house with his father half an hour earlier, following Colin in the station wagon. He had apparently witnessed the arrest, returned to the house, and called Tony Merchant.

As the police entered the Thatcher home, nineteen-year-old Greg turned to fifteen-year-old Regan and ten-year-old Stephanie and commanded: "All right you guys, don't anybody say anything." The cops were shocked at the hardness of the youth.

Greg had Merchant on the telephone and Stusek spoke briefly to the lawyer, explaining what was up.

Great care had been taken to anticipate problems. Constable Ed Pearson, from the identification section, photographed every room before the search commenced. Another photographer with another camera, Constable Walter Frykland, repeated the process after the search was complete. There would be no accusations later that the search had been conducted in anything but a circumspect manner.

Staff Sergeant Nel Silzer was assigned to Colin's multi-purpose office on the first floor. The ten-by-ten-foot room was filled with paper — personal, political and business. There were the constituency records, correspondence and lists. There were the farm accounts, bank statements, books of account, etc. Everything was there, including files on the estate of Ross Thatcher.

Silzer was there all morning, sifting carefully through the mounds of documents. In the bottom drawer of a filing cabinet he found two cancelled cheques written by Colin Thatcher on an account he maintained at the California Canadian Bank, 4230 Bob Hope Drive, Rancho Mirage, California. One was dated January 29, 1982, in the amount of $272.95 and the other was dated March 6, 1982, in the amount of $72.82. Both were payable to the Frontier Gun Shop. The Frontier Gun Shop, it was soon learned, is in Palm Springs, California, Colin's winter playground.

More pay dirt was hit by other members of the search team. In

178

two closets off Colin's bedroom, Corporal Bird found a doll shower and a June 25, 1982, copy of the *Los Angeles Times,* a Crown Royal bag containing a loaded Rohm .38 Special revolver, and a wig box with a wig holder.

One wall of the garage was stacked with split firewood. Not far down in this pile Sergeant Stusek came up with a Remington .38 Special ammunition box holding twenty-five live rounds and twenty spent shell casings. In a closet off the garage entry he found two toques, one blue and one brown.

The .38 Special revolver was, of course, unregistered. It was to have a lot to do with Colin Thatcher's remaining in jail for the next six months.

After completing their examination of the Redland Avenue residence, the members of the search team covered the Caron ranch, Colin's farm buildings five miles north of the ranch, and the deserted farmyard where the meeting with Anderson had taken place. Nothing of interest was found at any of these locations.

Another carefully planned day had gone off without a hitch. The tired searchers and the weary Winnebago returned to Regina.

Colin Thatcher was arraigned before Provincial Judge D.E. Fenwick and remanded in custody a week, until May 14, 1984. As Colin was taken out to the Regina Correctional Centre, Tony Merchant, who had appeared in court with him, got busy arranging a bail application. It was unthinkable that Colin Thatcher would spend any time in jail. In the hurry to spring Colin, some serious errors were made that would haunt the defence, and, to a lesser extent, the Crown at trial.

Queen's Bench Justice G.A.F. Maurice was available and, before noon, Merchant and Kujawa were before him arranging a time for a bail hearing. Merchant wanted the application dealt with that afternoon, and made a major concession to enable it to be dealt with immediately.

Bail applications are known as "show cause" hearings because that is what the accused must do in explaining "why his detention in custody is not justified." The usual procedure is for the Crown, when resisting bail, to produce some of its witnesses to describe the offence and the likelihood of conviction. An accused will be kept in custody if the court finds that his appearance to the charge is questionable or if it is thought necessary "for the safety or protection of the public."

Merchant, supremely confident that no court would hold Colin Thatcher, waived his right to hear the Crown evidence and undertook to accept Kujawa's description of the case as binding on all concerned. In doing so he delivered himself into the Crown's hands. Kujawa would have no difficulty presenting a more complete outline of the Crown case through his own mouth than he would be able to by examining witnesses. Merchant was assuming that the prosecution had a thin case since it had taken fifteen months to lay a charge. He did not know about the tape.

Even with the defence concession, it was not possible to hear the bail application before the next afternoon. Colin would have to spend a night in jail.

As the news of Colin's arrest for murder reverberated throughout Saskatchewan, the shocked public began to ask the question, Would this particular murder accused be allowed free on bail?

Most people think bail is not granted in murder cases, although it sometimes is. Even so, few expected that standard rules would be applied to the Thunder Creek MLA. The issue of "even justice for all" arose and soon made its way to the Saskatchewan Legislature. Later in the month Opposition Leader Allan Blakeney demanded (and got) from Justice Minister Gary Lane an assurance that the accused Thatcher "will receive no special privilege."

Merchant was stunned when he heard Kujawa describe to Mr. Justice Maurice the tape recording of his client, containing, Kujawa said, conversation about the actual killing and threats to three people. The lawyer said later that at that point he should have suspended the hearing and called for a new deal, even if that meant walking out of the courtroom and risking a contempt of court citation. The defence knew then that it had been had, and that all its submissions about Colin Thatcher's wealth and position, and his excellent (and well-travelled) track record of showing up for his court appearances, might not be enough.

Merchant and Thatcher had aimed high on the bail application.

Release on bail usually involves some restrictive conditions, such as regular reporting to the police and limited travel. Some such conditions were recommended in a Bail Verification Report prepared for the court by a Saskatchewan probation officer. Reporting to the police, Merchant said, was unnecessary for his client who was not "a run-of-the-mill sort of person." Thatcher, he said, was so well known in Moose Jaw that if he "weren't there for two days some policeman would notice it."

Travel restrictions would impede the accused's ability to travel to Palm Springs, and both Colin and Merchant thought he should continue to enjoy that right.

In spite of the surprise of the tape, when Merchant was finished with his submission he thought he had succeeded. Kujawa had challenged Mr. Justice Maurice. If Colin Thatcher was to be released at all, the Crown had no concern about conditions, he said. That put it on an all or nothing basis.

Donna Weisshaar, who had prepared the Bail Verification Report and had consulted with Colin in the process, had recommended against any release of this accused. There was "some question in respect of the subject's attitude," she said.

Mr. Justice Maurice held against Merchant. He found that Thatcher had not satisfied the onus on him to show that his detention was not necessary to ensure his attendance in court "to be dealt with according to law." The judge also found that keeping Colin in jail was required "for the protection or safety of the public." He mentioned the threats Kujawa said were on the tape and the unregistered .38 found in Colin's home.

The bail refusal was quickly taken to the Saskatchewan Court of Appeal. Tony Merchant, who had learned, to his surprise he said, that it was part of the Crown's allegation that Colin Thatcher had performed the murder himself and was not charged just with arranging the death, decided that he would be an alibi witness and could no longer act as counsel. He arranged for Gerry Allbright to come down from Saskatoon and handle the appeal which was heard on May 24 by Chief Justice Bayda and Justices Hall and Tallis.

"Given the material filed before him, we find that the Chamber Judge had little choice but to do what he did," said the court.

181

Colin would stay in jail at least until the preliminary inquiry, but the court authorized a further bail application then "in the light of the evidence adduced at the preliminary."

Allbright, who had found the defence stuck with Merchant's agreement in front of Mr. Justice Maurice to accept Kujawa's summary, attempted to counter with some evidence of Colin's innocence. A flurry of affidavits was exchanged between the defence and the Crown just before the appeal, unnecessarily it turned out, because the Court of Appeal declined to accept them.

Affidavits were sworn by Colin, Tony Merchant, the Thatcher housekeeper, Sandra Hammond, Sandra's brother, Pat Hammond, Greg and Regan Thatcher, and Barbara Wright from the ranch. All had to do with an alibi for Colin. The affidavits were hastily drawn and the times they identified were to cause the defence difficulty at the trial.

Merchant and Thatcher stated in their affidavits that the lawyer had telephoned Thatcher twice on the evening of the murder, the first time advising "that there was some problem at the Wilson home" and the second time advising of the killing. Merchant estimated the time of the first call at "sometime before 6:30 p.m." and the second at "some time after 7:00." Thatcher swore that his knowledge of the death came from Merchant's second call.

At the time of the bail application, the Crown believed that Colin had been speaking to Lynne Dally at 6:24 p.m. and had then told her of JoAnn's death. Wondering how he had acquired the knowledge by 6:24, the Crown filed an affidavit by Wally Beaton disclosing the call.

It was an error. As it turned out, there was no real proof that Colin had been a party to the 6:24 call, but he promptly seized upon it as part of his alibi.

The preliminary inquiry, initially scheduled for September, was moved up to commence June 25, partly to accommodate the accused who had to wait in jail and partly to ensure that he did. The Court of Appeal would have been more reluctant to refuse bail to Thatcher if he faced a long wait.

At the preliminary inquiry the Crown would have to come up with more than Serge Kujawa's say-so that it had a case against Colin Thatcher.

Gerry Allbright of Saskatoon had been retained to defend both Thatcher and Merchant on the charges of abduction and mischief which had been laid the day following the murder. Merchant had approved of Allbright's handling of those matters and it was natural to use him again on the bail appeal.

Thatcher and Merchant considered and rejected the idea of bringing in a high-profile criminal defence specialist from Toronto. That might not sit well with a Saskatchewan jury.

There are not many prominent defence lawyers in Saskatchewan, and almost all of them have been active politically. That was an eliminating factor to Merchant and his client. They decided to go with Allbright.

The thirty-seven-year-old Saskatoon litigation lawyer had a strong background in spite of his relative youth. A native of Prince Albert, Saskatchewan, Allbright had graduated from the University of Saskatchewan Law School in 1970 and was admitted to the bar the following year.

Working out of his home town, Allbright spent three years prosecuting throughout northern Saskatchewan, an excellent way to acquire a feel for the courtroom. A couple of years working in government civil litigation and the developing Saskatchewan Legal Aid Commission rounded out his early experience. He had been in private practice in Saskatoon for seven years, mostly specializing in civil and criminal litigation. He had formed his own firm earlier in 1984 and welcomed the Thatcher case as an opportunity to firmly establish himself.

Well regarded by his fellow lawyers, Allbright had been elected a bencher of the Law Society in 1979. Three years later, he became the youngest ever to be selected president. He had been appointed a Queen's Counsel in 1981 after only the required minimum ten years at the bar.

Not tall, but Hollywood-handsome, Allbright has a mellifluous baritone voice and is confidently articulate. He has no difficulty acquiring and holding attention. Hard-working and ambitious, the lawyer is also athletic and musical. Good at tennis (he once instructed) and curling, his guitar playing and singing will hold an audience.

A member of the Pentecostal Church, Allbright is a deeply committed Christian. But the lawyer's religious beliefs would not interfere with those being developed by his client as Colin Thatcher, pondering his fate in the Regina Correctional Centre, considered the teachings of Christ in a new light.

With Colin Thatcher safely arrested and tucked away on remand in the Regina Correctional Centre, the team got busy cleaning up loose ends and running down the leads that had been uncovered during the search of the Redland Avenue home.

The machinist who had built silencers for the .357 magnum on Garry Anderson's instructions was interviewed. He had made at least four out of pipe and washers and threaded them on the end of the gun's barrel.

Anderson claimed that he (and Thatcher) had test-fired the silencer-equipped .357 on a fence post at the abandoned farm north of Caronport. Bob Murton took specialists from the RCMP crime lab to the site. A piece of the fence post was removed for laboratory examination and, with the aid of a metal detector, a spent bullet was dug out of the earth near the post.

Garry Anderson had burned the items left in his Mercury that Colin Thatcher had borrowed in a barrel used for that purpose on his mother's farm. Murton and Street sifted through the trash in the barrel and took anything that seemed identifiable to the crime lab. Microscopic examination established the presence of sunglasses made by Revue, fibres of the sort found in wigs, and some clothing. A zipper was identified as coming from jeans of a size appropriate to Colin Thatcher.

The team decided to check once more with Colin's lady friends in the hope that they might feel more comfortable about discussing the case now that he was in jail. The young woman who had been told that the first shooting had been done by Colin's hired assassin now reported she had also been told an even more bizarre tale about the killing. JoAnn had been dealing in narcotics — mostly cocaine — in a large way, Colin told her, and had been killed by a competitor from Vancouver. Colin, upset because of the beating JoAnn had received, went to Vancouver. There he arranged and witnessed the beating and killing of the offender, he claimed.

Another former intimate recalled that Colin, speaking of the murder, had said: ''If she would have given up the children, none

184

of this would have happened."

Although the investigators encountered more cooperation than they had on previous interviews, nothing of real value was secured.

The American authorities were asked to attempt a trace on the Rohm .38 revolver that had been seized in Colin's bedroom closet. The report came back that the gun, manufactured in Germany, had been exported to New York in 1968 and then shipped to Dave's House of Guns in Dallas, Texas. There it disappeared into private hands.

It was in Palm Springs that the real evidence was located. The FBI was asked to look into the Frontier Gun Shop named in the cheques found in Thatcher's home. The bureau quickly reported that, on January 29, 1982, one Wilbert Colin Thatcher had purchased a Ruger Security Six .357 revolver from the Palm Springs gun shop. After the required fifteen-day waiting period he had picked it up and bought quite a lot of ammunition. On February 20, he had taken 100 rounds of .38 specials and on March 6, 300 rounds more of the same. The .357 will handle ammunition designated either .357 or .38.

On March 6, Thatcher had also purchased two boxes of Western Winchester ammunition, one in .357 calibre and one in .38 calibre. Both were aluminum-jacketed, hollow-point bullets. The .357 bullets weighed 145 grains and the .38 weighed 95 grains.

Ron Williams, the Frontier Gun Shop employee who had handled the sales, remembered Colin Thatcher well. He had also sold Colin a holster for the .357. The buyer had a local address and a California driver's licence, qualifying as a resident for the purchase. As to Colin's apparent suitability to acquire a gun, Williams later said: "He wasn't a straight arrow, but he wasn't bent badly enough not to sell him a gun."

In early June, with the bail appeals settled and the preliminary inquiry set for the end of the month, Ed Swayze decided to make a trip to Palm Springs. He needed to have a search made of Colin's condominium and to talk to Ron Williams about coming to Canada to testify.

There was someone else in Palm Springs Swayze wanted to meet, also. Although Lynne Dally had told Wally Beaton more than a year before that she would not come to Canada to testify at a murder trial, and could not be compelled to come, Swayze still wanted to see what the possibilities were.

Rereading the statement Colin's former girlfriend had given Wally Beaton in the light of the evidence that had since been acquired, made Lynne look like a much more interesting witness than had at first appeared. She had told Beaton of watching Colin pack a handgun in a doll shower box stuffed with a newspaper. Such a box and such a newspaper had been seized from the closet off Colin's bedroom.

Swayze asked Serge Kujawa to accompany him to Palm Springs. Nothing loath, the prosecutor replied that this was an investigation decision and, if the chief investigator wanted him in Palm Springs, he would go to Palm Springs. Kujawa did, however, want to know what Swayze had in mind.

Swayze explained that obtaining search warrants in the United States was technically difficult and that it would be helpful to have the senior prosecutor along.

But the real reason was that Swayze wanted some assistance with Lynne Dally, now Lynne Mendell by reason of her marriage. "It's because of that special way you have with flakey females," he told Kujawa.

On Wednesday, June 6, Kujawa, Swayze and Gene Stusek were in Palm Springs. The inspector and the prosecutor had a long chat with Lynne Mendell in her father's Sheraton Oasis Hotel. The prospective witness was as frank and revealing as she had been in her second interview with Wally Beaton in April 1983, but was no more inclined to participate in the trial. She agreed to discuss the proposal with her husband and her attorney father.

The next day Swayze phoned Lynne and was told that her husband and father had advised her to stay out of the murder case; she would be following that advice.

Swayze did not give up. On Friday he phoned Lynne again and asked to be allowed to speak with her and her father. Lynne gave the investigator her father's number. Swayze called it and left his number, but his call was not returned.

Still the investigator persisted. On Saturday he spoke with Lynne's husband, Bill Mendell, then vice-president and general

186

manager of a Palm Springs television station, who agreed to bring Lynne over to the Canadians' hotel room for a further discussion. They came, spent more than two hours examining all the considerations, and finally decided that Lynne would appear as a Crown witness at the preliminary inquiry in Regina two weeks and two days later.

Kujawa was impressed with the persuasiveness of the chief investigator and his unwavering confidence that this witness, so essential to his case, would eventually recognize and respond to her duty.

Swayze, in turn, recognized in Lynne Mendell a special need for reassurance and was to keep in close touch with her, right up to the trial and after. When Lynne began to receive telephoned threats, the policeman's concern became of real importance.

Kujawa was equally impressed with Bill Mendell's sense of civic responsibility. The TV executive had changed his initial view about his wife's participation and spoke with simple eloquence and sincerity of the duty and sacrifice necessary to preserve the freedoms of society. Lynne's husband obviously made a considerable impression upon her and had much to do with her eventual decision.

Ron Williams had been a sheriff's officer in California for sixteen years and related quickly to the murder investigation. A former Albertan, he willingly agreed to testify in Canada.

Williams told Swayze and Stusek that Colin Thatcher had asked for a gun to protect his condominium. For ammunition Williams, a firearms expert, had recommended the Winchester aluminum-jacketed hollow-points as a "people stopper." The silver-tipped bullets were new on the market and the Frontier Gun Shop carried them only in the .357 and .38 special calibre.

The warrant for the search of Colin Thatcher's condominium had been secured and the search was conducted with the assistance of the Palm Springs Police Department and the FBI. Nothing of evidentiary value was found, but the investigators from Regina were startled by what they spotted on the hat rack just inside the door. Hanging with a variety of other baseball-style caps was one with the name and insignia: "Regina Police Service K-9."

CHAPTER 14

The Preliminary Inquiry

Colin Thatcher would admit at his trial that he had been "disappointed" to see Lynne Mendell appear at the preliminary inquiry. But that must have been an understatement of his emotions as he watched his Palm Springs mistress enter the Regina courtroom that June morning. He had learned from Gerry Allbright the day before that Lynne would be called, but her actual presence as a Crown witness was still a shock. Colin was not accustomed to having his intimate friends turn against him and Lynne had indeed been an intimate.

Kujawa had been prepared to bet on his Palm Springs witness showing up in Regina, but had not been willing to jeopardize the Crown's credibility by making an advance billing that he might have to retract. Time and distance might have worn down the commitment he and Swayze had come home with two weeks earlier, and the practical prosecutor waited until his witness was in town before disclosing her imminent appearance to the defence. As it turned out, Mendell had changed her mind about coming to Regina, but had "changed it back."

When Lynne Mendell quoted Colin as having said, "It's a strange feeling to blow your wife away," the court clerk swivelled in her chair and fixed the accused with a venomous glare. The first revelation of the bitter passions contained in the Thatcher murder case caused shock waves in the crowded courtroom.

On Monday, June 25, the preliminary inquiry opened in the largest courtroom Regina's courthouse could provide. Two dozen members of the media, selected under a novel arrangement designed to eliminate elbow contests for seats, filled the first two rows. The remainder of the 100 seats were available to the public, which, as the inquiry progressed, began to arrive early and in large numbers, presaging the line-ups which later would be seen at the trial.

Muzzled by the usual order prohibiting the publication of the evidence, in this case extending even to the names of the witnesses, the reporters were hard pressed for copy as Saskatchewan's biggest story of the year unfolded before them.

Security was tight and all reporters and spectators were electronically scanned as they entered the courtroom. Provincial Court Judge Marion Wedge of Saskatoon had been selected to preside.

The theoretical purpose of a preliminary inquiry is the judicial testing of the Crown case to determine if it justifies putting the accused on trial. In practice that feature is nearly automatic as the provincial court judges who preside at this stage rarely find the evidence insufficient to put before a jury. In effect, then, the real purpose of the preliminary is to expose the prosecution's evidence to the defence, which uses the opportunity as a form of discovery, probing to prevent later surprise and to identify potential weaknesses.

Kujawa produced Lynne Mendell on Tuesday morning. When he was finished, Allbright, not unreasonably, asked if she could stand over until the following morning so that he could confer with Colin before cross-examining. Kujawa objected, wanting Mendell's entire testimony to be taken while she was before the court. He felt he had no right to hold the witness in Canada and, if she failed to return for the trial, he would be able to use her transcribed evidence only if it had been tested in cross-examination.

Suggesting that Allbright should be able to proceed without preparation, Kujawa offered some gratuitous advice on the defence conduct at a preliminary. Allbright took offence and replied that Kujawa ''obviously doesn't know how a defence should be conducted.''

Hidden behind the angry exchange was the fact that Allbright does have an unconventional theory that he was to put into practice at the Thatcher preliminary. He believes that it is possible to cause a Crown witness so much discomfort upon this

189

first appearance in the witness stand that he or she will choose not to show up for the trial or, at least, will avoid repeating sensitive testimony. In few cases do the witnesses enjoy the luxury of deciding to stay home, but in the Thatcher preliminary the Allbright strategy might have worked with Lynne Mendell. It nearly succeeded, Allbright claims, with Garry Anderson.

Allbright's attack on Lynne Mendell was characterized by his use of the impersonal "witness" as a form of address when speaking to her, a technique he employs when seeking an extra degree of intimidation. But Mendell was not intimidated. She denied that she was a woman scorned, wanting retribution for the years she had wasted on Colin that did not end in marriage. Allbright suggested that Mendell's story was "a flight of imagination" and that the reward was a motivation for her being in Regina. Bright and articulate, Mendell stood her ground, and Allbright backed away, catching Kujawa by surprise and without a witness ready.

Lynne Mendell, billed as a "surprise witness" by the media, had the spotlight at the preliminary, but it was Garry Anderson who would make or break the Crown case. Allbright perceived this and threw his best effort at the accomplice, spending more than half of the fourth and last day of the hearing trying to destroy the believability of his story.

Garry Anderson continued to be a problem to Ed Swayze, even after the success of the taping encounter with Colin Thatcher. The accomplice had been relocated west of Saskatchewan but had become unhappy with the RCMP, who were supervising his change of identity. Swayze feared that Anderson was losing his will to continue through to the end of the case, and he conscripted Serge Kujawa for a clandestine trip to Edmonton to confer with the witness.

Their meeting, in a downtown hotel, was the first between the prosecutor and the Crown's number one witness. They shared a common country background and a strong rapport between the two developed immediately. Kujawa helped to restore some confidence to Anderson, and Swayze was to call upon Kujawa again for similar help.

The next time was Tuesday night of the second day of the preliminary. Anderson, due to testify the next day, had been ensconed at St. Michael's, a Franciscan retreat house at Lumsden, a few miles out of Regina. The accomplice had lost control of his emotions, was ranting about the treatment he was receiving and threatening not to testify.

Subpoenas have only a limited use with truly recalcitrant witnesses, so Swayze once more enlisted Kujawa and the two made a late-night trip out to the retreat. There they met with Anderson and Lloyd Balicki, still acting as counsel to the witness but who, because of a misunderstanding, would be discharged by his client later in the summer.

This time it was Swayze who broke the ice — by referring to the well-fed look that he and Anderson shared — and restored the situation. To placate Anderson, Swayze had him removed to a Regina hotel, and he appeared ready to testify on the morrow.

On Wednesday, Garry Anderson took the witness stand and, with Lloyd Balicki watching, spent the afternoon being led by Serge Kujawa through his years of involvement with Colin Thatcher. His stress was apparent but his story was told. The real test would come when he faced Gerry Allbright in the morning.

Allbright had Wednesday night to consider Anderson's testimony and prepare his cross-examination. In the morning he handed the accomplice a glass of water, saying "you may need this," and began.

What followed was three hours of pure theatre. Allbright plays his role as defence counsel to the fullest and against Anderson he pulled out all the stops. With word, tone and gesture he heaped scorn and disbelief upon the story of assisting with murder. Sometimes seeming to almost climb into the witness box with the large Anderson, he thrust his face within inches of the witness as he "suggested" the entire tale was a fabrication.

Anderson was so careful and deliberate with his responses that Allbright accused him of having been coached. Why the pause, he wanted to know, before answering the simple question, "How old are you?"

If the defence lawyer discerned the terror seething below the surface, he failed to capitalize on it. He suggested that Anderson's immunity deal was dependent upon his testimony, that he was motivated by the reward in "concocting" his evidence. But the accomplice survived.

191

Allbright probably did not know how desperately determined Anderson was to succeed in his ordeal. When he did, his feeling of triumph was obvious to Kujawa who met his witness briefly outside the courtroom. At their earlier encounters, Anderson's handshake had been limp and lifeless. That afternoon Kujawa was fortunate to be braced for the powerful grip he received.

Charlie Wilde took the clean-up position of the major Crown witnesses. Unlike Garry Anderson, Charlie was under no stress whatever. He freely admitted his criminal record and drug addiction, but would not agree with Allbright that his mental faculties had been affected by his habit. "Pretty fair memory for a drug addict," he claimed. Charlie Wilde would present the most difficulty to Allbright as he prepared his cross-examination for trial.

Both Colin Thatcher and Gerry Allbright seemed well aware that they were on display at the preliminary and that their conduct and deportment would be scrutinized carefully by the hungry press corps. Colin masked any surprise or concern he may have felt as he watched Lynne Mendell, Garry Anderson and Charlie Wilde parade his secrets through the witness box. Allbright went further. Frequently during the Crown testimony he would rear back in mock horror at the dastardly concoctions that were coming forward, or turn and share a wink with the audience.

At the conclusion of the Crown evidence Allbright asked for a dismissal. His concern, however, was not so much for the merit of his motion as for the impression it would make on the media and the public. He could not be seen to concede any part of the strength of the Crown case.

Allbright argued that the test to warrant putting Colin Thatcher or anyone to trial was evidence that showed that he was "probably guilty." This evidence, he submitted, failed to meet that test.

Judge Wedge disagreed. The test, she held, was whether "a reasonable jury properly instructed could infer guilt from that evidence." The Crown evidence met that test, she held, and Colin Thatcher was committed for trial "at a judge and jury sittings of the Queen's Bench at Regina."

"I will be exonerated," said Colin Thatcher as he left the courthouse to return to the Regina Correctional Centre.

Nine court reporters went to work transcribing the recording of the evidence at the preliminary and, with unusual dispatch, the four volumes of the transcripts were completed and available within days. Almost immediately it became known that they were public court documents and could be purchased by anyone for the fee of $153.00. Dozens were sold, passed from hand to hand, and photocopied by a public hungry for details of the murder evidence. Coffee-break debate became more precise as some knowledge of the actual happenings in the case seeped through Regina and out into the rest of Saskatchewan.

Allbright promptly accepted the invitation of the Court of Appeal and made another application for bail for Colin Thatcher. On July 10 it came before Mr. Justice K.R. Halvorson who was not at all sure that the Court of Appeal had the jurisdiction to authorize the second bail hearing. Reluctantly undertaking to hear the matter, he accepted the affidavits that the defence and the Crown had put together for the first bail appeal but which had not been accepted by the Court of Appeal.

It may have been a questionable second chance, but a second chance it was, and Allbright was not going to make any mistakes this time. He put everything he had forward. Now that the Crown case was out in the open, he was able to point out supposed areas of weakness, and dispute Kujawa's claim that the tape contained admissions and threats. Allbright emphasized the difficulty he and Thatcher were having conferring privately, and was willing to accept severe restrictions on Colin's movements if he was released.

Kujawa had mentioned in the first bail hearing that the public was watching to see if Colin Thatcher received any special considerations. Allbright agreed, but argued that the special consideration his client was getting was the unreasonable refusal of bail; the public was being given the message that the courts thought Thatcher guilty.

Mr. Justice Halvorson asked Kujawa to specifically identify the threats he saw contained in the transcript of the tape. As the prosecutor did so, some unusual exchanges took place between the Crown and the Bench.

Kujawa pointed out Thatcher's reference to Gerry Gerrand as "a guy I could do." The judge wondered how the lawyer could be "at risk," since he was not, at least yet, even a witness.

"The fact seems to be that whether Gerrand was around or not wouldn't make a whole lot of difference to this case or you'd have called him on the preliminary," Mr. Justice Halvorson continued.

"It would make a great deal of difference to Gerrand," Kujawa observed.

Mr. Justice Halvorson reminded Kujawa that the evidence from the preliminary could be used at the trial if a witness went missing, and asked what the accused could "do between now and the trial to assist his case?" Lynne Mendell's evidence was "already on the record anyway; it will serve no purpose to rub her out."

As Mr. Justice Halvorson reserved his decision for a week, it looked as if Colin Thatcher might finally make it home from the Regina Correctional Centre he hated. But on July 17, when the judgment came down, bail was again denied, again on both grounds. Mr. Justice Halvorson found a "substantial likelihood that the accused would, if released, commit a criminal offence or an interference with the administration of justice."

Allbright tried again in the Court of Appeal, but achieved nothing but some impetus that helped him secure a transfer of his client to the Saskatoon Correctional Centre where he could more easily confer with him. On September 7, after considering the matter for a week, the Appeal Court handed down its decision denying bail to the accused Thatcher.

Two days later, Colin Thatcher was taken to Regina's Plains Hospital for medical investigation of possible heart attack symptoms. After a quick blaze of publicity and two nights in hospital, Colin was pronounced well and returned to the Regina Correctional Centre. Later Colin claimed that there was nothing to it; he had not wanted to go to the hospital, but the jail staff insisted.

Colin Thatcher was very unhappy with Serge Kujawa. As he told the prosecutor at the trial, he considered the description of the tape on the first bail application appeal to be "a gross misrepresentation" and responsible for his continued incarceration.

Kujawa telephoned Gerry Gerrand and told the other lawyer:

194

"Talent will surface. It took you three years to make it to the top of Colin's hit list and I did it in six weeks."

"That's not funny, Serge," Gerrand replied.

Any thoughts Allbright had had about not attempting to move the trial out of Regina were gone as soon as he saw the crowds at the preliminary. There was too much interest and gossip in the capital to risk hoping for a "clean" jury there. The public dissemination of the transcripts gave him the argument for a change of venue if, indeed, much argument was needed.

In mid-August, Allbright brought his motion for a change of venue before Madam Chief Justice Batten of the Saskatchewan Court of Queen's Bench who, as Mary Batten, Liberal MLA from Humboldt, had been in Ross Thatcher's "caucus" when he became Liberal leader in 1959. To support his motion, Allbright filed an affidavit sworn by Colin Thatcher complaining of the crowds at the preliminary and the wide circulation of the transcripts. For some reason Allbright found it appropriate to have Thatcher allege that the transcripts were being passed around "for reading purposes throughout the government circles surrounding the Legislative Assembly."

Kujawa's view was that the Crown's chances were improved by removing the trial from Regina and he had no real opposition to the request. He thought that those who were connected to or supportive of Colin or his late father, Ross, were concentrated in the Regina-Moose Jaw area from which a jury would be drawn if no move was made.

Allbright would have preferred Halifax if it was available but, within Saskatchewan, Prince Albert or North Battleford. Logistically, however, Saskatoon was the only city other than Regina that could accommodate all the participants, and Chief Justice Batten so ordered.

October 15 was chosen as the date for the commencement of the trial.

The defence made one further attempt to improve its tactical position. A month before the trial Allbright was in front of Mr. Justice John Maher, by then the designated trial judge, asking for particulars of the charge and disclosure of telephone taps.

The defence was bothered by the way in which the indictment

was framed. Allbright asked for particulars of "the means by which the accused herein is alleged to have caused the death."

The charge against Colin Thatcher was that he "did unlawfully cause the death of JoAnn Wilson and did thereby commit first degree murder." This would cover having done the deed personally or having arranged for someone else to perform the actual killing. Allbright wanted to limit the Crown down to one allegation or the other, feeling sure that the prosecution would then choose to go with a charge of actually performing the killing.

Mr. Justice Maher refused the request. Particulars, he said, "are to enable a defendant to fairly defend himself, but are not to fetter the prosecution."

Colin Thatcher would thus be tried upon what came to be known as the "two-pronged indictment" and the propriety of this charge would be argued at the trial, in the Court of Appeal, and all over Saskatchewan for some time to come.

The invasion of privacy sections of the Criminal Code which permit wire taps, the "interception of communications," under very restrictive conditions, prohibit the use or disclosure of any such communication "without the express consent of the originator thereof or of the person intended by the originator thereof to receive it." Without such consent, it is an offence to even "disclose the existence" of such an interception or wire tap.

On his other motion Allbright succeeded. Noting that "the Crown admits that numerous conversations were intercepted over a period of eighteen months or more," Mr. Justice Maher ordered the disclosure to the defence of all "intercepted telephone conversations of witnesses who testified at the preliminary inquiry or whom the Crown intends to call at trial." It was the last time telephone taps were mentioned in the case, although Allbright was to complain bitterly that telephone monitoring severely hampered him in the preparation of the defence.

196

III
The
Trial

''Charlie Bronson you're not.''
— Serge Kujawa to Colin Thatcher,
October 30, 1984

CHAPTER 15

Regina v. Thatcher

It was Gerry Allbright who declared that the trial of Colin Thatcher had attracted more public attention than any such event since the trial of Louis Riel, ninety-nine years earlier. Certainly the arrangements for the trial of Colin Thatcher devoted more attention to security and publicity than any similar event in prairie history.

In August, Ed Swayze and Inspector Nel Silzer assessed the security conditions of three of Saskatoon's downtown hotels. They were looking for accommodation for the Crown witnesses they considered to be possibly in jeopardy. They chose the recently constructed Ramada Renaissance and booked the top floor, the 19th, for the duration of the trial. When the police, prosecutors and Crown witnesses moved in, a guard was on 24-hour duty to prevent unauthorized access. Large mirrors were angled in three corners of the corridor providing an uninterrupted view of the hallway and stairway entrances.

A room in the northeast corner of the floor gave a clear view of the back of the courthouse, half a block away. It was equipped with RCMP and city police radios and binoculars which were used to maintain surveillance of the rear garage area of the courthouse where the witnesses and the accused entered and departed. One of the functions of the observers was to coordinate arrivals so that the Colin Thatcher and the Crown witnesses did not encounter each other.

The Saskatoon courthouse was placed under even more stringent security requirements. The building itself was thoroughly checked and some windows covered to prevent possible assassination attempts. The staff was issued identification cards bearing their photographs. During the trial, the courthouse was secured each night by the sheriff's officers after the cleaning staff had left.

Twenty-four-hour surveillance of the courthouse was provided by the RCMP and Saskatoon City Police. The sheriff's office coordinated the activities of the RCMP, Saskatoon and Regina police, and the commissionaires who covered the courthouse entrances, elevator and the courtroom. At the courtroom door, metal detectors and bag searches would face all observers allowed to enter.

For Colin Thatcher a temporary prisoner's dock was placed against the wall facing the jury instead of the regular one in the centre of the courtroom facing the judge. This move, also, was made to ensure better security. Colin's back would be to the wall instead of the watching audience. As it turned out, Thatcher would spend little time in the dock.

Following the successful arrangements at the preliminary, formal media accreditation was adopted under the direction of Pat Bugera, director of communications with the Department of Justice. Thirty-five local and national journalists were accredited. They represented eight papers, eight television stations, eight radio stations, and an assortment of wire services, magazines and book publishers.

With all this preparation, the defence felt that it was being prejudiced, that the public perception of the activity must be a prejudging of the guilt of Colin Thatcher. But no counteraction was taken or, perhaps, could have been.

Not many of the nearly thirty members of Saskatchewan's Court of Queen's Bench met all the eligibility requirements to preside over the trial of Colin Thatcher. Experience, a certain seniority with its attendant lengthy period of divorce from the hurly-burly of legal practice (and political activity), and a not-too-close acquaintance with the accused's family narrowed the choice to a few. Chief Justice Mary Batten's selection of the Honourable Mr. Justice John Hayes Maher was no surprise.

First appointed to the Bench in 1966, "Jack" Maher had served eleven years as a District Court judge before being elevated to the Queen's Bench in 1977. He graduated in 1942 from the University of Saskatchewan Law School in a wartime class of seven that included another jurist, W.Z. (Bud) Estey, formerly Chief Justice of Ontario's High Court of Justice and now a member of the Supreme Court of Canada.

Jack Maher had made major in the Ottawa echelon of the Canadian Army before returning to his hometown of North Battleford to practise law. Seven of Judge Maher's years as a District Court judge had been served in the rural area of Humboldt before he moved to Saskatoon in 1973. Four years later he was elevated to the Court of Queen's Bench, then only a ten-member court, where he continued an emphasis on criminal trials.

As a practising lawyer, Jack Maher had been an active Liberal and had known Ross Thatcher in the early years of his party leadership. There had been a disagreement with Ross over Maher's account for successfully contesting an election result in one riding in 1961, but no hard feelings lingered, and Premier Thatcher had been happy to endorse Maher's selection for appointment to the Bench.

Adjusting well to life as a jurist, Jack Maher had not lost interest in the world outside the judicial corridors. He had headed several commissions of inquiry into such diverse topics as police brutality, wilderness welfare camps and libraries.

The legal acumen of Mr. Justice Maher was no secret to the province's courtroom lawyers. His experience, personality and stature would easily enable him to maintain control over what promised to be a turbulent trial.

The panel from which the jury for the Thatcher trial would be picked had first reported to the Saskatoon courthouse on September 10. Six trials had preceded the Thatcher case on the fall jury sittings and, as the fifty-nine members of the panel assembled on Monday, October 15, they greeted each other with familiarity. They had been randomly selected by computer from the Saskatchewan hospitalization register of residents of Saskatoon and within a sixty-mile radius of the city.

Many observers expected the defence to conduct a lengthy jury selection complete with psychological screening and in-depth examinations of prospective jurors. Neither Allbright nor Kujawa are exponents of this American-style innovation.

Kujawa had been known to offer the defence, "I'll take the first twelve jurors called if you will," and quotes a response he received from John Matthew, QC, a very senior British prosecutor, who had handled a number of illustrious trials. Kujawa had asked how many jurors his English counterpart had "stood aside" in his career. "I should expect some dozen and a half," was the dry reply, expected from one who practised in a system where juries are taken as they come.

Both the Crown and the defence had researched the age, occupation, reputation and possible criminal background of each of the potential jurors, however. It is a standard procedure, but was performed more thoroughly for this particular case.

One unusual precaution had been taken with the jury panel before the selection process began. It had been agreed at the pre-trial conference the week before that the entire panel would be screened for anyone who had read the transcript from the preliminary. When Mr. Justice Maher asked anyone who had read it to stand up, none did.

Court clerk David Sinclair shook the wooden box of cards, each containing the name of a panel member and selected one. "The juror look at the accused and the accused look at the juror," Sinclair intoned. Neither Allbright nor Kujawa spoke and the first juror was chosen.

Thirty-five names and twenty-five minutes later the seven-man, five-woman jury was complete. "Bush league," a Toronto reporter snarled in disappointment.

Until the late 1960s, sequestering a jury from the beginning of a murder trial had been automatic in Saskatchewan, but neither counsel requested isolation of the Thatcher jury. There is the risk of incurring the jury's resentment. Kujawa had raised the matter at the pre-trial conference the preceding week, but Allbright had strenuously objected on the grounds that it would be a departure from the norm. Mr. Justice Maher had sided with the defence.

In open court the trial judge advised the new jury that he hoped it would not be necessary to order them sequestered until they began their deliberations. This would enable them to enjoy press coverage of the trial, although they were instructed to ignore it, but the media was warned not to publish anything that was said or done in the absence of the jury. An order was made prohibiting the publishing of the names of the jurors so as to protect them from anyone attempting to speak to or influence them. It was not to be entirely effective when a newshound interpreted the order as not applying to a juror's family.

Kujawa opened the case for the Crown, briefly outlining the evidence he proposed to call. His case, he said, would fall into four parts. The first, the "physical part," would consist of cars, a holster, a credit card slip, wounds and bullets. The second would be Lynne Mendell. The third would be Garry Anderson and Charlie Wilde, the accomplices. The fourth would be the tape.

It was not yet noon when the preliminaries were finished and the case was ready to go. The court adjourned until two o'clock.

When the court reassembled, Peggy Thatcher sat at the right edge of the public gallery with her grandson Greg. It was the first time she had appeared at any of the proceedings since Colin's arrest. An overcoat covered her navy skirt and sweater, and her hair was neatly coiffed. The sixty-nine-year-old woman was composed and alert.

Peggy Thatcher had sat at the side of her husband Ross through thirty years of political ups and downs, and now she resumed her role on behalf of her son Colin. The ease and dignity with which she conducted herself throughout the trial was the subject of much remark. In fact, as the drama deepened, some wondered if there was not such a thing as being too dignified under certain circumstances.

Accommodating the Thatcher family in the courtroom caused the officials considerable diplomatic concern. The media had been assigned to the first two rows and part of the third which they shared with the family, who thought they should have been in the first row. Colin's supporters liberally utilized the privilege of assigned seating, sometimes taking twelve of the fourteen seats in the row by including friends. No one wanted to interfere, but the entourage was finally reined back to six seats.

The seating of the Thatcher family, and the later presence of young Stephanie, became such an issue that it intruded into the cross-examination of Colin, and Allbright thought it worthy of mention in his jury address.

Allbright, having tested the water in the absence of the jury and finding no objection, now formally requested permission to have his client sit with him at the counsel table rather than remain in the prisoner's dock. This is not an unusual request, particularly in less serious criminal matters, but the stature of the accused improved as Colin joined his counsel. Allbright's assistant was displaced and relegated to a corner chair beside the prisoner's dock.

The first Crown witness was called. Craig Dotson, the only person to have seen the killer of JoAnn Wilson, took the stand.

It is axiomatic in trial work that the witnesses who present a problem be put on the stand as early as possible in the case, in the hope that any negative aspects in their testimony will be overshadowed by subsequent evidence. Kujawa was adhering to this theory by calling Craig Dotson on the first day of the trial.

Dotson was the only witness to have seen JoAnn Wilson's assailant. Now was the time for the Crown to pay the penalty for his being locked into a description that did not fit the accused. A personal identification based on the fleeting glimpse Dotson had given the figure leaving the Wilson garage would be useless for purposes of conviction. There would be no point in the prosecution trying to explain to the jury that the reverse should also hold true and that Dotson's description was not strong enough to dictate an acquittal. The only thing to do was to put the witness forward, let the defence make its point as best it could, and hope that the impact would fade as the trial progressed.

Eyewitness testimony has been the greatest single cause of the miscarriages of justice which have occurred in the legal history of Canada, the United States and England. Still the most famous of these is the English case of Adolph Beck who was twice wrongfully convicted, the first time upon the personal identification of twelve witnesses, the second time upon identification by four. When the error became manifest, a committee of inquiry was set up to discover the cause. Its report, made in 1904, began from the premise that ". . . evidence as to identity based upon personal impressions, however bona fide, is perhaps of all classes of evidence the least to be relied upon. . ."

In more recent years, studies and experiments by forensic psychologists have proven the unreliability of and the danger inherent in eyewitness testimony. Simulated acts of violence performed before unsuspecting test groups have produced such a variation of descriptions as to show that accurate recall in personal identification is the exception and not the rule. Still there is almost nothing, except fingerprint evidence, that carries more weight with juries.

Kujawa knew this, and so did Allbright, as the one played his weak card first and the other sought to capitalize upon it.

Allbright regarded Craig Dotson as the Crown witness most crucial to the defence. "He had the most to give me." He also thought, from his experience with the witness at the preliminary, that he might even be partial to the defence case. That was not to be so.

The examination-in-chief of the eyewitness was handled by thirty-six-year-old Alistair Johnston who had been assigned to assist Kujawa. Johnston had been with the prosecuting arm of the Department of Justice for eight years. For six months he had been involved with nothing else but the morass of evidence amassed by the Regina police. Johnston's pleasant personality endured the "all-hours" requirements of the case.

As Johnston took Dotson quickly through a description of the events, it was obvious that the witness knew what was sensitive about his testimony.

"As I looked to my left, I saw a person emerge from the garage that's there. The person did nothing to attract my attention. I didn't dwell on looking at this person."

"How long did you look at this person?"

"I didn't look at the person. I saw the person."

"Okay."

"Just a second. Just a fraction of a second or just momentarily. Nothing, the person did nothing to attract my attention. Not running, wasn't shielding himself from me. Wasn't moving in any way that attracted my attention. Didn't look like a child that had been screaming, which is what I was looking for. And I paid the person no particular attention."

Craig Dotson was not going to establish himself as an eyewitness who had made a careful observation of the suspect and whose identification could be relied upon.

Allbright had something else he wanted from Dotson in

205

addition to a description of the assailant as someone other than his client, and that was the fixing of the time of the murder. The later the better for the purpose of his alibi defence. After some pleasantries, and an unsuccessful attempt to induce the witness to agree that traffic on Albert Street was heavy at that time on a Friday night (thus taking longer to cross), Allbright went to the time Dotson had left work. He found the witness leaning to an earlier departure rather than a later and quickly left that feature, going to the more important observation of the assailant.

The defence counsel's planning for this examination had produced the strategy that he establish that Craig Dotson, as he retraced his steps on 20th Avenue searching for the cries of distress, was anxious and alert. In that state his powers of observation should be heightened and his description more accurate and reliable.

Dotson preferred "concerned" as a description of his state of mind. Allbright accepted that and, somewhat unctuously, began to expand.

"You're going home unconcerned and you hear cries and screams that persist and, Mr. Dotson, to your credit, you became concerned at least to start inquiring into the source of those cries and screams. And don't be modest, Mr. Dotson, but you became concerned, did you not?"

"Yes, I did."

"In fact, Mr. Dotson, your concern, the level of your concern began to rise because, in fact, those cries persisted, did they not?"

"Yes, Sir, they did."

"And you became concerned enough, as a citizen, and I commend you again for turning around and going back to try and locate the source of the cries and the screams to see what you could do to alleviate them, you would agree with that, Sir?"

"Yes."

"Now, I have no doubt whatever, human nature what it is, Mr. Dotson, that at this stage your, your level of anticipation or anxiousness, if I can put it that way, is rising even more. These are unusual things, Mr. Dotson, would you agree?"

"Yes."

206

Dotson agreed with Allbright that he was "looking," admittedly for a child, but "looking" when ". . .a man came out of the garage and . . . he looked directly at you, Mr. Dotson."

"Yes."

"Directly at you. And while you got but a short view of that man, would you agree, on that occasion?"

"Very short, yes."

Allbright then made the point, with Dotson's agreement, that just a few seconds later, when he found the body, the witness knew that the man he had just seen had some importance, suggesting that his recollection would be fixed because of that.

Dotson admitted that the composite he had helped Donna Hodgins-Locke prepare on the night of the murder "looks to you, to the best of your ability, always remembering that, like the man you saw coming out of the garage." And finally, he admitted that the drawing and the description he had given the police of a man approximately thirty years old, five foot nine to five foot eleven in height and "of medium to slim build," "doesn't look like Colin Thatcher," a man he knew and had seen over a hundred times.

Allbright had all he could get and he had quite a bit. It would be hard for the jury to believe that the murderer could have been Colin Thatcher, disguise or no disguise. The beard and the hair might have been artificial, but the age, the height and the build did not fit the six-foot, 185-pound, forty-six-year-old accused sitting confidently at the counsel table beside his lawyer.

Dotson's testimony ended the first day of the trial. Both sides retired from the courtroom with some feeling of satisfaction. For the Crown, it was enough that the jury was in place, the case opened, and the evidence under way. For the defence, strong points had been made with Dotson for the jury to mull over the first night.

The Regina police in the Renaissance Hotel had some developing concerns. By the week's end they were to have another melodrama on their hands second only to the one unfolding in the courtroom.

Garry Anderson had been subpoenaed to appear at the opening

of the trial. He had been in Saskatoon that day, had been seen driving past the courthouse, but, ominously, had also been seen later, far south of Saskatoon, driving towards Moose Jaw.

During the night an early blizzard reached Saskatoon. Coincidentally, it originated in Iowa, first home of the deceased JoAnn Wilson, and extended far enough north to disrupt the trial over her death, and as far south as Denver where two witnesses from Palm Springs were making connecting flights.

On Tuesday morning at the Correctional Centre, the RCMP cruiser carrying Colin Thatcher to court got stuck in the snow. The camera crew from Saskatoon's CFQC-TV had to put down their equipment and push the police and the accused free.

In the courtroom two rows of spectators were missing, the only time in three weeks that this was to occur. As Kujawa and Johnston led the jury through the initial police findings at the scene of the crime, the credit card slip and its identification by Jack Janzen, the gas station attendant who have given it to Colin Thatcher, the storm raged outside. Highway travel was impossible, and by afternoon city streets were bĕcoming clogged.

The Crown's witness from the Central Vehicle Agency was stormbound in Regina. Allbright accommodated the prosecution by admitting that his client had signed out the blue Oldsmobile KDW 292 on January 10, 1983 and kept it until January 23.

Gene Stusek put in evidence some photographs of the blue Oldsmobile KDW 292, the money Colin had left at the abandoned farm for Garry Anderson, and the holster. Allbright was interested in Stusek's knowledge of a 6:24 p.m. phone call between Palm Springs and the Redland Avenue residence, but Stusek had none.

Bob Murton went onto the stand to put in evidence a homemade silencer he had received from Garry Anderson. Allbright took the opportunity to show him Wally Beaton's affidavit from the bail appeal referring to the 6:24 p.m. phone call between Colin Thatcher and Lynne Mendell, trying to get confirmation of the fact of the call. Murton, too, had no personal knowledge of the matter and declined. But the jury was now aware of the call.

Margaret Johannsson, Joan Hasz and Dwayne Adams told the jury of the blue car with the bearded occupant they had observed on 20th Avenue the days preceding the murder.

In the afternoon an RCMP officer interrupted the proceedings and approached Mr. Justice Maher. He gently explained to the jurist that he had accidentally triggered his "panic button," an emergency alarm switch behind the judge's bench, a standard precautionary measure in Saskatchewan courtrooms.

At three o'clock, with the storm continuing, Judge Maher adjourned the trial for the day. Sheriff Siemens reported that the city buses were no longer running and many telephones were down, and wondered if he should be seeking emergency hotel accommodation for the jury. The judge left it to the jurors to find their own ways home, but directed them to call the sheriff if they had difficulty or had trouble getting back in the morning.

As the blizzard worsened Tuesday evening, the police on the 19th floor of the Renaissance Hotel became very concerned about their witnesses. Garry Anderson had left the city and was a guaranteed problem. Charlie Wilde was now "whereabouts unknown," presumably lost in the storm. He and Dawn Trickett had left Winnipeg by car the day before. Lynne Mendell and Ron Williams were to fly from Palm Springs via Frontier Airlines out of Denver, and airports were closing all over the West.

Late that night everyone who was coming voluntarily made it through to Saskatoon. Charlie and Dawn had been fortunate. Losing a wheel from their car not far out of Winnipeg, they had returned and caught a train. Mendell and Williams also were lucky. Their Frontier flight had a scheduled stop in Regina before going on to Saskatoon, but Regina airport was closed and they missed that stop, flying straight to Saskatoon which accepted their late landing and then closed also. The storm had been so severe in Denver that they had worried that Stapleton Field would close before they could get away.

Lynne Mendell had received two telephone calls threatening her life and that of her husband if she testified. The last call had been just a week before the trial. Ed Swayze's constant reassurance had been crucial in maintaining her confidence.

In case anyone had plans to intercept Lynne on the journey to the trial, Ron Williams was doubling as bodyguard. At six foot one and 300 pounds, and once a deputy sheriff, he was well qualified. Mendell and Williams were happy that their flight had bypassed Regina. If they were to meet trouble, they had expected it to come aboard at that stop.

At the Renaissance Hotel, Mendell was ensconced in the presidential suite on the 19th floor behind the police security lines.

Since June, when she had decided in favour of testifying against Colin Thatcher and had appeared at the preliminary inquiry, Lynne Mendell had lived in daily fear of harm coming to her and her husband. She swam and sunbathed at her parents' condominium because a guardhouse was near. When the Mexican gardeners on her condo grounds were replaced with workers of lighter complexions, she imagined that the newcomers had Canadian accents and was relieved when the Mexicans reappeared after a few days. The two threatening phone calls had confirmed her fears.

Mendell was desperate to be believed. Her story was strange, she knew, and subject to criticism. If she was not convincing, the guilt she carried for her involvement with Colin during the years of his murder planning would not be expiated and the fear of his reprisals would remain.

More than once Serge Kujawa had been importuned by his witness: "You do believe me, don't you?" The prosecutor did, and said so.

On Wednesday morning Serge Kujawa swiftly and skilfully took Lynne Mendell through her relationship with the Canadian politician from their meeting in the fall of 1980 until their break-up in early 1983 after the murder. That consumed only forty-five minutes, and the court broke early for lunch so as not to interrupt Allbright's cross-examination.

Thatcher's former Palm Springs girlfriend had been a surprise to Allbright at the preliminary and he had had only one evening to prepare his attack upon her. On this afternoon he was ready.

The defence counsel's strategy was two-pronged. He would attempt to establish that Mendell was emotionally and, perhaps, mentally unstable; that only such a person would continue an intimate relationship with someone who was supposedly plotting, and actually committing, murder. Also, he would contend that, bitter because the expected marriage had not come to pass, she was twisting the oblique conversations she described and applying meanings that were never intended.

Allbright spent the entire afternoon with Mendell. He grilled her about the plausibility of one who knew what she claimed about a murder she did not support, did nothing to prevent it, and carried on normally.

"It doesn't ring true until it happens," was the essence of her repeated description of the unreality of the pre-murder events.

Mendell did not attempt to justify her behaviour, merely to convince her listeners that it was conceivable and human. She succeeded.

As Allbright repeatedly accused Mendell of abnormal acquies-cence in the incriminating actions and statements she described, an acceptance of the truth of those events grew and seemed to be shared by the lawyer himself. It was a dangerous course the defender had chosen, to cast doubt upon the cause by questioning the effect, and he paid the penalty of reinforcing the first.

Mendell was articulate and candid and frequently turned Allbright's thrusts into opportunities to elaborate on her character and that of Colin Thatcher. When the defence counsel pointed out that the alleged beatings she had received from Colin conveniently seemed to have always occurred in private, without witnesses, she replied:

> I don't like the picture it makes of me to admit that I stayed with someone who had hit me, even once. I look at that person and I don't like that kind of person. So, it is difficult for me to say that. I wouldn't make that up. That was a weakness I had and I don't know what else to tell you. Of course, he wouldn't do it in front of witnesses.

When Allbright brought up Mendell's suicide attempt in the Moose Jaw home and tried to suggest that it was representative of emotional instability characteristic of her, she sought and received leave from Mr. Justice Maher to explain the circum-stances. She delivered such a compelling description of what Colin had put her through, and of his nonchalantly going to bed

211

and to sleep after beating her to the floor, that the jury might have been left more sympathetic of her plight than critical of her weakness.

Mendell had testified that on the day of the murder she had received two phone calls from Colin, "maybe one around five or six and maybe one around eight, nine." In the first Colin had said he was "going into Regina now," and in the second he told her he had just heard of JoAnn's killing.

Allbright pointed out the two-hour time difference between California and Saskatchewan and the fact that, if the first call was at 5:00 p.m., it was already 7:00 p.m. in Regina and JoAnn had been dead an hour. He accused her of suffering from "Palm Springs time warp."

If Allbright had hoped to expose Lynne Mendell as flighty and unstable, he was disappointed. How the jury would regard her and her testimony would never really be known, whatever the verdict, but neither would be totally dismissed. When it came time to address the jury he would ask, "You going to put him away for the duration because of her evidence?" but, in Lynne Mendell's words, "it didn't ring true."

Allbright questioned Mendell about the admissions Colin had made to her about his handling of the first shooting and the murder and her possible misinterpretations of them. She repeated her contention that Colin had denied to her that he had beaten JoAnn. Observers noted that no question was put to Lynne Mendell about the comment Colin had made: "It's a strange feeling to blow your wife away."

Colin Thatcher's Palm Springs playmate was the media hit of the week. Ignoring her security, she accommodated the frantic photographers by posing outside the courthouse and at the Renaissance Hotel. Her security escorts were frustrated and annoyed.

On Friday, Lynne Mendell, still escorted by Ron Williams, returned to Palm Springs.

The public in Saskatchewan, and across Canada, were now becoming fully aware of what was going on inside the Saskatoon courthouse. The evidence, which had been suppressed at the preliminary inquiry, was, for the first time, fully exposed to the newspapers, television and radio. It was a lead story in every newspaper and on every newscast in the province. Outlines of the testimony and commentary by the reporters in attendance were devoured in every home in the province. The Saskatchewan Roughriders, teetering on the edge of another disastrous football season, were forgotten as the armchair quarterbacks turned their attention to murder. Saskatoon, Regina and Moose Jaw, the province's three major cities, are all one-newspaper towns, and each paper increased its press runs to accommodate the demand for news of the trial. The *Star-Phoenix* in Saskatoon began running pages of actual testimony. Coffee-break chatter was about nothing else and the remote spectators began adopting partisan positions almost from the beginning.

The opening-day evidence of Craig Dotson, widely interpreted to mean that Colin Thatcher could not have been the actual murderer, was the end of it for many. Few understood the implications of the double-barrelled charge in the indictment. On the other hand, Lynne Mendell's story, with the lurid comment, "It's a strange feeling to blow your wife away," was all the evidence others required to conclude that the accused Colin was guilty.

Saskatchewan is not a passionless province, and as the trial of Colin Thatcher aroused the emotions of its fascinated observers, objectivity was forgotten. This was a contest and, in the way of spectators everywhere, favourites were chosen early. Only later did more than a few discern that much more than the guilt or innocence of Colin Thatcher was at issue, that what was on trial in Saskatoon in this fall of 1984 was justice itself.

CHAPTER 16

Ammunition Capers and a Missing Witness

On Thursday morning, pathologist Dr. John Vetters described to the shocked jury the injuries JoAnn Wilson had received and the cause of her death, the bullet to the head. During his autopsy Vetters had removed what he could of the bullet fragments and turned them over to Sergeant A.J. Somers of the RCMP forensic laboratory at Regina.

Somers then told the court that his examination of the fragments led him to the conclusion that the bullet "was probably Winchester .38 Special Plus P, aluminum-jacketed ammunition, ninety-five grain [in weight]." The bullet was a hollow-point "intended to facilitate rapid expansion . . . upon striking an object." The firearms expert was further of the opinion that the bullet had most likely been fired from a Ruger, although he "would not rule out other possibilities, such as Smith & Wesson or possibly Colt."

Somers claimed that the ammunition had been manufactured for only two or three years prior to 1983 and that "definitely it would not be available in the retail market in Canada as an over-the-counter item for anyone; just anyone to go and purchase."

Gerry Allbright is something of a gun collector and is knowledgeable about firearms and ballistics. At the preliminary he had accepted Somers's evidence at face value but since then had lost some respect for the witness's expertise. As a result, the issue of the ammunition's uniqueness and its supposed unavailability in Canada became contentious and confused.

Somers contended that Canada's Explosives Act prohibited the importation of hollow-point ammunition except for use in a rifle or by police, presumably because it has no non-lethal use. In the case of ammunition of .22 calibre, which is completely interchangeable between rifle and handgun, the distinction was meaningless. With heavier calibre ammunition not suitable for a rifle, such as .38 or .357, it would not have been lawful to import into Canada the bullet which killed JoAnn Wilson.

It was an important point, because the ammunition Ron Williams had sold Colin Thatcher in Palm Springs was identical to what Somers said had been found in the victim. If it was not available in Canada, an incriminating inference would be drawn.

Friends of Colin Thatcher had told Allbright that the ammunition could be made available in Canada and that they could get him some. "Fine," he said, "do so, as long as it's legal." They arranged to acquire some ammunition for the lawyer.

Allbright was then able to attack the firearms expert. "I suggest you're partially right, and partially, witness, very much in error. I can buy that right here in Saskatchewan, and I can assure you I'm not a police officer; I can legally buy it, sir."

The defence counsel then slapped down two boxes of Winchester Silvertip hollow-point ammunition of .38 calibre. One was .38 automatic in 125 grain, but the other was the .38 Special Plus P 95 grain that Somers had identified as causing the death. Allbright also produced an invoice for the ammunition, made out to him, from The Gun Rack, Drinkwater, a small town in the accused's Thunder Creek constituency. The invoice was dated October 11, exactly one week earlier.

It was grandstanding but impressive, even though it was technically improper. To prove the purchase Allbright would have to take the witness stand himself, or have the vendor do so. He was putting in evidence out of his own mouth while not under oath, something Kujawa was to complain about throughout the trial.

Allbright was contemptuous of Somers for not being able to tell him how much the bullet fragments from JoAnn's skull weighed. Somers had weighed them, but had not recorded the weight. How, then, Allbright demanded, could he identify the bullet as being 95 grain?

Kujawa responded with some grandstanding of his own. He had Somers acquire a scale over the lunch break and bring it to the courtroom. The witness weighed the bullet fragments in front of the jury and announced the total to be 83.6 grains. The missing grains, he explained, were in the fragments too small to remove from the skull, although they showed on the x-ray.

Somers reconfirmed for Kujawa that, of the ammunition Allbright had produced, only the .38 Special Plus had the aluminum jacket of the kind found in the fragments.

Ron Williams followed Somers. He was something of a firearms expert himself, owned thirty guns, and had loaded personally, or under his direction, some one million rounds of ammunition. He told the jury that he had recommended the .38 Special Silvertip hollow-point ammunition to Colin Thatcher "because it's designed to stop people."

To Allbright, Williams conceded that it was common in California to buy and sell firearms privately and that such transactions were not recorded. Colin, however, had purchased the .357 Ruger from a licensed dealer and, accordingly, there was a record of the sale.

More would be heard on the ammunition question, but the rest of Thursday was spent listening to Tony Wilson.

Kujawa took JoAnn Wilson's second husband as delicately as possible through the story of the litigation, the first shooting, the eventual property settlement and, finally, the murder. The prosecutor was not acting entirely out of consideration for the witness. Wilson was bitter — this had showed at the preliminary — and the Crown did not want his testimony before the jury tainted by this. Fearing that Wilson might overplay his strange conversation with Colin Thatcher following the first shooting, and that it might be more prejudicial than admissible, Kujawa did not bring it out.

Wilson was easily the most emotionally involved of the Crown witnesses. Though he managed to disguise his resentment better than he had at the preliminary inquiry, his dislike for Colin Thatcher slipped into view. Commenting during cross-examination on the property dispute between JoAnn and Colin, Wilson grumbled, "He could have kept on fighting it for the next ten years and never paid, knowing him."

Later he told Allbright that ". . .JoAnn was extremely frightened of her life." The defence counsel jumped at this.

"You don't like Colin Thatcher at all, do you?"

"No."

"Would I be correct in saying that you wouldn't mind seeing Colin Thatcher to be convicted for this, would you?"

"I would not mind."

"In fact, that's exactly what you'd like to see happen, isn't it?"

But Mr. Justice Maher interjected at this point and stopped the line of questioning.

Allbright often showed little or no consideration for Wilson as a bereaved husband, but somehow seemed hesitant to fully drive home the accusations he unleashed. If the defence was to try to divert the attention of the jury from Colin Thatcher by casting suspicion on another, Tony Wilson probably had to be that other. In his address to the jury Allbright would suggest that Wilson could be seen as a suspect, but in his cross-examination of the man he did little to lay a foundation for such an accusation.

Allbright did ask about marital problems between Wilson and JoAnn concerning the presence of the young housekeeper, but received the expected forthright denial. He drew out the fact that the housekeeper, now without duties since Stephanie had left a year before, still lived in the Wilson home, but went no further. He established that Wilson, home with the flu the afternoon of the murder, had opportunity and also some financial motive under the terms of JoAnn's will, and again went no further.

Allbright questioned Wilson about why the garage lights were not working the night of the murder in such a way as to suggest that he might have been the cause of the malfunction. He had ascertained earlier that the witness did not know Garry Anderson, and had never even seen him, but closed with the last cynical question:

"And you don't know Garry Anderson, witness?"

"No."

217

It was as if the defence counsel had been unable to decide whether to examine the widower viciously or sympathetically and had compromised on meanly.

As the court closed for the day, several members of the Regina police and the RCMP were already out of Saskatoon and heading south. They were going for witnesses, Gene Stusek and Al Lyons to the American border for a customs officer, and Ed Swayze, Jim Street and Jim Card to Caron for Garry Anderson. A lot of sleep would be lost that night.

On Wednesday, Garry Anderson had phoned the Saskatoon courthouse. Ed Swayze spoke to the missing witness, who was at his mother's farm at Caron. Anderson was wild and furious. He cursed the chief investigator and everyone involved with the case. He told Swayze to come and get him and threatened to kill him if he did.

It is an understatement to say that Swayze concluded that his witness was not going to honour his subpoena. The RCMP were keeping an eye on the Anderson farm and Swayze arranged with them to go and get the witness the following day. The RCMP Emergency Response Team was assembled.

On Thursday afternoon the RCMP flew Swayze and Street down to Moose Jaw, where they joined forces with the ERT and planned an assault on the Anderson farm.

On the way down in the plane, Street convinced Swayze that, rather than an assault in force, he had an excellent chance of talking Garry out of the house. Swayze agreed that the SWAT-trained Street could chance the single-man approach.

Anderson and his current girlfriend, Linda, were alone in the house. Mrs. Anderson and sister Barbara had been intercepted away from the farm and convinced not to return.

Street went into the house, an act of great personal courage in the face of an enraged and, apparently, deranged Anderson, who was armed with a loaded shotgun. Street, who had spent a lot of time with Anderson planning Operation Wire, felt he knew his man and was confident that he could control the situation. There was a wild card present, though, in the person of Linda, whom Street did not know, and her movements towards him each time Anderson waved the shotgun towards Street seemed strange to the policeman and interfered with his concentration on the problem before him.

Street could not get past the kitchen into the living room where Anderson remained with the gun, and he retreated.

That left the problem with the RCMP tactical specialists who had the house surrounded. They, in turn, were perplexed as to how they were to remove Anderson without harm, a matter upon which Swayze was adamant. His orders, he said, were to produce that witness in the courtroom in the morning in shape to testify.

Anderson refused to be engaged in conversation. Attempts to talk to him by telephone were met with furious profanity and the banging down of the receiver.

The Emergency Response Team was the RCMP version of SWAT. Not wanting to adopt the acronym used by so many other forces, the famous Mounties came perilously close to naming their unit Technical Weapons And Tactics.

The ERT that had been assembled on the Anderson farm was well equipped with modern gadgetry, including tear gas and grenade projectiles and launchers, interesting explosive devices and even a remote-controlled mechanical robot. Time, however, the team commanders regarded as their most effective weapon.

Time Swayze did not have. Garry Anderson was due on the stand in Saskatoon at 10:00 a.m. The chief investigator's patience was pushed to its limit as he waited at the temporary command post that had been set up a quarter of a mile from the farmhouse. First the tear gas, and then the grenades, were decided upon, sent forward, and then called back at the last moment in the hope that some less drastic action would appear as an alternative. The tear-gas-equipped robot went into action, but did not have enough cable to reach the house from the protective cover required by its handler.

The siege continued from dusk until well past midnight. Finally, Swayze could stand it no longer and left for Regina to find a psychiatrist, instructing the others to bring Anderson along if and when they succeeded in securing him. Not long after Swayze left, at almost 3:00 a.m., one of the explosive devices was detonated near the house. Although it had almost no destructive capacity, it produced an impressive explosion.

219

It did the trick. Anderson and Linda came out of the house, were taken into custody without physical harm, and were conveyed immediately to Moose Jaw, en route to Regina. At Moose Jaw, Anderson demanded a lawyer, was given a telephone, and called William J. Gardner, QC, roommate of Ross Thatcher's at Queen's University, fifty-one years before.

Marguerite Gardner screens her husband's late night calls and nearly rejected the hyper-excited Anderson before her intuition told her that this was one caller who really did need a lawyer in the middle of the night.

In Regina, Garry Anderson was hospitalized and examined by Dr. Charles Messer, a prominent psychiatrist who had responded to Ed Swayze's plea. If he could not put his witness on the stand, the inspector intended to have a reason. If Garry Anderson was diagnosed as insane, that would support an application to the court in Saskatoon to read before the jury the evidence he had given at the preliminary inquiry.

The psychiatrist did not find the witness to be insane. The alcoholic Anderson had removed liquor from his life but had a tendency to substitute Tylenol in times of stress. He had consumed a great deal of the pain killer during the days leading up to his apprehension and, he would testify, some three dozen capsules on that Thursday. He had achieved a superb state of intoxication and a temporary suspension of his brain's ability to function. His mental processes would be back to normal in a day or two.

Anderson was flown to Saskatoon and, certainly in no condition to testify in spite of Swayze's caution, placed in a hospital to rest and recover. Bill Gardner, retained to advise the accomplice during his testimony, drove to Saskatoon. As additional support for the upset witness Gardner took with him Linda and Anderson's mother, Katie, and settled them into the Bessborough Hotel across from the courthouse.

The temperamental Garry Anderson had thrown quite a tantrum and had attracted to himself a lot of attention.

Kujawa had been incensed at what he considered improper tendering of evidence by Allbright in what came to be called ''the ammunition caper.'' During the noon break on Thursday, while his expert was hunting up a scale, the angry Crown prosecutor accosted the defence counsel and demanded the admission of some facts. Specifically, Kujawa insisted that Allbright admit to the court that he had not routinely discovered the ammunition in Drinkwater, that it had been imported especially for him, and that, on importation, it had not been disclosed to Canada Customs that it was hollow-point ammunition.

Allbright agreed to the first two conditions but not the third. His information, he said, was that the hollow-point feature had been disclosed to Customs.

With that, warrants and subpoenas were secured and Gene Stusek headed for Regway, a border crossing 245 miles southeast of Saskatoon. He stopped in Regina and picked up Al Lyons. At 2:30 a.m. Friday they were back in Saskatoon with Customs Officer Larry Piller and his files.

Al Lyons and his wife Delores had been on a ten-day cruise to the Virgin Islands. Scheduled to be back in Regina on Wednesday, their flight had run into weather problems. The couple had been in Winnipeg and Vancouver, neither place on their tickets, and had just reached home more than a day late when Stusek arrived with the orders for Regway.

When the sleepwalking and well-travelled Lyons arrived at the Renaissance Hotel with Stusek and the customs officer, Swayze mischievously snarled at him, ''Where the hell have you been?''

Friday morning in court began with further confusing testimony and debate about the legality of importing hollow-point handgun ammunition into Canada. Allbright admitted that the Drinkwater gun dealer had gone down to Montana to purchase the .38 Special cartridges on October 10, the day before they were sold to him. Customs Officer Piller then testified that the importation of hollow-point handgun ammunition above .22 calibre was prohibited and that the hollow-point feature of Allbright's ammunition was not declared to him.

Allbright promptly confronted Piller with some .357 hollow-point ammunition which, he said, had been purchased in Saskatoon the day before by his partner. Kujawa was again incensed.

It was a low point in the trial and tempers were short. When

Kujawa explained to the court that his next witness, Garry Anderson, was unavailable and asked for an adjournment until Monday morning, Allbright objected strenuously. Upset that his word was questioned, Kujawa replied, "My reliability is, of course, absolutely destroyed. I will call evidence to show he's not available. I will call evidence that I couldn't help it, if that is required. I don't mind being part of a new low."

It was time to break for the weekend and Mr. Justice Maher adjourned the proceedings until Monday morning. The first week was over.

The jury, press and spectators were thoroughly confused by now about the ammunition issue. It would arise once more before the end of the trial.

On Saturday evening the *Star-Phoenix*'s Doug McConachie and his wife hosted a party at his home for the media corps. There was much black humour as the press, which had suffered under the strain of the week's events, harmlessly vented their emotions. Mike Ward of Canadian Press, who had covered the highly publicized Demeter trial in Ontario, discussed the numerous parallels between the two cases. Michael Tenszen of the *Globe and Mail* took a straw vote on the simple question, "Guilty or Innocent?" There was one vote for "innocent" out of the approximately twenty polled, even though the Crown's case was not all in and the defence had not yet been heard from.

Garry Anderson had spent the weekend resting in Saskatoon's City Hospital and by Monday morning was calmed enough to testify. His emotions and fears were under control. Bill Gardner had spent some time with Anderson and, although the two had not met before Friday, they both knew many of the people around Caron and Moose Jaw and got along well together. Kujawa had dropped in on his witness and provided some additional reassurance.

Several of the police were contemptuous of what they felt was Anderson's infantile behaviour. He did need a high degree of support and that was what he had as he entered the witness stand on the morning of Monday, October 22. His greatest source of strength this morning was his examiner, Serge Kujawa, who had by now travelled to Edmonton, the Caron farm and the City

Hospital to assist his witness in carrying out his commitment to testify.

By this second week of the trial the public demand for seats had produced protests and problems in the early morning line-ups outside the courthouse. Arrivals had begun earlier, and 6:00 a.m. became the latest time to ensure admittance. The demand produced a market for places in the queue and the profit takers were able to boost their prices from $20 in the first week to $50 on Monday morning and $100 by the afternoon.

Sitting unobtrusively among the spectators that Monday, undetected by the reporters in front of him, was Garry Anderson's lawyer, the former roommate of the accused's father.

In his examination of Anderson, Kujawa required only an hour to lead the witness through his story of two and a half years of murder planning with Colin Thatcher. The big, bearded accomplice told the jury of the initial contact by Thatcher in the fall of 1980, of the meetings with Charlie Wilde, the passing of the money, his providing of cars on three occasions, the inspections of the Wilson home and back alley, the .357 and its silencers, and the final cleanup.

When Kujawa came to the May 1 meeting and the recording, the jury retired while the lawyers and the judge settled the question of the admissibility of the tape. A *voir dire*, commonly defined as a "trial within a trial," was held to determine if Garry Anderson had "expressly consented" to the recording and its use as evidence. This is the requirement of the Criminal Code's wiretapping provisions.

Allbright had an opportunity to cross-examine Anderson on the issue of consent and he used it to suggest that the accomplice was afraid of losing his immunity deal if he did not cooperate in the taping. Anderson insisted that he understood at Besant Park that he had the right to refuse to undertake the mission and that he understood today that he could refuse to permit the tape to be played in court. Mr. Justice Maher had no difficulty in finding that consent existed and directed that the tape be accepted into evidence.

Kujawa and Johnston were expecting more resistance from Allbright to the admission of the recording. At the pre-trial conference on the Wednesday before the case opened, the defence had told Mr. Justice Maher and the Crown that it would be calling two expert witnesses on the subject of the tape. The prosecution had scrambled in reaction, lining up its own experts to prove that the recorded conversation was actually between Thatcher and Anderson. They had not forgotten that Allbright, in the Court of Appeal on the first bail application, had described the tape as "inaudible and fabricated." The Crown was ready with specialists in the recently developed technique of voice print identification.

In fact, Allbright had some concerns about the "totality" of the tape and had considered calling some evidence on its completeness or lack of it. In the end, he raised no technical objections.

After quickly learning that the quality of the reproduction made it difficult to follow, Mr. Justice Maher allowed the jury to have transcripts so that they could more easily understand what was being said. Allbright had initially expressed to the court the hope that this would not be necessary, as he did not want the jury to think that the conversation had "a significance beyond a normal piece of evidence." It was a brave comment and a fond hope. No one piece of evidence in the entire case would have more significance to the jury than the taped conversation the jury listened to that day and a number of additional times later when they began their deliberations.

When the playing of the tape was completed, Kujawa had Anderson explain his absence on Friday, his behaviour during the whole week, including the Tylenol and the police siege of his mother's farm. He needed to take the sting out of his witness's aberrant actions before turning him over to Allbright. Allbright reserved his cross-examination until the following morning.

The prosecution and the Regina police relaxed. Garry Anderson's evidence was in. They had waited more than a year for the accomplice to talk at all and, after they had secured his supposed cooperation, he had given them more difficulty than any witness they had ever dealt with. It remained to be seen how he fared under cross-examination, but there was nothing more they could do.

Because the press corps had discovered that Anderson was staying in a hospital and were prowling through every one in the city, the witness was moved over to the RCMP Detention Centre after his first day's testimony. On Tuesday morning he was better dressed. The Emergency Response Team that yanked him off his mother's farm Friday morning had not given him time to pack a bag and he had arrived in Saskatoon wearing jeans and a down vest. He had testified in these on Monday. Some minor items of clothing had been purchased for him and he was attired in a jacket and trousers borrowed from Bill Gardner.

Anderson had added to the heavy security provided for him, hoping to preserve some anonymity. When travelling to and from the courthouse garage, he lay on the back seat of the police cruiser covered with a blanket to foil the photographers. This morning Jeff Vinnick of the *Star-Phoenix* had outwitted the witness and the security screen of Sheriff Siemens. Scrambling up a ladder, Vinnick pointed an automatic camera through a gap in the covering over a garage window and came away with several recognizable pictures of the bearded Anderson alighting from a police car.

When Gerry Allbright rose to his feet on Tuesday morning he faced two staggering challenges: he had to destroy the credibility of this alleged accomplice who had described in chilling detail his long involvement in murder with the accused; and he must transform the recorded conversation from a near confession by his client into an innocuous discussion of events unrelated to crime.

"Thou shalt not kill."

Allbright's choice of a dramatic opening to his cross-examination of Anderson had less impact than he might have hoped for. A devout man, the defence counsel was making a conscious effort to keep his Christian beliefs out of the trial. This was not an exception but an attempt to throw Anderson off balance. It may have served only to make the witness more frank.

Anderson conceded that it was wrong to kill, wrong to help another to kill, and suggested that one who did so is a fool.

"Were you a fool, Mr. Anderson?"

"Yes, I was."

Anderson went on to agree that his immunity deal meant that

225

he could never be prosecuted for this murder, could never "sit where the accused sits," and had nothing to lose in the witness stand.

Allbright took Anderson through his early denials to Regina police, his talking to a lawyer, his thinking process that led up to the immunity deal in February 1984. The accomplice admitted that the possibility that he might be charged himself was part of that thinking.

Anderson confirmed that all he had received from Colin Thatcher was $1,000 to $1,200, which, he agreed, was about two months' earnings for him. Allbright suggested that for the $50,000 reward the witness "might be prepared to say that you had done something which you really hadn't, and that you really weren't involved in a murder at all?"

Anderson told the lawyer that he had gone to the May 1 meeting with Colin Thatcher "to try and obtain a confession," and that, to do so, he was prepared to say some things to Colin that were not true. Certainly the accomplice had exaggerated his end of the work, attempting to provoke Thatcher into more damaging admissions. He had said that he "had a bitch of a time gettin' blood and stuff off" the car and Colin had merely replied, "Yeah. Is there no chance that it can ever surface?" Now Anderson admitted to Allbright that "I didn't get any blood off."

The accomplice admitted he was nervous at the meeting. Strangely, Allbright asked if he was "nervous because you feared for your safety?" He should not have been surprised at the cynical reply: "That thought had crossed my mind."

Allbright's strategy with the tape, to explain it as innocent conversation having nothing to do with murder, was probably the only one open to him. Certainly, he knew Colin Thatcher would be attempting to do the same when his turn came. Since neither the word "murder" nor the name "JoAnn" appeared on the tape, perhaps something could be made of that. Along the way he would make the accusation that Anderson, with his eye on the reward, was trying to frame his client.

Reminding Anderson that his stated purpose in meeting with Thatcher had been to get a confession, the lawyer pointed out that "you don't ask and insert one question that could unequivocally be said to relate directly to JoAnn Wilson's

226

murder and put it to Thatcher.''

Referring to examples in the transcript where Colin had given straight answers to Anderson's questions, he then said: "You're walking a tightrope because if you ask the wrong question you're going to get an answer that shows he had nothing to do with this matter, and that's an answer you can't afford the police to hear." Anderson explained that, early in his conversation with Thatcher, he had been afraid to ask a direct question because "it would spook him."

Allbright took the accomplice to places in the transcript that he termed "golden opportunities" to "put the nail in" Thatcher and where Anderson failed to do so. The witness candidly agreed with the lawyer on most of the examples put to him. For example, instead of having said "I got rid of the stuff outta' the car," Allbright suggested to Anderson that he might have stated, "I got rid of the clothes that you wore the night of the murder; I got rid of the bloody clothes; I got rid of the stuff you used to kill JoAnn Wilson.''

Although Allbright was working on Anderson's credibility, he was highlighting the natural strength of the Crown's version of the taped conversation. Anderson had walked as close to the edge as was possible without, as he said, "spooking" Thatcher. The jury members' imaginations must have boggled at the vision of an alleged murderer and his accomplice speaking in the clear, unequivocal terms suggested by Allbright.

When Thatcher had asked Anderson "Do you need some bread?" the accomplice had replied "Yeah. I can use some. I can use some for that car." That had been a "golden opportunity," Allbright submitted, for Anderson to have removed all doubt by saying, "I can use some for that car that you used that night to kill JoAnn Wilson."

Allbright's efforts to emphasize what the tape did not say may have served instead to underscore what it actually did say, a problem he faced with the tape throughout the trial. The euphemistic jargon of two conspirators speaking guardedly in fear of being overheard (". . .when we talk, just assume the bastards are listening.") contained a mass of assumed and implied incrimination.

"I'm glad it went down," Anderson had said to Thatcher.

Why "it"? Allbright asked. Why not "the killing," or "the death of JoAnn Wilson"?

"I'm glad you got her," Anderson told Thatcher at the end of their conversation. He agreed with Allbright that he could have said "I'm glad you killed her."

Garry Anderson was being careful with his responses. Slow, even plodding, but sure, he gave the defence counsel cautious and brief responses, even when he had an opportunity to clarify or explain.

Allbright suggested that Anderson had been instructed on how to handle the encounter with Thatcher, and gave an example: "Someone told you you'd better get the name Tony Merchant into the conversation somehow; were you instructed to do that by anyone?"

"Could have been discussed that the name Merchant was to be mentioned." A laconic reply.

Allbright accused Anderson of having failed in his mission "to get a confession, or a direct admission, from Colin Thatcher that he killed his wife."

"I don't know if I failed." Still laconic.

Allbright, carefully selecting his examples from the transcript, succeeded against the odds in making his listeners wonder what might have happened if Garry Anderson had put just one accusation of JoAnn's murder straight to Colin Thatcher. The defence lawyer had a thin theme but he raised some curiosity with it.

The work of the defence that morning, obviously painstakingly prepared, was somewhat impaired by its own actions on another front. Everyone in the courtroom was uncomfortably distracted by the presence, for the first time, of ten-year-old Stephanie Thatcher sitting with her grandmother, Peggy, and brothers Greg and Regan. First on Peggy's knee, and then perched on an RCMP jacket, the bright, pretty child aroused indignation so universal among the media and spectators that the jury must have been similarly affected.

Stephanie had arrived at court wearing the coat purchased for her in Paris by Lynne Mendell. It was the same coat she had worn to her mother's funeral.

Allbright had not agreed with the decision to bring Stephanie

228

into the courtroom. He knew how it looked and was worried about the potential displeasure among the jury. He did not put his foot down, however, because he felt that Colin needed the moral support of having all his family present.

Allbright spent the afternoon in a more pedestrian re-examination of Anderson's activities as assistant to Thatcher. There was little sparkle.

The defence counsel was interested in the colour of the .357. Was it a blue finish or a nickel type of finish?

"I believe it had a blue finish."

Allbright seemed puzzled why Anderson had returned the holster to Thatcher when it seemed more reasonable to keep it with the gun. He suggested that the accomplice added this to his story to fit the fact that a holster had been found in Colin's CVA car.

"I gave it back because I didn't need it."

The time of Anderson's accidental meeting with Thatcher the day before the murder was important. Someone had been watching JoAnn's home in Regina that afternoon. If Colin had been with Anderson in the late afternoon, he could not have been watching the Wilson home in Regina.

Anderson told Allbright that he came down from La Ronge that Thursday and met Colin "between 2 and 3 o'clock."

"Could it have been around 3:00, 3:30 that day?"

"It may have."

Allbright made the mistake of pressing the point. He thought it would be late in the day when Anderson reached Caron from La Ronge and Anderson said it was 360 miles on the route he drove. Allbright asked again if the witness "would be comfortable with it being perhaps 3:00 to 3:30 on that Thursday afternoon that you encountered him around Caron."

Anderson said he started out early in the morning and "if I recall, I believe it was between 2 and 3 o'clock."

Anderson remained consistent and unshaken and sometimes gave as good as he got. Allbright accused that Anderson, a poor man, "would concoct a story to frame this man, Colin Thatcher" in order to get the $50,000 reward. The witness reminded the lawyer, referring to Thatcher's early proposition to him, "I believe I was offered fifty thousand and I turned it down."

229

In closing, Anderson agreed with Allbright that he did not think his 1974 Mercury, with a 400 cubic inch engine, could be driven from "the heart of Regina to the heart of Moose Jaw in twenty minutes." Allbright had the 6:24 phone call in mind.

Kujawa thought some re-examination was in order. "There was one reason for you going out in that field and meeting with the accused and that reason was to get a confession if you can; a confession to the murder of JoAnn Wilson?"

"Yes."

"Why did you pick on Colin Thatcher? Why didn't you choose to extract the confession from someone else?"

"Because I believed it was him."

The prosecutor took his witness back through some of the taped conversation, making sure that the jury knew that Anderson understood the references to mean police, money and murder. Referring to the last bit of conversation on the tape, Anderson told him: "When I said 'I'm glad you got her,' I, at that point, was still trying to get him to admit that he killed JoAnn Wilson."

"Did he appear to understand what you were talking about?"

"I believe he did." (Thatcher responded, "Okay.")

Garry Anderson's ordeal was over. The accomplice with the troubled conscience and the tumultuous emotions left the courtroom four years after he went to Charlie Wilde on behalf of Colin Thatcher. That night he did not return to the City Hospital or the detention centre. Nor did he join his mother and Linda, who, looking for some peace and solitude, had moved to a motel to avoid being identified by the media. Garry Anderson spent a quiet night with an old friend.

The tape recording of his last conversation with Colin Thatcher remained in the courtroom. On it, missed by the Crown in re-examination, was proof of Anderson's reason for not using the words "murder" or "killing." Early in the discussion the accomplice had tried the word "gun" and got a severe reaction from Thatcher, paranoid about hidden microphones: "Don't even talk like that. Don't — don't even — walk out this way a little further."

On Wednesday morning the Thatcher entourage of family and

friends had risen to nine people, again including Stephanie. As the crowd and participants settled in for the day's proceedings, the little girl went up to her father seated at the counsel table and kissed him on the cheek. It was a heart-rending scene that mixed with the continued indignation at the child's presence.

Later, in the corridor during a break, grandmother Peggy suggested to Stephanie that she did not have to remain if she did not want to. "Greg says I have to be here," Stephanie explained.

As the case continued, the Crown cleaned up some tie-ins respecting the tape, calling SWAT men McKee and Golemba and Special "O" operatives Waelz and Britton. Waelz and Britton had also covered the money drop on the Friday morning.

Jim Street told the jury of sweeping the farmyard Thursday night and finding the garbage bag containing $550 the next morning.

A month before the trial, anticipating the defence that Colin had been at home at the time of the 6:24 phone call, Street had done a test run from the Wilson garage in Regina to Colin Thatcher's back door in Moose Jaw. Street testified that his total time, running to and from the car and driving at 100 to 110 miles per hour, was twenty-eight minutes and nineteen seconds. Unfortunately, Street had used Lewvan Drive to get out of Regina, and Lewvan had not been opened in January 1983. Street claimed that his route was no faster than Pasqua Street which would have been used in 1983, only safer.

(That was undoubtedly true for Street, whose driving is something of a legend around the Regina Police Department. The previous week, when the airports were closed, Street had driven pathologist Vetters up from Regina through the storm. Street's heavy foot made no concession at all to the weather, and the shaken Vetters made some colourful comments while demanding alternative transportation home.)

With Street on the stand, Allbright tried one more time to get the 6:24 phone call into evidence and failed again. The defence lawyer was searching for some way to establish that Colin had been at home on the telephone at that time.

Charlie Wilde wrapped up the Crown case against Colin Thatcher. Nattily dressed, handsome, almost urbane, the distinguished-looking Charlie appeared more like a banker than

231

the drug addict/junkie/confidence man he admitted he was.

As Charlie told his story, it was easy to picture this debonair dude meeting the Thunder Creek MLA in front of the Legislative Buildings, stepping into Colin's yellow Corvette and driving with him around south Regina while murder and money were discussed.

Allbright attacked Charlie in the standard way, emphasizing his lengthy criminal record (which included one conviction for impersonation) and his addiction. He suggested that Charlie's mind was fried by narcotics and that he might easily be "playing a role" in front of the jury.

Charlie admitted that he was not "above a little blackmail" but, when asked why, then, he did not run some blackmail on Thatcher he replied: "You don't go to the well too often."

It was a sensible answer and Mr. Justice Maher later pointed it out as such in his charge to the jury.

And that was it. Kujawa closed the Crown case against Colin Thatcher. Allbright asked to have until morning to decide whether he would call evidence and, although it was early in the afternoon, Mr. Justice Maher adjourned court until the next day.

That evening on the 19th floor of the Renaissance there was no relaxation of the tension that had been building since the trial had begun. Rather, as the prosecutors began to anticipate and predict the defence which would come against their case, the anxiety level heightened until it became almost palpable. Security was still on and would remain until Charlie Wilde left the next day, but responsibilities had diminished and there was little left to do but worry.

CHAPTER 17

The Alibi

Gathered in Kujawa's suite (he had claimed seniority and succeeded to the presidential suite vacated by Lynne Mendell), the Crown team of prosecutors and police debated every theory and suggestion. Ken MacKay, Director of Prosecutions, joined the discussion. He had just finished his negotiations with Bill Gardner over the details of the relocation and assistance granted to Garry Anderson.

No one doubted that Allbright would call evidence. His defence was known to be alibi and that meant witnesses. The debate was over who would lead off for the defence, Colin Thatcher or Tony Merchant. Although it did not make sense in traditional terms, the consensus was that Kujawa would face Thatcher's civil lawyer in the morning. But would Thatcher himself testify at all? An alibi defence would force him into the stand, for the courts have almost no regard for alibis that are not supported from the witness box by the accused. But Thatcher was vulnerable, so vulnerable. How could he possibly explain all the incriminating activities that had been proven against him?

Allbright did not need the early adjournment to decide whether or not to put Colin Thatcher in the witness box. He had known from the beginning that the accused would have to testify. Although one who is accused of a criminal offence is not obliged to answer the case against him but can remain silent and ask that the charge be proven beyond a reasonable doubt, in practice that right sometimes has limited application. Allbright knew that this case was one of those times. He also knew that there had not been a major Canadian murder trial in years where the accused had remained silent and been acquitted.

Like the Irish juror who, looking at the accused in the prisoner's box, said, "Sure, and if you're not guilty, what are you doing in there?," the Saskatoon jury would wonder why Colin Thatcher would choose not to step forward and explain himself. No matter how carefully instructed they were to disregard the accused's silence, the question would remain in their reasoning or their subconscious.

The alibi defence Allbright was planning made the question academic in any event. He would try to prove that Colin Thatcher was somewhere else at the time of the murder, and he had witnesses who would say so. If Colin Thatcher declined to testify also to that effect, the law required the presiding judge to instruct the jury so critically respecting the alibi that it would be next to worthless.

Allbright was using the early adjournment to prepare his examination-in-chief of the six witnesses he would be calling in support of Thatcher's alibi. One of these was Tony Merchant, and the lawyer was proposing to use him to lead off his defence. Traditionally, an accused would be called first in such a situation, followed by those who corroborated his story. Allbright was saving Thatcher to the end.

The next morning, Thursday, Kujawa had been teasing Al Johnston in the Renaissance. Telling the junior prosecutor that he was "stuck here with the old guru, so pay attention and you might learn something," he was giving Johnston a lecture on predestination when they were joined in the hotel elevator by Richard Collver. Kujawa seized on Collver's presence as an example. When the prosecutors laughingly told the story to Swayze before they went into court, the detective did not join in the laughter. Instead, his antenna went up. Swayze does not believe in predestination, but he does not believe in coincidences, either. He went looking for Collver.

As Allbright walked into court Thursday morning, he handed a subpoena to Wayne Mantyka in the media seats and a few moments later the reporter was in the witness stand. Mantyka, a reporter with CKCK-TV in Regina, not noted for his reluctance to take positions on newsworthy items, had decided to inject himself into the dispute between the Crown and the defence over the availability in Canada of the hollow-point ammunition.

234

Taking his cue from Allbright's reference to a local gun shop, Mantyka had, the day before, gone over to the store and had himself filmed handling a Ruger Security Six .357 and buying a box of .357 Winchester Silvertip hollow-points. On advice the feature had not been shown, but Allbright was happy with the opportunity to have someone unconnected with the defence support his theory of the availability of the ammunition.

Kujawa was incensed and angrily attacked Mantyka for not knowing that the issue was the illegality of the importation. "I sure wish you had listened to the evidence more carefully," he told the reporter as he sat down. The following Thursday when the jury was being addressed, Mantyka, adhering to his usual schedule, left the courtroom before Kujawa began speaking and covered only the defence address. The Crown address to the jury was missing from CKCK-TV newscasts for some hours and then was supplied by another reporter.

Allbright, in advising the court that morning that he would be calling witnesses, stated in a very matter-of-fact way that he did not think it was "necessary to make an opening statement to the jury."

It was probably a mistake. Although his alibi defence was simple and the jury would have no difficulty in understanding it, Allbright passed up an opportunity to emphasize what he was setting about to prove. Having abdicated his right to open, Allbright used Tony Merchant to introduce his case. Thatcher's civil lawyer would make an impressive beginning but, as things worked out, the strategy produced results less positive than might have been hoped for.

It was Merchant's morning, beginning with his entrance. Never one to run with the common herd, the lawyer declined to use the witnessroom door at the front of the courtroom but instead entered from the barristers' lounge at the very back. The point that there was a difference between this witness and those the Crown had been calling for ten days was quickly made.

Looking much younger than his forty years, and dressed as usual in a double-breasted suit that he seems to affect in disguise of his slight frame, Merchant handed some papers to Allbright and took the stand.

In a very unconventional introduction of a witness, Allbright

235

then led Merchant through an obviously rehearsed description of the Regina lawyer's family background, professional and business achievements, and political and community activities. The jury heard of the success and position of the witness's maternal grandfather, his father, his mother and his sister. They were told in detail of his education and professional career, including the number of lawyers in his firm and his position as third senior partner. The lawyer went on to outline an impressive list of businesses and properties, with sales figures, of which he owned "a part" or "a piece." A diploma Merchant received from the University of Regina was elevated to a Bachelor's degree, although he declined the Master's Allbright tried to confer upon him.

Merchant's unusual emphasis of the positive aspects of his career was illustrated by his carefully edited version of his political career. He twice told the jury that he had been elected to the Saskatchewan Legislature in 1975, "the only time that I ran." No mention was made of his three political defeats, once running for the leadership of the Saskatchewan Liberal Party and twice for Parliament.

Merchant was to maintain in cross-examination by Kujawa that this sort of character introduction of a witness was common in his practice, but watching lawyers were amazed at his performance.

Finally getting closer to the matter at hand, Merchant told of coming to know Colin Thatcher, at first politically and then as his solicitor, during the four years of his marital dispute.

Merchant's purpose that morning was to establish an alibi for his client on the occasion of each shooting. In the process he would cast imputations of professional incompetence at Kujawa and criminal activity at the Regina police.

Merchant told the jury about telephoning his client on the evening of May 17, 1981, immediately upon learning of the shooting of JoAnn, and then driving madly to Moose Jaw. Merchant said he later searched out his long distance telephone records for both that day and January 21, 1983. After disclosing the existence of these telephone records in court on the first bail application (but not presenting them), Merchant discovered they had disappeared from his office which had suffered several "mysterious" break-ins. His suggestion was that the police had criminally appropriated the records which were not available to them by search warrant because of solicitor-client privilege.

Because he had been "concerned that records might disappear" Merchant had made copies of the telephone records but, for some reason, Allbright did not tender them in evidence.

Merchant's allegation that the Regina police had burgled his office, raided his Thatcher files, and stolen his telephone records, was reminiscent of such sensational occurrences as the CIA's snooping in the office of Daniel Ellsberg's psychiatrist. Curiously, it did not provoke much reaction, even in the media, perhaps because of the characteristically casual and offhand way in which the lawyer tossed it out.

Mr. Justice Maher, in his charge to the jury, described Merchant's accusation as "incredible." It was indeed incredible, and made the more so the next morning when Allbright advised the court that his lawyer witness had telephoned him half an hour earlier to explain that, upon checking with his partners, he had discovered that the break-ins to their offices had occurred before Colin Thatcher's arrest. That meant before the bail application and before the disclosure of the existence of the telephone records which, he had alleged, had caused their disappearance. Months after the trial, Merchant said that the records were likely tucked away for safekeeping and lost within his own office.

Merchant's evidence of his activities on May 17, 1981 was no more carefully considered and, to his surprise, quite useless in establishing an alibi for his client for the first shooting. He estimated his driving time to Moose Jaw at thirty-five minutes immediately following his telephone call to Thatcher. That had been as soon as he learned of the event from the police at his home and was, he obviously thought, early enough to establish that Colin could not have done the shooting. When Kujawa told him the police he had seen in front of the Thatcher home had recorded his arrival at 12:45 a.m., and that the shooting had occurred at 10:10 p.m., he explained that he had not known the time of the shooting. He had never inquired.

Thatcher's divorce lawyer had a more solid recollection of what he had done on January 21, 1983, and when he had done it. He had, as before, telephoned Thatcher immediately upon

237

learning of the shooting, and found him at home. This, said Merchant, was at 6:15 p.m., a time he was quite positive of, in spite of his affidavit filed on the bail application and shown to him by Kujawa, which put the time at "some time prior to 6:30." With the murder having occurred at six o'clock or slightly before, if Colin was home in Moose Jaw at 6:15, he could not be the murderer.

Merchant said he called Thatcher again about 7:00 p.m. and once again, later yet, from a restaurant. The first two calls, he was careful to explain, were made from a home extension of a separate phone he maintained in his office, number 525-2880, not from his normal residence phone.

Merchant said he had met Lynne Mendell half a dozen times in the company of Colin Thatcher. He was about to respond to Allbright's question about "his observation as to his [Colin's] reaction to her" when Kujawa rose. He objected, saying, "This witness who has done about everything else is now going to give us character evidence on Mrs. Mendell."

Mr. Justice Maher upheld the objection. Allbright withdrew the question "if you feel that it's an improper area," and closed his examination of the lawyer.

"Mr. Merchant, tell me. Was your father an eagle scout?" Kujawa did not propose to be kind to his fellow lawyer as he opened his cross-examination.

"Actually, I think he was," Merchant replied.

"I'm absolutely amazed that you left that out because you put in everything else."

Complaining about the lengthy and glowing introduction Merchant had given himself, Kujawa asked, "As a lawyer, surely you know that you can't call character evidence to bolster the credibility of a witness or do you ever read any law?" Although Allbright objected, Merchant was not insulted and admitted he did not know "the answer to the question of criminal law that you addressed to me."

The lawyer had testified during Allbright's examination that, on the day of his arrest for the snatching of Stephanie, the Crown had not known that the Criminal Code sections dealing with abduction had been repealed and replaced. He now told Kujawa

238

that he did not "want to criticize your lack of knowledge in your field." Since it was Merchant who had not known of the change in the law and Kujawa who had brought it to his attention, the prosecutor told the witness: "I resent that."

The exchange between the two lawyers was becoming heated and threatening to become unseemly. Mr. Justice Maher suggested it was time for lunch.

Kujawa had only begun his cross-examination. Over sandwiches in his suite in the Renaissance he agonized with Al Johnston and the police about how to handle the curious matter of Merchant's telephone records.

Allbright, after introducing Merchant's story of the break-ins to explain the loss of the original telephone billing records, had not put in the copies, although he had waved them around the courtroom. Why not? They were perfectly acceptable evidence.

Kujawa knew, however, that the long distance billing records that SaskTel gives its customers were not precise enough to prove anything: they show only the hour in which a call is made, a span of fifty-nine minutes. The question was, then, why not take the records out of Merchant's hand and put them in as a Crown exhibit? They should show only that a call was made between 6:00 and 7:00 and thus would not corroborate Merchant's assertion that his call was at 6:15.

The difficulty was that there should be no phone call at all showing on the billing records. Early in the investigation the police had checked Merchant's telephone number 525-2880 with SaskTel computer records, and found no record of the phone call he described. Merchant, the police knew from SaskTel, was under the impression that no such check had been made and that, since the computer tape had been erased as a matter of routine, it was not now possible to definitively confirm or deny what calls had been made, or when.

A rule of evidence, known as "the best evidence rule," requires that, before copies of documents can be accepted as evidence, the unavailability of the originals must be explained. The widespread use of photocopying has relaxed this requirement somewhat, but the reason for the rule remains. Alterations in the original document often do not show as such on the copy.

On the theory that, if the documents in Merchant's hands

239

showed anything particularly supportive of his story, Allbright would have put them in evidence, Kujawa decided to do so himself. He was right. Merchant's copies showed a call to Redland, but identified it only as some time between 6:00 and 7:00.

Merchant agreed with Kujawa that "so far as the bill shows, the call could have been made now or fifty-nine minutes from now." How, then, the prosecutor wanted to know, could anybody "get any profit, gain or advantage by stealing those bills?"

"I'm not sure that in the middle of the night someone would have thought of that," Merchant responded. He had referred to the bills in his affidavit as "telephone records" without specifying that they were SaskTel bills.

In that affidavit Merchant had put the time of his call to Thatcher at "some time prior to six-thirty." "How did you shave about twenty minutes [actually only fifteen] off that today?" asked Kujawa. Merchant explained that when drawing the affidavit he decided not to be specific "because I was just going by recollection at that time."

Merchant and Kujawa were making each other nervous. The witness sipped frequently from his glass of water and the prosecutor was halting as his mind searched for the questions.

Merchant refused to agree with Kujawa that the Thatcher divorce proceedings had been "extremely bitter." "Bitter" he would accept, but not "extreme."

"In the real extreme ones, how many people get killed?" Kujawa asked, and then withdrew the question.

Kujawa brought up Mr. Justice Noble's judgment in which he had fined Colin for contempt of court. The judge had been critical of Merchant's behaviour on that occasion, describing it as "an affront to the court." Kujawa read the further statement, "This shows how far Mr. Thatcher, with the active assistance of his counsel, is prepared to go to prevent the mother of Regan Thatcher from gaining lawful custody." Merchant thought that Mr. Justice Noble was merely disagreeing with his "tactics."

Merchant stated that during the period of Regan's absence he did not know where the child was, but was forced by Kujawa to admit that when he saw Regan in the Thatcher home on May 17,

1981, he then "knew where he was." The lawyer conceded that, although he knew Regan was supposed to be in JoAnn's custody and that the police and authorities were looking for him, he did not report his whereabouts, nor advise Colin to. Instead, he explained, he had launched another custody application.

Lawyers following the case conjectured as to whether Tony Merchant's performance in the witness box had helped or hurt his client. Four days later Tony Merchant wrote a memorandum to one of his partners explaining his testimony. He said: "It is strange the way a case comes together when people read about it in the newspaper. It demonstrates how ineffective the criminal justice system probably really is." The memo discloses that some of his impressions of the night of the first shooting were based upon what he had been told by a friend at a radio station.

During lunch hour, while Kujawa was wrestling with Tony Merchant's testimony, Ed Swayze tried to get the prosecutor's attention concerning a chat Swayze had had that morning with one Richard Collver. The man had something interesting to say, said Swayze, and he thought the prosecutor should talk to him. Kujawa waved Swayze off. "We'll have to talk about it later," he said.

After Tony Merchant left the stand, Allbright swung into more direct evidence of his client's alibi, calling two witnesses who claimed to have seen Colin Thatcher at his ranch and in Moose Jaw at times conflicting with the time of the murder. They gave the sort of testimony that has given rise to the somewhat jaundiced view courts take of alibis.

Barbara Wright now remembered that, on the day of the murder, she looked out the window of the ranch house kitchen and saw Colin Thatcher checking his cattle, not leaving until almost 5:30 p.m. Wally Beaton listened sadly as the witness denied having told him anything different when he had interviewed her and other residents of the Thatcher ranch, shortly after the murder. At that time, she stated flatly that she hadn't been at the ranch until 6:00 p.m. and did not see Thatcher at all that day.

Kujawa brought out the fact that, having not considered the

241

event for more than a year, Wright had sworn an affidavit the previous May describing her observation. The night before giving the affidavit she had received telephone calls from Colin Thatcher, Greg Thatcher, Tony Merchant and Gerry Allbright.

Pat Hammond, twenty-four-year-old brother of Sandra, and Colin Thatcher's mechanic, said he had driven past Colin, each in their own trucks, at the intersection near Thatcher's home "very close to 5:30 . . . within five minutes either way."

Hammond, also, had talked to the police shortly after the murder, had not mentioned anything of having seen Colin that afternoon, and had not known that Colin's whereabouts at that time would be important until the arrest in May. Then he, too, had sworn an affidavit, which Kujawa showed him, putting the time of seeing Colin at "between 5 and 5:30 p.m."

Allbright attempted to repair the damage, but Kujawa objected and Mr. Justice Maher upheld the Crown, saying, "Mr. Kujawa discredits that evidence by an affidavit, isn't that the end of it? Isn't it up to the jury now?"

The judge's use of the word "discredit" struck the trial watchers with unusual impact. It was taken by many as a sign of judicial favouritism.

Pat Hammond was followed by his sister, Sandra Silversides. After it was over, Serge Kujawa said that she had been the toughest witness he had ever met in his career.

Pristine and demure in a blue sailor dress, the blonde twenty-two-year-old major domo of the Redland Avenue residence was immediately introduced by Allbright as being "nervous" and unable to withstand much courtroom stress. Some watchers agreed; others thought they saw a very skilful and calculating role being performed.

Sandra, a graduate of a two-year business administration course given by the Saskatchewan Technical Institute in Moose Jaw, was employed by Saskatchewan Tourism and Small Business, a government job arranged by Thatcher. She received "a salary for being Colin Thatcher's constituency secretary," looked after the household chores in the Redland Avenue home, and ran her own house. She told the jury that on January 21 she had gone to the Thatcher home at 5:00 p.m., made dinner (she

242

remembered that it was Hamburger Helper) for Colin and his two sons, ate with them, and left about 6:15 p.m.

Learning of the murder, the young woman had returned to Redland Avenue about 7:30 p.m., telephoned the news to some of Colin's constituency executive members, stocked the house up with some mix and left again.

At 6:00 p.m. that evening Colin Thatcher had been sitting across the table from her at dinner, she said.

A month before the trial the police, interested in the money transactions that Blaine Mathieson had described Sandra handling for Colin, had seized the housekeeper's bank statements and other financial records. Knowing this, Allbright brought out that Sandra had run a housekeeping account through which she purchased groceries and other "odds and ends," and was reimbursed by Colin.

Kujawa was looking at Sandra's bank statement for the period four years earlier, November 1980 through February 1981, when she was still a high school student being paid $500 a month to help around the Thatcher house. The statement showed that more than $10,000 had passed through the girl's bank account in those months when money had been paid to Charlie Wilde and Cody Crutcher.

Sandra did not remember that much money or many of the specific deposits and withdrawals Kujawa put to her, but did not deny them either. She admitted that she had sometimes cleared Colin's cheques through her account and given him cash. So, Kujawa said, "During the period that I mentioned, it could have happened that you handled all of that that way?"

"Probably, yes."

Sandra agreed with Kujawa that, while she had been running the Thatcher house since JoAnn had left, she had "had a lot of other women come into that house — always girlfriends of Colin's."

The girl was adamant about the Mustang car. She had never seen one around the Thatcher house or in the garage.

Kujawa was in a spot. The girl was threatening to break down on him and, sincere or not, it was going to be a good enough job to make him look like a bully to the jury. They had been told that

243

Sandra had been arrested the same day Colin was, advised she was being charged with being an accessory, and then released. She was suing the police. The prosecutor tried coming straight out.

"Are you playing a bit of a role, Sandra?"

"Pardon?"

"You are playing a bit of a role here, aren't you?"

"I don't think so, no."

Kujawa decided to try one more tack and then run for home. The long distance telephone log covering the phones in the Thatcher house showed that on January 21 Sandra had been talking to Blaine Mathieson in Saskatoon from the constituency office phone in the house for twenty-six minutes, right up until two minutes to six. That did not give her much time to have dinner on the table at six. Sandra did not remember the call, "but I wouldn't deny it, no."

While the entranced courtroom had been listening to Tony Merchant, Swayze and Beaton had been looking for Dick Collver. They found the former Saskatchewan Conservative leader, who was in town only by sheer coincidence on a family visit, in Saskatoon's YMCA.

Swayze wondered if Collver knew anything that might be useful to him. Collver thought he probably did, but wanted to talk to his lawyer, R.L. Barclay, QC, of MacPherson, Leslie and Tyerman in Regina. Swayze went off to call Barclay.

Barclay's office told Swayze that the lawyer was, by more coincidence, in Saskatoon, attending a meeting of the Benchers of the Law Society. By noon Swayze had Collver's story and was trying, unsuccessfully, to get Kujawa's attention.

Dick Collver had been about as close a friend as Colin Thatcher ever had and had recruited the Thunder Creek MLA to his Conservative caucus in 1977. At New Year's 1980, Thatcher had visited Collver at his mentor's Arizona ranch and asked for assistance in locating someone to murder his estranged wife. Collver, on the advice of his counsel, had said nothing of the event at the time, after the first shooting, or even after the murder. Now, he said, he wanted to get it off his chest. He would testify.

244

Swayze collared Kujawa when court adjourned for the day, after his cross-examination of Sandra Silversides. The prosecutor agreed that Collver would have to be called, but there was a problem as to when and how. The Crown's case had been closed for a day.

The prosecution was already planning to call some evidence in rebuttal to the testimony heard from the defence that day, particularly Wally Beaton concerning Barbara Wright and Blaine Mathieson concerning Sandra Silversides. It seemed natural and proper to include Collver as a rebuttal witness, since Thatcher's testimony would surely give them the opening.

Kujawa talked to Collver late Thursday night, and then made his decision, overruling Al Johnston and others. He would not hold Collver to call in rebuttal, but would apply to reopen the Crown case and call him as he had his other witnesses.

In the morning Allbright was told of the Crown's intention. Collver's presence in Saskatoon and his potential testimony was by now fairly widely known in the legal community and the defence counsel had heard the story the night before.

Allbright could not object to Kujawa's choice of attempting to reopen rather than calling Collver in rebuttal, although he would, of course, oppose the application.

Kujawa was proposing to bring Collver forward at the end of the trial. Perhaps because Allbright was nicely into his defence and did not want his segment of the trial interrupted, he did not insist that Kujawa make his application to reopen immediately. Dick Collver, accordingly, would not testify until the next week, after the defence, including Colin Thatcher's testimony, was all in.

That arrangement was to have a serious impact upon the trial, particularly when Colin Thatcher tried to cope in the witness box with the witness waiting to follow.

Before the jury, Allbright continued presenting his alibi defence. He called Colin Thatcher's two sons, Regan and Greg.

Fifteen-year-old Regan, in jacket and tie, told the jury of living with his grandmother in Palm Springs to avoid the custody order directing that he be with JoAnn. Regan said he had been back in his father's home in Moose Jaw two weeks when the first shooting of his mother took place on May 17, 1981. On that day

245

he had been home the entire day and so had Colin, working on the swimming pool. Regan had taken a phone call from Tony Merchant and called his father to the phone. Merchant later arrived at the home.

On the day of the murder, Regan said, he came home after school. Greg was at home. Sandra came to cook supper (Hamburger Helper) and Colin arrived at 5:30 p.m. All four sat down to dinner at 6:00, Regan knew, because Colin always took his supper to the TV room to watch the news.

Once again Regan had taken a call from Tony Merchant and called his father to the telephone. That call came "between ten after six and a quarter after six." Another call from Merchant came later.

Regan told Kujawa that, when Colin came down to Palm Springs while he was living there, he would move over to his father's condominium. When asked if he ever saw Tony Merchant in Palm Springs, the boy explained that he "was not supposed to go around the condominium, so Mr. Merchant couldn't see me and to the best of my knowledge he never knew I was down there at the time."

Wondering how a phrase like "to the best of my knowledge" got into the vocabulary of a fifteen-year-old, Kujawa asked where it had come from, "from your own head right now?"

"Yes."

"Very well done."

In the witness stand, Regan's recollection of the times of the events he had described happening on May 17, 1981, was hazy. He thought Tony Merchant was at the house "right up until I went to bed . . . at roughly ten o'clock. Nine-thirty, ten o'clock." It was a tough spot for the boy who had been but twelve on the night he was trying to remember, and the courtroom was full of compassion for him.

Regan was another who had sworn an affidavit during the application to have his father released on bail the previous May. The affidavit, drawn by Gerry Allbright, made no mention of the time of the Merchant telephone call on January 21 that Regan was now fixing precisely at 6:10 to 6:15 p.m. Regan could not explain this. Like other defence witnesses, his recollection had become more specific with the passage of time.

"Yes." Regan agreed with Kujawa when he asked, "In the dealings between your father and your mother, you were clearly on your father's side?" Also on Colin's side, said Regan, were Greg and Sandra.

Gregory Ross Thatcher, nineteen, had shouldered a lot of family responsibility since his father's arrest. In addition to directing operations on the cattle ranch and grain farm, he had served as go-between, interviewing his imprisoned father for the Saskatoon lawyer who examined him this morning. Given a special, pseudo para-legal status with better access to the Regina and Saskatoon correctional centres, Greg had been deeply involved in the preparation of the defence.

A tall, handsome, well-dressed youth, Greg, as had Regan, affected a casual, even nonchalant air as Allbright led him through his description of the Thatcher household and the events of May 17, 1981 and January 21, 1983.

On the first occasion, Greg told the court, he had been out with friends but came home at 10:00 p.m. He was there when Tony Merchant's telephone call came, but did not think he had answered it. He remembered the lawyer coming to the house and arranging for Colin and Greg to give statements to the police the next day.

Greg, also, recalled that dinner on the evening of the murder had been Hamburger Helper. It had been served to Sandra, Colin, Regan and himself promptly at 6:00 p.m. The telephone call from Tony Merchant that night had come at "quarter after six, a little earlier, one or two minutes earlier, one or two minutes later, about that." The second call had come later, "forty-five minutes, maybe."

He spoke quickly, rushing his words so that the court reporter asked Mr. Justice Maher for help in slowing him down.

Greg was very defensive in response to Kujawa. When shown the statement he had given Regina police the day after the first shooting, when he said he had returned home at 10:30 p.m., and asked "how you remember so much better now than you did right after it happened?," he replied: "I'm just saying that's the way I remember it happened now. I'm not arguing. I'm not arguing with that. I may have said the time was ten-thirty. As I remember now, it was ten o'clock."

247

Kujawa had been told by Dick Collver that Colin and his family had expressed bitter remarks about JoAnn during a New Year's visit to his Arizona ranch at the end of 1980. The prosecutor was stonewalled when he asked Greg about possible bad feelings that might have been evident at that time.

Curiously, the prosecutor did not ask Greg of his possible involvement in helping Colin avoid Regan's custody order. The statement in Kujawa's hand said clearly that Greg had taken Merchant's call on May 17, when Tony Merchant had discovered that the missing Regan was at home. In his statement Greg had made no mention of Regan's presence in the house.

The alibi evidence was all in. The scene had been set for the main actor. The question would be whether the supports that had been put in place were firm enough to carry Colin.

The defence so far was not such as to be above cynical comment. Every one of the witnesses was in some way dependent upon Colin Thatcher: two were his sons; Sandra was his employee twice over; Sandra's brother, Pat Hammond, was his mechanic; Barbara Wright was his ranch hand's wife and lived in the ranch house. Even Tony Merchant had had to acknowledge past favours.

In spite of the length of time back to the night of the murder, each witness was able to recall with precision the essential feature of the alibi — when they had seen or spoken to Colin Thatcher that night. Yet, six months earlier, their recollections had been different and less supportive of the alibi. Sandra had overlooked a long telephone call that would have interfered with her making supper as she described.

It is natural and to be expected that inconsistencies and even contradictions would appear in such a collection of recollections so long after the event. Experience has taught judges and lawyers to view pat testimony with suspicion. Thus, the conflict between Regan and Sandra as to whether Colin ate his supper in the kitchen or the TV room is alone of little concern. However, when coupled with the insistence of everyone at Redland Avenue that night on such a forgettable fact that Hamburger Helper was the menu, the conflict takes on different meaning.

Apparently unnoticed, an interesting anomaly was peering out

248

of the evidence. Did it mean that the defence had not come forward exactly as intended by the accused?

Colin had told Garry Anderson: "I was just lucky that night. I was home with four people. Four people. Pretty solid, and that's pretty hard."

Three had testified. Who was the fourth?

After Greg Thatcher left the stand, Allbright requested an adjournment until Monday morning. Wanting for some reason to maintain suspense, his next witness, he said, would be a "very, very major witness" and "a long witness." He did not want the weekend to interrupt the testimony. Although it was not yet noon, the court adjourned to Monday morning.

Outside the courtroom Allbright refused to give reporters any indication of who his "major witness" would be. Colin, when asked if it would be him, shook his head "no."

It made for a weekend of wild speculation. By now Dick Collver's presence in Saskatoon and the fact that he might be a witness in the trial was an open secret. The possibility that the former Conservative leader could be the unknown defence witness led to tantalizing conjecture of what he might contribute on behalf of Colin Thatcher.

Knowing better, Serge Kujawa was not distracted by the speculation. He went down to Regina for the weekend and prepared for his cross-examination of Colin Thatcher. In Saskatoon, the lights burned late in the offices of Gerry Allbright, visible from the courthouse.

Kujawa had a concern. The Thatcher civil trials had exposed a very unpleasant side to Colin Thatcher, as Mr. Justice M.A. MacPherson had determined. In his testimony before the jury Colin was unlikely to volunteer any damaging description of himself. In fact, if in cross-examination he denied matters that had been previously proven, as Kujawa expected he would, the prosecutor would be bound by his answers. JoAnn would never testify again, and her earlier evidence could not be used in front of the jury.

Thatcher could, of course, be confronted with his previous testimony where it differed from what he might choose to tell the jury, but Kujawa did not know his way around the thousands of pages of civil transcripts well enough to make the necessary quick references. Probably no one did any more, not even Gerry Gerrand who had lived through those trials with JoAnn.

It would be best if Colin would be honest, but how to ensure that? On Sunday morning Kujawa telephoned Gerry Gerrand.

Gerrand understood the problem immediately. That afternoon he gathered up the several volumes of transcripts containing Colin Thatcher's testimony in the civil actions and drove up to Saskatoon. He would sit in the courtroom while Colin testified and be a signal that the truth was at hand.

The spectators began arriving to hear Allbright's "major witness" at midnight. By 2:00 a.m. Monday morning the courthouse corridor was full and the line-up began to form outside in the minus 19°C cold. By now the regulars were using numbers to ensure order and places in line according to time of arrival.

CHAPTER 18

The Accused Takes the Stand

Colin Thatcher had spent a lot of time in witness stands in the five years leading up to his appearance — the "major witness," after all — before the jury on Monday morning. The "first-time" nervousness was gone but the pressure he was under showed in the flippancy he was not quite able to conceal.

Gerry Allbright had put a lot of effort into preparing his presentation of the accused politician to the jury. He had not read the hundreds of pages of transcripts of the testimony in the divorce, property and custody trials, but the criminal lawyer led his client through a history of the Thatcher family very similar to that heard in other courts.

Taking Thatcher through his relationship with JoAnn and the first sixteen years of their marriage, Allbright came to 1979 and Ron Graham. Colin said that in early 1979 JoAnn became "very troubled," "very down" and that, out of concern that "things were slipping away," he was for the last eight months of their marriage "an excellent husband."

He detailed the growing affair between JoAnn and Graham, which he had not believed until after the separation. He told of JoAnn's leaving, his search for her and the children, and, on finding them in Brampton, Ontario, his taking Sandra Hammond and going for them. Colin told the startled jury that Sandra's mother's suggestion that her eighteen-year-old daughter accompany him on the mission was "the greatest compliment that I have ever received in my life or probably ever will receive."

Moving carefully through the chronology of the events of the fall of 1979, including the first custody trial, Allbright and

251

Thatcher came to Christmas of that year and the family trip, without JoAnn but with Blaine Mathieson, to Palm Springs.

Then followed one of the most surprising features of the trial. Thatcher began to discredit the waiting witness, Dick Collver, and the story he had not yet told.

Colin had discussed his troubles with Collver in Regina earlier in 1979, and his caucus mate had tried to convince JoAnn to be reconciled with Colin. Collver had suggested that Colin visit him at his ranch at Wickenburg, Arizona, about forty miles out of Phoenix, during the holiday season.

Allbright led Thatcher into the strange testimony. "Can you tell us what that visit was like, the circumstances surrounding it? I understand it may become important later, Mr. Thatcher."

And Colin did. He told of spending New Year's at the Collver ranch, dining and drinking on New Year's Eve, and of not having an opportunity to talk to Collver until the next morning. He described Collver's condition on that morning-after as "that never-never land when you are still half drunk and hung over." Collver, Colin said, was "the cheapest drunk in the world," meaning that he had no capacity for liquor.

All that, and more, was Colin Thatcher's in-advance explanation of how his conversation with Dick Collver that New Year's morning included references to killing JoAnn and hiring "hit men." The suggestions, he said, came from Collver, but only to illustrate the unacceptability of that option and the necessity of settling his dispute with JoAnn.

It was rebuttal evidence before its time. The jury had not yet heard of Dick Collver as part of the case, much less any allegation of murder intentions as early as New Year's 1980. By putting his version of the incident forward at this time, Thatcher was doing much to ensure that Collver's would come later and, perhaps, come with a vengeance.

Turning to Regan, Colin admitted that, in spite of the custody orders, he had arranged for his son to live with his grandmother, Peggy, in Palm Springs, and attend a private school.

He moved on to the property dispute with JoAnn and stated that he, Tony Wilson and JoAnn had been working on a settlement before the May 1981 shooting and had agreed in principle. "I knew we were going to make a deal before the shooting." The suggestion was clear. He had no motive to take JoAnn's life at that time.

Colin's activities on May 17, 1981 had been as described by Greg and Regan. He had been opening the Redland Avenue pool. Colin was prepared to put some time estimates on Tony Merchant's telephone call and arrival at the house: 11:00 p.m. for the call and 11:45 p.m. for the arrival, he thought. By now he had heard from Kujawa's cross-examination of Merchant that the police had recorded the lawyer's arrival at 12:45 a.m. With the shooting at 10:00 p.m., even Colin's closer estimates were useless for purposes of an alibi.

The final agreement settling the property action, made in February 1982, was outlined. It provided that Colin was to receive title to the Redland Avenue house and, he told the jury, that had not yet happened in January 1983. Because, he alleged, the title had not been transferred, Colin felt he was not obligated to make the $87,500 payment due on February 1. This seemed to be an attempt to destroy the motive that might be found in the moratorium clause of the agreement.

Coming up to the week of the murder, Colin told of his ouster from the cabinet on the preceding Friday. Except for attending a funeral in Regina on Monday, he claimed to have spent the entire week at home and at the ranch, avoiding people, "licking my political wounds." He denied seeing Garry Anderson at all that week, contradicting Anderson's testimony that they had met on Thursday and twice on Friday. Al Johnston arranged to alert Corporal Ken Hagerty of Moose Jaw who had seen Anderson and Colin intersect at the Caronport Gulf station the morning of the murder.

On the day of the murder, Colin said, he spent the morning at the ranch, returning home at noon. There he worked in his office "a good portion of the afternoon" before going back to the ranch "between four and four-thirty."

Driving back to Moose Jaw for supper, Colin said he met Pat Hammond at the same intersection, Redland Avenue and Saskatchewan Street, that his mechanic had described. They waved to each other.

Thatcher testified that he returned to his home at a "quarter to six, give or take. I can't give you an exact minute." He said he

253

did not leave his house again until 7:30 p.m. when he went jogging.

At 6:00 p.m., he went on, he was having dinner, in his kitchen, with Sandra, Greg and Regan. "Between six-fifteen and six-twenty" the call came from Tony Merchant with the first news of the shooting of JoAnn. After telling the news to his sons, Colin said he telephoned Lynne Mendell in Palm Springs, "in direct response to Tony Merchant's call." Merchant, he said, had called again about 7:00 and once more later in the evening from a restaurant.

Despite "shock" and "a feeling of sickness" at learning of JoAnn's death, Colin said he put on a jogging suit and went for a ten- or fifteen-minute run. He had "to think," he said, "or maybe I wanted some fresh air." The police outside his residence were "obvious." The police, however, who had been recording arrivals and departures since 7:10, did not see Colin.

Thatcher, for whom "it had been one blazes of a tough week," then settled in for the evening with his personal and political friends who had come over to be with him. "Yes," he said, "we did do some drinking that night. I could not have felt worse." Colin did not tell the jury, but among those with him that evening were Lyle Stewart, Robert Barrie and Terry Burgen, of his riding executive, Gerald Clarke, Chuck Guillaume, and, quite by accident, Constable Marvin Taylor of the Regina City Police.

The next day, concerned about Stephanie's safety, he said, and after consulting with Tony Merchant, Colin had removed her from the Kohli home and taken her back to Moose Jaw. Later he had been arrested and returned to Regina.

Allbright took this opportunity to ask his client about the credit card slip found near JoAnn's body. Colin had acknowledged to the police on that Saturday that the invoice was his and bore his signature. His lawyer asked if he had "any idea how it got to be where it was found."

"I have no explanation at all."

The credit card slip was to be about the only item of incriminating evidence for which Colin Thatcher did not have an explanation, although he said he was careless with gas slips, usually leaving them in the vehicle or stuffing them in a pocket.

Allbright then had his witness tell the jury his perspective of his affair with Lynne Mendell. Colin described the relationship much as the girl had, except that he thought she was far more interested in marriage than he was.

When he phoned with the news on the night of the first shooting of JoAnn, Colin said that Lynne had inquired, "Is she alive?" and, when told "Yes," replied, "Oh shit."

Colin denied having told Lynne about "donning a disguise and driving through the country and road blocks" on the night of the first shooting. He thought she might have picked up some of that story from her mother who received clippings from Canadian newspapers. Also, he suggested that she might have mis-construed his telling her of Tony Merchant's experience with road blocks on his drive to Moose Jaw that night.

On his feelings for Lynne Dally/Mendell, Colin said: "There were times when I cared for her, but I never trusted her."

The .357 Ruger had been bought from Ron Williams and the purchase recorded because "I may very well have to use that gun some day. And I was thinking from the point of view of a non-citizen; that gun better be registered and better be up front." Colin knew, he said, that an unregistered gun could just as easily have been acquired.

He had bought a holster from Williams, too, but it was not the one in evidence, found by Chuck Guillaume in his CVA car. The one purchased in California he had identified with his name and address written with a marking pencil. Also, it was a darker brown and a different make.

The .357 had gone missing from the Palm Springs con-dominium in 1982 and Colin changed his cleaning woman.

Colin denied having any arrangements with Lynne Mendell regarding regular telephone calls. They spoke from time to time, usually in the evening, but there was "no set pattern."

He had seen Wally Beaton's affidavit about the 6:24 p.m. telephone call at the bail application. "That put a lot of things into direct perspective. Until that time I could not put a direct, to the minute, time on the phone call from Tony Merchant. But I remember very clearly making that phone call to Lynne immediately after I had received it from Tony . . . and that enabled me to pinpoint the time of Tony's call to me." It also, of

255

course, enabled him to pinpoint the time of the call with Lynne Dally.

Interestingly, Beaton's affidavit discloses only a "suppertime phone call . . . made at 6:24 p.m.," and not where it was made from. In fact, the telephone call originated in Palm Springs instead of Redland Avenue and was not placed by Thatcher at all.

The reason why Allbright had not cross-examined Lynne Mendell about the statement she claimed Colin had made: "It's a strange feeling to blow your wife away," now became apparent. Colin explained that something similar, but much less sinister, had been said. Lynne had asked, "Did you blow her away?" and he had replied, "I cannot imagine what a strange feeling that would be. No, of course not."

Colin denied he had ever told Lynne that he had killed JoAnn. He also denied her quote about the beating, but again had a different version. She had asked, "Christ, why would they beat her and then shoot her?" He had replied, "I have no idea," and then added, "Whoever was in there was an animal anyway. He wasn't a — nobody could to that to another human being."

Allbright and Colin Thatcher consumed an entire day in putting this much explanation before the jury. They still had Garry Anderson, Charlie Wilde and the tape to go as Mr. Justice Maher adjourned the court until Tuesday morning.

The rush for seats in the courtroom to hear the testimony of the Thunder Creek MLA brought the commissionaires out at 2:00 a.m. Tuesday to supervise the line-up. Forty-five people were already standing in the cold, and the numbering system was not solving all the problems. A mobile canteen was now serving coffee to the shivering spectators.

Colin began the second day of his testimony with a version of events that, whether clever concoction or the truth, touched just on the edge of the evidence already given by Garry Anderson and Charlie Wilde. The accused admitted a very minor connection with the alleged accomplices, one that was barely enough to explain the incontrovertible facts in their accounts but not so much as to be compromising on their main accusations.

In the fall of 1980, Colin said, he had approached Garry about a possible deal on some land. He said they spoke again in early

256

1981 when Anderson, quite incidentally, brought up a suggestion that he knew someone who might be able to help Colin cause some trouble for Ron Graham. Thatcher was interested enough to agree to meet Anderson's contact and to cover Garry's expenses.

In the spring of 1981, when Anderson reported that "two fellows from Calgary" would be coming the next day, Colin said he told him to being them to the abandoned farm where he would be working.

Anderson showed up the next day with one man. Colin did not think it was Charlie Wilde, although there were similarities in appearance. He said that the stranger had a proposal, supposedly having to do with a lady friend of Graham's, that Colin found distasteful and refused to have anything to do with. He cut short the meeting but, before the others left, the stranger offered to do harm to Colin's wife, saying, "I know you are having problems there" and "We're in the business."

A few days later, Colin said he ran into Anderson who told him that he had spent $500 arranging the meeting. Colin agreed to pay, but told Anderson he would have to wait for the money.

Colin even included a reference that would include Cody Crutcher, who had not testified and who, on the evidence, he had never seen. A year after the meeting, just before the 1982 provincial election, Colin said he received a telephoned blackmail threat at his office in the Legislature from someone who identified himself as a friend of Garry Anderson's and who had not been able to "make a meeting a year earlier."

Colin told of encountering Anderson in the grounds of the Legislature in the fall of 1982. Garry's car had been seized for overparking and Colin, or his secretary, recovered it from the Wascana Centre Authority. Here Colin had to be prompted by Allbright to tell of leaving his topcoat, scarf and gloves in Anderson's car, "an old, brown Dodge." The topcoat had Colin's name on the label, he said.

Thatcher testified that he had not seen Garry Anderson again, at least to speak to, until May 1, 1984. By then "the rumour was everywhere in the Caron, Caronport, Mortlach area that I had hired Garry Anderson to kill JoAnn. That I had arranged to get Garry Anderson a job in northern Saskatchewan."

What was strange, Colin said, was that the Regina police

257

"were almost deliberately sending me the message to make me think this was their theory . . . the Regina police wanted me to know that they thought Garry Anderson had committed the murder after being hired by me."

Thatcher said he was very concerned about these rumours when he encountered Anderson on the morning of May 1. When Garry came up to Colin in the ranch yard and wanted to meet at the abandoned farm, he was gone before Colin could say "Wait a minute. Talk to you right here." That overlooked Colin's own words on the tape telling Anderson to "head up to the nuisance ground."

Colin said he followed Anderson to the farmyard because he wanted to know what the Regina police "were doing and saying to him." Also, there was the $500 "Anderson felt that I owed him." "I didn't need any haystacks burning or any outlying granaries on fire."

Had Colin had any suspicions, "I would not have been there." He said he was afraid that the Regina police "were going to try to hang this on me." Tony Merchant had told him a year before: "If they can't solve it, they will ultimately try to hang it on you."

But Colin had gone to the farmyard, he had talked to Garry Anderson, and the Regina police had recorded the conversation. Now he and Gerry Allbright were going to explain to the jury that the conversation had nothing to do with the murder of JoAnn Wilson on January 21, 1983. It was a tall order.

Colin, very articulate in the courtroom, explained to Allbright that he sounded different on the tape because he was using "Caron slang," something he "falls into" when out at the ranch or in the Caron area. Tony Merchant later said he had found the Colin he listened to on the tape a Colin he had not heard before. He perceived a different vernacular and a profanity that he thought were foreign to his client.

Allbright took Thatcher through the transcript of the tape recording almost line by line, having him explain to the jury what each strange statement actually meant in the context of the conversation he remembered. Thatcher insisted throughout that his main concern was the desire of the Regina police to link him with Garry Anderson and with Garry Anderson's government job.

"Have you been hassled?" meant "Have the Regina police come down heavily on you?"

Anderson's question, "Everything went okay though, eh?" and Colin's reply, "Yeah, there's no connection back" was only in reference to the government job.

"I got rid of the stuff out of the car" was taken only to refer to Colin's topcoat, scarf and gloves accidentally left in Anderson's car at the Legislative Buildings in the fall of 1982.

Colin's pleased response, "Good," meant that he did not care to have his topcoat found in Anderson's car. "Something sinister could be made out of something that was very innocent."

"I didn't know what the hell you'd done with the gun" had been said by Anderson "with a smile on his face." Colin "took it to be a very ill attempt at humour, a very poor attempt at humour." What Thatcher had actually said was cited earlier: "Don't even talk like that, don't — don't even — walk out this way a little, away from the car."

Colin's statement that "there are no loose ends" was "a poor choice of words . . . but this is an unguarded conversation. I'm being very candid. I'm talking the way I do when I'm at Caron."

"Is there any way a loose end from a couple of years ago can ever resurface?" referred to the man Anderson had produced three years earlier and the blackmail caller.

"Son-of-a-bitch" was not Charlie Wilde, the conman, but Tansy Mustard, a weed. The jury learned that "that's a term that many farmers refer to Tansy Mustard as." Colin, the farmer, was checking his field as they talked and thinking about seeding his crop.

"Do you need some bread?" was Colin's way of asking Anderson about the $500 which had never been paid. The discussion about where to leave the money was because the farmyard was "convenient" for Colin and he "really didn't care whether it was convenient or not for Anderson."

"We got no problem. There is no problem. You and I have any distance; keep a distance" meant that Thatcher and Anderson had done nothing wrong but should avoid giving the police "anything which enables them to proceed on something that isn't true."

Colin's concern about the car — "Has it disappeared," the one "the stuff that was left, you know?" — was an inquiry into the car Anderson had at the Legislative Buildings in the fall of 1982.

Although his response on the tape was "Okay," Thatcher said he did not know what Anderson meant when he said, "The car was cleaned and sold." Nor did he understand "That really screwed me because at that time I needed the money," though at the time he answered "Yeah." (The tape actually has him responding, "Yeah. Is there no chance that it can ever surface?")

Colin's assertion "It ain't coming to that 'cause there's only two places to put the connection together and they got zero else," was Caron slang meaning "We have done nothing wrong and nothing is going to happen."

"It's just always deny, deny, deny" meant "When you have done nothing wrong, I see nothing wrong with denying it."

Colin's reference to his alibi, his statement that "I was just lucky that night. I was home with four people," meant that, in view of the police pressure, he was "fortunate" to have "very substantial corroboration of my whereabouts."

Anderson's statement that he "had a hell of a time getting the blood and stuff off" the car was another attempt at humour. Colin "saw nothing humorous about it at all."

Allbright, with an unusual delicacy, was editing out Colin's mild profanity, declining to use the word "bastards" when asking about "I don't trust the bastards for bugs . . . when we talk just assume the bastards are listening." The statement, Colin said, was merely a suggestion that "the investigation will never be closed until it is solved . . . there's a possibility we could be overheard."

"Don't give them any information. You taught me that. Remember, they got that one guy three years later" was a reference to another attempt at humour which had taken place in the Caronport coffee shop. One of Colin's friends had mentioned a news story about finding a wife-killer three years later. Colin

260

had endured several "distasteful" jokes since the first shooting of JoAnn.

In his farmyard conversation with Anderson, Colin had boasted of recovering his political prominence, of "falling back into favour again." He said that Premier Devine "likes to talk to an old pro again" and had called him in California.

For some reason it was important to the accused to set that straight also. Colin explained that it referred only to some recent teasing of him by Stephanie who had said "the premier is calling." "It was just a private joke." It was a convoluted explanation of a minor point having nothing to do with crime. Perhaps Colin was remembering that Premier Devine had nearly been called against him in his civil trials and wanted to avoid provoking his appearance here.

On the subject of Tony Merchant, Colin had told Anderson that the lawyer "knows zero. Knows zero." About what? Merchant knew nothing about the "silly meeting" three years earlier, the blackmail attempt, or Colin's owing Anderson $500.

Caron slang, apparently, did not enable Colin to understand Anderson when he said, "I'm glad it went down," and the accused had not understood until the preliminary inquiry that Anderson had been talking about murder.

"I'm glad it's over," to which he likewise responded affirmatively, referred to the investigation, which, to Colin, "appeared to be dormant."

"A guy I could do, that guy I could do," in reference to Gerry Gerrand, was slang. However, "it means nothing. And at the best could be called running off at the mouth."

Anderson's closing comment to Colin, "I'm glad you got her," was taken as a reference to Stephanie and her custody.

Allbright left the tape recording and its transcript and asked Colin Thatcher if he had, in fact, left money for Garry Anderson. Yes, he had, admitted the accused.

Curiously, however, Colin, who had listened to the Special "O" operatives describe his trip to the farmyard Friday morning, and to Jim Street, who had swept it Thursday night, said he had made the money drop just before 9:30 p.m. on Thursday. Fred Waelz, who had been watching through binoculars, had

261

positively identified Colin Thatcher as the driver of his truck on Friday.

On Friday morning, Colin told the jury, he had not been driving his GMC three-quarter-ton. He had left between 5:30 and 6:00 a.m. in Greg's vehicle, checked some cows at the ranch, returned home and then driven to the Legislature where he was in time for Question Period.

Who, then, had been driving the GMC that had been so carefully watched as it visited the abandoned farmyard? "Greg was driving my truck," said Colin.

Why would Colin deny that the money drop had been made on Friday morning as it so surely had been? He had admitted the fact of the placing of the money. Was this feature of his testimony a vestige of a once-intended denial of the entire Anderson connection? A denial of the meeting, the conversation, the recording, the money? Had Colin's memory played a trick on him at the end of a long and demanding exercise, allowing him to overlook the fact that this denial was no longer necessary?

Allbright had one last question for Colin Thatcher: "Mr. Thatcher, did you have anything whatever to do with the death of JoAnn Wilson?"

"No, I did not."

It was 11:30 Tuesday morning when Allbright finished. Thatcher had taken nearly a day and a half in making his explanations to the jury. Kujawa asked to be allowed to begin his cross-examination after lunch and the court adjourned.

Kujawa had known from the beginning that the Crown case would run squarely into Colin Thatcher's credibility; that either the confrontation in cross-examination would pierce that credibility or Colin likely would go free, and that this make-or-break point in the case would be a far more personal duel between the prosecutor and the accused than usually found in a criminal court.

Both men had been preparing for the event about the same length of time, since the preliminary inquiry, although Kujawa had been aware of the impending contest since before Thatcher's arrest.

The prosecutor had attempted to acquire an understanding of

262

the psychology and personality of Colin Thatcher. He had never met the politician but eagerly questioned those he encountered and trusted who knew Colin. Kujawa wanted to find the weak point. As he rose to begin his assault, his main operating conclusion was that his opponent was an extremely skilful liar. JoAnn's father, Harlan Geiger, had told police that Colin was "the most accomplished liar I have ever met." Lynne Mendell described him as "a pathological liar." Kujawa also expected to face a man of supreme confidence and swollen ego, but with an Achilles heel in an uncontrollable temper.

Colin Thatcher, in his evidence-in-chief, had laid himself wide open to Kujawa by asserting that he had been an "excellent husband" in the last months of his marriage to JoAnn and by alluding to the perfidy of his wife and his best friend, Ron Graham. Gerry Allbright, not fully familiar with all Thatcher's divorce, property and custody trials, could not prevent this mistake. Certainly, Thatcher must have seen JoAnn's lawyer, Gerry Gerrand, in the courtroom but, either not wishing to deviate from a set piece, or too confident of his ability to pull it off, he gave the jury an easily destroyed description of himself as the wronged husband. When Kujawa ripped the facade away, he had the upper hand.

It was like an inquisition. Kujawa hurled his accusations against Thatcher and hostility ripped and flowed between the two. Subtle it was not.

It began with the revelation that Colin had female company with him in California when his wife left him, a girl who had been named in the divorce action, and that a different one had accompanied him on a previous trip. "And you were cheating and laughing and boozing up and making smark-aleck remarks about how you were cheating on the old bag at home," Kujawa summarized.

"A bachelor's holiday," Colin called it.

That the accused had not disclosed to his counsel the infidelity that took place during the Palm Springs holiday was evident from the obvious shock with which Gerry Allbright learned the truth. Perhaps Colin thought his lawyer would know. "That is public knowledge. It's been in *Maclean's* magazine," he told Kujawa almost proudly.

263

Colin admitted that he had not conveyed to the jury an accurate impression of his behaviour on that trip.

Kujawa forced Thatcher to admit that, if his actions the day after the shooting had been out of concern for Stephanie's safety, he had not shown much the night of the murder. He had made no inquiries about the safety or condition of his daugher, although he claimed to have mentioned it to Merchant. He then accused Colin of seeking to "get her and the other members of the family into the front row of this courtroom." Colin replied that "they should have been sitting closer to me."

The prosecutor continued pressing on Colin's personal affairs, questioning him about his financial difficulties and his ability to make the payment due shortly after JoAnn's death. He suggested that, quoting Lynne Mendell, Thatcher was "the kind of person who was always blaming somebody for your troubles" and, after losing his cabinet position, was "out to get" JoAnn.

"Do you think you're in touch with reality?" he put to Thatcher.

"I guess that's what we're here to find out," was the response.

When Colin complained of his six months in jail, Kujawa accused: "You sounded pretty smug here for the last couple of days at the story you made up and told so beautifully. I think you made good use of those six months myself, wouldn't you agree?" Colin disagreed.

The prosecutor turned to the hard evidence, beginning with the gun. Colin claimed he had reported its loss in California but acknowledged that no record of his report existed. "Bad luck," suggested Kujawa.

More "bad luck" in the finding of a holster in Thatcher's government car.

"Good trick," not "bad luck," was Colin's answer to the doll shower box and the *Los Angeles Times* found in his bedroom. On the date on the newspaper Lynne Mendell had been in Moose Jaw, he said, and could not have been watching Colin wrap a gun with it in Palm Springs.

"Extremely bad luck," Colin agreed on the finding of the credit card slip near JoAnn's body.

Colin denied that his CVA Oldsmobile, KDW 292, had been

the car seen near the Wilson home on the days previous to the murder.

"You've taken 'deny, deny, deny' to new heights already and we haven't even got going good yet," said Kujawa.

The prosecutor went on to Barbara Wright and Pat Hammond and the pre-affidavit conversations Colin had with them. The Thatcher temper came loose. His witnesses, the alibi supporters, Colin said, "testified under The Perjury Act [sic] . . . They're vulnerable. They didn't have immunity like your witnesses [Anderson and Wilde]."

"Mr. Thatcher, keep calm," said Kujawa.

But Colin's temper had come loose. His face contorted and he strained towards his tormentor. Although Greg and Regan had not been mentioned, he snarled: "It's very easy to say that my sons have lied. Why don't you step out on the courthouse steps and say that, where you don't have the immunity?"

Thatcher was furious but was not, as many thought, challenging Kujawa to physical combat. Resorting to a form of intimidation more common to the Legislature, the invitation to "step outside and say that" was the MLA's way of daring his opponent to shed his privilege respecting defamatory statements. It may also have been a cunning attempt to project himself as a protective father.

Kujawa chose to receive the challenge as physical. "How about the fourth green on the golf course?" Kujawa shot back in reference to Colin's threats to Ron Graham five years earlier.

"Charlie Bronson you're not," he added, a retort that the press seized upon and which became one of the descriptive catch-phrases of the duel.

The outburst did Thatcher no good. His temper had been exposed. It was the only feature of the entire cross-examination that Allbright had Colin explain in re-examination.

Kujawa carried on to the other defence witnesses. "Sandra is a very special person to me," Colin said, but he denied that she "laundered" money for him. There had been no Mustang car in May 1981.

The prosecutor questioned Colin about what he called the "time shifts" in the evidence of Greg, Tony Merchant and Barbara Wright, referring to the discrepancies between their affidavits and testimony in court. The accused replied that "everybody told the truth and if you don't think they did, you know what to do about it far better than I do."

Why did Lynne Mendell come to testify? She and Colin had still a friendly relationship? "Not friendly enough I guess," Colin suggested.

"This is real bad luck?"

"I was disappointed to see her on the stand at the preliminary, yes."

"Where did she [Mendell] get the idea about the disguise and the going through fields to avoid the police on the way back to Moose Jaw?" Kujawa asked. "Out of some fantasy, obviously," Colin replied.

"You pretty much live by deny, deny, deny, don't you?" Kujawa accused the witness.

Leaving Mendell, Kujawa took Colin back to the Court of Appeal at the time of the bail hearing in May, when Allbright described the tape recording as a "fabrication."

Thatcher was waiting and ready. He counterattacked, accusing Kujawa of describing the tape on that occasion as a "confession," as containing "threats to at least three people." Thatcher called this a "gross misrepresentation" responsible for keeping him "six months in jail." "You bet I denied that that tape was the correct tape."

Thatcher's anger was again exposed. He was furious and yelling. But he seemed to be using it as a tactic, almost deliberately. Kujawa was losing control of the situation. Mr. Justice Maher interjected, questioning the relevance of what took place in the Court of Appeal.

Colin pressed his advantage. He accused Kujawa of having refused to allow Allbright to hear the tape in spite of "many" requests. "We had no idea what tape that you had. And the description that you were giving at that time . . . was grossly, grossly inaccurate . . . you bet we denied that tape."

Mr. Justice Maher admonished the prosecutor. "You've got to be fair, Mr. Kujawa." He also pointed out, "I suggest, and I think it's the law, that you're bound by his answers."

It was a good time for the afternoon recess and Mr. Justice Maher ordered a short adjournment.

Colin had managed a recovery with his attack on the prosecutor and, for the remainder of his cross-examination, was closer to being on equal terms with his inquisitor.

That Colin's outburst at Kujawa was not unintentional but rather his method of intimidation became clear when the prosecutor tried to turn it to advantage. Suggesting that JoAnn ''lived in great fear'' of Colin, which was denied, Kujawa went on: ''During arguments would you talk to her the way you talked to me just before the recess, or do you reserve that?''

''I reserve it,'' Colin replied. ''I reserve it for people that may be making misrepresentations. Generally she did not make misrepresentations.''

''I'm suggesting to you that when you get mad, you get wild, like you did a while ago?''

''I don't think that was getting wild.'' It was only part of the Colin Thatcher arsenal.

Allbright felt that Kujawa's cross-examination of the accused to this point had been ''brilliant.'' What followed he described only as ''average.''

After the break Kujawa secured admissions from Thatcher that he had been in possession of the loaded .38 found in his home, that it was unregistered, and that there had been no permit to acquire it. The prosecutor chose not to inquire into why the accused had the gun or where he had got it.

Kujawa wanted to know why Colin had told the jury about the New Year's visit to Dick Collver's ranch. ''Because my attorney asked me,'' replied Colin.

Kujawa persisted. ''What was your purpose in telling the story?''

''I was replying to a question from my attorney in the examination-in-chief.'' No more.

When the prosecutor came to the tape he hinted that, although it was not yet 4:00 p.m., an adjournment to the morning might be appropriate. The day ended.

On Wednesday morning, as Kujawa and Thatcher faced each other again, the hostility was much less evident. The accused appeared fully composed and confident.

The area in the centre of the courtroom vacated by the prisoner's dock, now moved over to the wall opposite the jury,

267

had been assigned to the police investigators. This enabled a few of the team members to sit just behind Kujawa and Johnston and be available for quick consultation. This morning Wally Beaton was seated with Ed Swayze and Al Lyons. It was Beaton's last day as a policeman. During the summer he had decided to retire and had handed in his notice, effective October 31, thinking that would encompass the trial in his last and biggest case. Now the trial was running over, but Beaton would stay to the end in case he was needed as a witness.

If Gerry Allbright was going to put the 6:24 p.m. telephone call into evidence, the man who could do it was sitting right behind him.

In the family section Stephanie was sitting on Greg's knee. As her father duelled with Kujawa, the little girl was contentedly reading a Nancy Drew mystery.

The prosecutor went almost immediately to the tape recording and its transcript. He announced his "purpose and intent": "My suggestion is that this tape talks about nothing but the killing of your wife."

"I categorically disagree with you," Thatcher replied. Colin said that he was having "an unguarded conversation," that he was "very relaxed," and "what you see is what you get."

As Kujawa took the accused, almost line by line, through that conversation, Colin repeated his explanation that he was talking about the rumour of his association with Anderson, not the fact. He disagreed with the prosecutor's interpretations. "If you want to take something out of context and zero in on it, you can probably find something to go any which direction. We have got people sitting in the first few rows [the reporters] that do this for a living."

The prosecutor was unable to force admissions from Thatcher. He had portions of the tape replayed, starting with Anderson's reference to the gun that Colin had taken as poor humour. Kujawa pointed out that Anderson was hyperventilating. "Wasn't he huffing and puffing?"

"Well, he may have been, but he had a grin on his face while he was doing it."

During the morning recess, members of the media and lawyers

among the spectators expressed disappointment at the lack of blood drawn by Kujawa. Sensing that Thatcher was vulnerable, they were critical of the prosecutor's apparent inability to fully expose him.

Kujawa returned to the absence of any statement of innocence in the taped conversation and Thatcher's advice to Anderson to "deny, deny, deny."

"This guy, is he so stupid he needs to be told not to confess to a murder that he didn't do?"

"Obviously, he is not stupid at all, Mr. Kujawa, because it appeared that he conned me that morning and I think perhaps he conned your department and the Regina police to some extent."

Referring to the cleaning of the car and Anderson's statement that he "had a bitch of a time gettin' blood and stuff off," Kujawa suggested Thatcher had fear in his voice when he asked, "There is a chance it can surface?" He played the tape again.

Colin disagreed. "But he was joking. I knew there had been no blood in the car."

Kujawa's frustration became evident in his attitude towards Thatcher. Allbright made an objection, saying that Kujawa was attempting to "belittle the witness." Mr. Justice Maher agreed, and the prosecutor apologized.

Reading the comment "I got no intention of giving them anything to trip on," Kujawa asked Thatcher: "Why didn't you just say 'We're innocent. Nothing can be done'?"

"Because, Mr. Kujawa, I am assuming that I — I have no idea that I'm going to be going over this conversation line by line at some subsequent date. And I was not trying to set the other party up for anything. That's why I didn't."

"You were talking about nothing but murder throughout this tape, isn't that a fact?"

"No, no, that is not a fact."

Thatcher denied again that he understood the meaning of Anderson's statement "I'm glad it went down." "It was obviously something that was meant for your consumption on the tape and I guess, unfortunately for him, I didn't pick up on it; I didn't understand what it meant." That was Colin's explanation, and he went on: "Let's bear in mind, I'm not the person there

269

that is to get somebody to confess. I'm not the person that has been instructed by the police to try and implicate an innocent person that had nothing whatsoever to do with this matter.''

Asked about his statement in connection with Gerry Gerrand, ''That guy I could do,'' Colin repeated: ''It means nothing. It is slang for nothing. I see Mr. Gerrand in the audience.''

Allbright objected, saying that Kujawa was ''editorializing'' with some of his critical comments. The prosecutor apologized, explaining, ''One does get involved.'' ''That's putting it mildly,'' Mr. Justice Maher agreed in admonishment.

Kujawa played the ''That guy I could do'' portion of the tape for the jury.

The prosecutor closed with the allegation to Thatcher that ''When your wife left, when your whole world tumbled, you had nothing but a hate for her which resulted in you killing her on January 21st?'' Colin replied that Kujawa had ''read far too many press reports which describe the animosity between JoAnn and myself to a much more intense degree than what it was. She never forgave me for her not being Mrs. Ron Graham. She blamed me for it.''

After assuring Allbright that he had not challenged Kujawa to physical combat with his ''step outside'' remark, Colin Thatcher left the witness stand at 2:30 in the afternoon. He had been testifying for nearly three full days.

He was intact. It had been a game performance by the politician, but his credibility had been badly damaged by his outburst and claims of fidelity. It was far from obvious whether he had sustained enough belief to survive. Would it be his last hurrah?

270

CHAPTER 19

The Final Witness

When Colin Thatcher left the witness stand, Gerry Allbright closed the case for the defence. Kujawa, in the absence of the jury, then brought up the matter of the waiting Dick Collver.

The prosecutor explained to Mr. Justice Maher how the proposed witness had appeared the previous Thursday, after the Crown case was closed. "It was sort of an act of God that brought the man here, and I now request leave to reopen the Crown's case to call this one witness."

Although Allbright objected, he was in a dilemma. By introducing the subject of Thatcher's New Year's conversation with Collver as part of the defence evidence, Allbright had opened the door to Collver's coming in as a witness in rebuttal. It was now, as Mr. Justice Maher said, "a clear case for rebuttal." Kujawa was applying to call Collver as part of the Crown case, but the distinction was for lawyers. Either way, the jury was going to hear the other side of the story of that New Year's in Wickenburg, Arizona. Allbright fell back on a defence counsel's last, and often best, argument — the "potentially significant prejudice" to his case if Collver was called.

The decision lay within the discretion of the trial judge. After retiring to consider the question, Mr. Justice Maher announced his decision:

> The defence chose to adduce evidence with respect to the involvement of Mr. Collver. I deem it a proper matter where the jury should have the benefit of all the evidence. I fail to see where this results in prejudice to the accused and, in the

interests of justice, I order that the Crown be permitted to reopen its case to permit the calling of Mr. Collver as a witness.

Again, a lawyer sat among the spectators and watched as his client took the stand as a Crown witness in the case of *The Queen v. Colin Thatcher*. Ronald Barclay, QC, had represented Dick Collver for several years. On this occasion his own interests as well as his client's would be of concern to him.

Richard Collver, a one-time Saskatoon management consultant, had acquired the leadership of the moribund Saskatchewan Conservative Party in 1973, a time when it had no members in the Legislature and had not been taken seriously for years. His flamboyance and organizational skills took the Conservatives to the position of official opposition but after the party's failure to defeat the NDP government in the 1978 general election, the disappointment centred on Collver. Embroiled in a number of highly publicized lawsuits and with a public stature exemplified by the nickname "Tricky Dick," Collver was not, it was felt, viewed by the voting public as acceptable to succeed to the office of premier.

In 1979 Collver resigned as leader, left the Conservative caucus and, with another Tory defector, formed a rump group dedicated to the annexation of western Canada to the United States. As a Western Unionist he sat out the remainder of his term in the Legislature. He moved his residence and business interests to Arizona.

In Colin Thatcher's words, Dick Collver was the man who had "convinced or cajoled" Thatcher into leaving the Liberals and joining his Conservatives.

Dick Collver faced the jury and began his story. He had been approached by Colin in the fall of 1979, when his fellow MLA's marital litigation had just begun. At Colin's request, Collver and his wife Elinor took JoAnn to dinner and "attempted to convince her to return to her husband." JoAnn refused, "said she was afraid to go home," and, apparently at the prospect, had become ill.

Colin and his children, baby-sitter Sandra and boyfriend Blaine Mathieson had visited at the Collver ranch at Wicken-

272

burg, Arizona, at New Year's 1980. Colin, feeling that his wife had run off with his best friend, "was more than hurt, he was stabbed inside."

During the visit Colin and Sandra, Collver said, continually referred to JoAnn as "the bitch," and did so in the presence of the children.

In Collver's description of the conversation on New Year's morning, Colin had said: "I have only one solution for the bitch. The only solution is, I've got to hire somebody to kill her." Colin, Collver said, then asked his friend to contact some lawyers he knew in Alberta with criminal practices, so that "he could find someone to assist him in killing his wife."

During the visit, Collver said, Colin had been encouraging his children to "phone long distance all over the world and charge it to Graham Construction" on a Graham credit card they had.

Collver had been so upset by Thatcher's behaviour that he had asked him to leave.

The next day Collver had telephoned his lawyer, Ron Barclay, and asked, "What I should do? Did I have any obligation? Should I come forward?"

Barclay, he said, had told him, "You have no legal obligation. Do what you think is right, but you have no legal obligation." Collver had "let it slide."

Back in the Saskatchewan Legislature in the spring of 1980, Colin seemed to have recovered from his obsession and never again mentioned to Collver the killing of JoAnn. He did, however, ask his friend to attempt to negotiate a settlement of his dispute with JoAnn. Colin, said Collver, was prepared to pay $400,000, no more.

Collver said he met with JoAnn and her then friend, Tony Wilson. He secured their approval to a settlement of $230,000 to JoAnn and custody of Stephanie, the two boys to stay with Colin.

Collver was "ecstatic"; he thought the matter was settled. Colin, however, according to Collver, rejected the deal, saying, "The bitch isn't going to get anything."

Collver withdrew and had no further personal involvement with Colin or JoAnn.

In May 1981, when he heard of the first shooting of JoAnn, Collver said he telephoned Ron Barclay again. He asked: "What are my obligations now? A crime has been committed.'' Barclay again told Collver that he "had no legal obligation to come forward whatsoever" and gave him a copy of a brief prepared by his firm.

After the murder of JoAnn, Collver said he telephoned Barclay a third time "and got the same advice again."

In cross-examination, Allbright was naturally curious about the sudden appearance of the witness. Collver explained that he had not come to Saskatoon "to come forward at the eleventh hour," but "once the police asked, I had to tell the truth, and that was my understanding as well."

Allbright was also curious about what considerations were "more important to you than trying to help another human being stay alive?"

Collver's answer was frank and reminiscent of Lynne Mendell's testimony. "It's a matter of belief as time goes on. It's a matter of how serious does it get. Maybe I was wrong. Instead of phoning Ron Barclay in 1979, if I had phoned someone else, perhaps another human life would be saved."

Allbright suggested that "you put the legal opinion ahead of any moral obligation you might have had."

"Unfortunately, yes, I did."

Collver agreed that, in retrospect, he was "criticizing" himself "a little bit."

Dick Collver's last comment was to agree with Allbright that Colin Thatcher considered him "one of his better friends." "I think we both feel the same way," he said with obvious sincerity.

With Dick Collver to close his case, Serge Kujawa discarded all thoughts of calling any evidence in rebuttal to the defence testimony. He had been thinking of calling Wally Beaton in response to Barbara Wright, and Blaine Mathieson to contradict Sandra Silversides. Ken Hagerty of the Moose Jaw Police Department, who had seen Anderson and Thatcher briefly connect on the morning of the day of the murder, which did not fit with Colin's story, was also on hand.

To the prosecutor this was "nit-picking" and he was not about to lessen the dramatic impact that Collver had obviously made. The Crown closed its case completely. "For the second time," observed Mr. Justice Maher.

Allbright was not sure what to do. He told the court that he had "one or two witnesses" he would like to "put back on the stand" in the morning. Mr. Justice Maher told the defence counsel that "whatever evidence you wish to lead that is relevant to this issue, either directly or indirectly, I propose to allow you to lead." Allbright thought he would require only the morning to do this and that they could proceed with addressing the jury in the afternoon.

Gerry Gerrand had stayed until the end of Colin Thatcher's testimony and then, naturally curious, had listened to Dick Collver's testimony. What he heard enraged him. According to Collver, some people had known for three years of Colin Thatcher's murderous designs upon JoAnn and had kept that knowledge to themselves. Included among those with that knowledge were the senior members of Ron Barclay's firm, MacPherson, Leslie and Tyerman. That meant that W.M. Elliott, QC, who had worked with Gerrand while mediating the settlement between Colin and JoAnn, possessed that knowledge.

Ron Barclay had flown up to Saskatoon to be present while Collver testified. That completed, he caught a ride back to Regina with Gerrand who, his task finished also, was returning to his office after a three-day absence.

It was a quarrelsome ride. Gerrand soundly berated the other lawyer for withholding the knowledge of Colin's intentions from both JoAnn and from himself. JoAnn might be alive if that information had been given to her, Gerrand felt. Barclay contended otherwise. He and his firm had carefully considered their position, he said, and were bound by the confidentiality requirements of the rule respecting solicitor and client privilege. They could not reveal what Dick Collver had told them. Besides, JoAnn was fully aware of Colin's intentions; certainly that was so since the first shooting.

The debate between the two lawyers would expand throughout the legal community and come to the attention of the Law Society of Saskatchewan, which concluded that Collver's law firm had not acted improperly.

In Saskatoon the Regina police investigators and the prosecutors took Wally Beaton out to dinner in celebration of his retirement. Kujawa asked Beaton to stay around in case Allbright wished to call him to prove the 6:24 p.m. telephone call he had referred to in his bail affidavit. Beaton was happy to oblige. He did not want to go home now.

It was Halloween. Duane Smith, the kindly commissionaire who guarded the back door of the Saskatoon courthouse, had felt his heart go out to Stephanie who was in a strange city without friends of her own age. Smith had suggested to Peggy that his daughter come downtown and provide some company for Colin's daughter. It was a great arrangement and the two girls had played happily in the Renaissance pool. This evening Stephanie was making the Halloween rounds in Saskatoon with her new friend.

On Thursday morning in the courtroom, Allbright advised Mr. Justice Maher that he had concluded that Collver's testimony "has been dealt with and I don't think it requires further evidence." The defence closed its case, Kujawa confirmed that he had nothing in rebuttal, and the evidence was all in.

Allbright made no attempt to call Wally Beaton or anyone else to prove the 6:24 p.m. telephone call. He said later that he considered it to be in evidence and that he certainly was not going to run the risk of putting a police witness on the stand and exposing him to Kujawa who, in cross-examination, might have brought out a great deal of damaging evidence. Kujawa insists he would have done no such thing and, if Beaton had testified on that one point only, it would not have been proper for him to expand his evidence. The prosecutor said he would have put Beaton on the stand himself and turned him over to Allbright if the defence had asked for this.

In any event, the fact of a telephone call to the Redland Avenue residence at 6:24 p.m. of the night of the murder was not part of the case, whether Colin Thatcher had been a party to that call or not.

The case now being complete, the court would adjourn until the afternoon when counsel would address the jury.

Before doing so, however, Mr. Justice Maher excused the jury and asked Kujawa and Allbright to outline for him "the theory of the Crown and the theory of the defence which might assist me in

276

my charge.'' He proposed, he said, to instruct the jury that they could convict Colin Thatcher of either having caused the death of JoAnn or having aided or abetted any person to do so.

Kujawa agreed but Allbright did not. In his view, ''the Crown's theory is a very clear, straightforward one — that it was on-site, firsthand murder committed by Mr. Thatcher.'' The defence counsel could not see where the evidence supported any suggestion that his client could be found to be a party to an offence committed by another. Then they adjourned until after lunch.

Allbright had not told Mr. Justice Maher what the ''theory of the defence'' was and, when he faced the jury that afternoon, he failed to tell them either. The defence counsel could feel immortality tugging at his gown; he had to find the right theme and play it perfectly. Instead, he touched every opportunity he saw in the case, developed as many concerns as he could, but presented no one predominant thrust. In the process he crossed some boundaries of content proper for comment to a jury by counsel.

The defence faced the inescapable fact of the murder of JoAnn Wilson. It needed some rational explanation of her death that was consistent with the innocence of Colin Thatcher to prevent the jury from merely concluding that it *had* to be Colin. Allbright never really got around to suggesting such an explanation.

As the jury settled in their seats to listen to Gerry Allbright on Thursday afternoon, Colin Thatcher, wearing a navy blue suit over a white shirt, was back seated in the prisoner's dock. He watched confidently and approvingly as his counsel undertook to convince the jury that the former Energy Minister had had nothing to do with the death of JoAnn Wilson, or at least raise enough doubts to secure an acquittal. Colin had plans to go down to Palm Springs as soon as this was all over and had made arrangements with his current girlfriend, Diane Stoner, who had been sitting with his family throughout the trial. Diane also watched as Gerry Allbright undertook the greatest challenge of his career. Stephanie was absent.

The public concern that the Saskatchewan, or Canadian, justice system might not be capable of coping with a prominent politician on trial for the murder of his ex-wife had not escaped the attention of Gerry Allbright. He converted that concern to his defence.

He opened by telling the jury that they were facing two trials — the trial of Colin Thatcher for murder, and the trial of "our very system of justice." The media coverage, the rumour, the speculation and the gossip made it, in the minds of many, "impossible" for Thatcher to get a fair trial. He recounted the "four bail refusals" and the "six months incarceration" as evidence that many concluded in advance that his client was guilty. "If Colin Thatcher, with all of that against him, can get a fair trial in this court, then, indeed, justice lives."

Allbright was giving it his all. His baritone voice was ideal for the script and he stood with his arm on the edge of the prisoner's dock where Colin Thatcher sat. He was already out of line, however, and the hackles were rising on Kujawa's neck. There was no evidence before the jury of the publicity the case had received or even of the unsuccessful attempts to have Thatcher released on bail.

The defence counsel continued at length. He asked the jury to ignore "the rumours, the gossip, the innuendo, the custody, the fact that four bail applications were heard and refused" and, sliding over his own contradiction, "to decide this case on the evidence."

Referring somewhat inaccurately to Kujawa's opening remarks at the beginning of the case when he outlined his evidence in four categories, Allbright quoted the Crown as saying that, if one of those four were proven, the case was made out. The comment led to Allbright's identification of what he called "four schools of thought" or "possibilities" he saw contained in the case. He stated them (in reality only three) to be: Colin Thatcher "did it himself; he didn't do it himself; he hired somebody else to do it; or he didn't have anything to do with it whatever."

Creating some confusion in the minds of his listeners as he did so, Allbright now moved on to another group of four elements of the case. Colin Thatcher was in Moose Jaw at 6:00 p.m., January 21, 1983, he said, and that was proved in "four different ways," two from the defence and two from the Crown.

Craig Dotson's description of the killer was not Colin

Thatcher. Neither was the Adams composite drawing. That was one way.

The 6:24 p.m. phone call was the second way. If Colin had been on the telephone then he could not have been at the scene of the murder.

The tape, with the statement by Colin that "I was home with four people," was the third way.

The fourth way was the alibi supported by six witnesses.

"If you accept any one of those four premises," Allbright continued, "then the solution is at hand." Allbright's premises were difficult to follow, but the presentation certainly was impressive.

The credit card slip, which had defied explanation, even by Thatcher, to Allbright was the single most important piece of evidence exonerating his client. As he now told the jury, no hired killer would take it with him and, if the killer was Colin himself, would you "take it out of your clothes that you wore a few days earlier and put it into your killing clothes?" Here Allbright took a small licence. There was no evidence and, of course, could not be, of different clothes.

To Allbright, this was "simple logic":

Whoever killed JoAnn Wilson planted a credit card slip, I suggest to you, eight feet from the corner of that garage so that Colin Thatcher would become the accused in these proceedings. Only a madman, only an insane person, would drop their own calling card at the scene of a murder where it's going to be found.

There was the explanation of the murder that was consistent with Thatcher's innocence, but was it "rational"? Allbright thought so, even though there was no suggestion anywhere in the case of anyone wanting to "frame Colin Thatcher." He invited the jury to find "one false premise in that series of logic." To begin with, there was the premise that the slip was left there on purpose and not accidentally dropped by Thatcher.

Allbright then went into another area that was to cause him some difficulty after he concluded his address. He complained of missing Crown witnesses, "conspicuous by their absence."

279

Stating that the Crown has "an obligation, a duty, to be impartial, to be unbiased, to present all the evidence to a court that is fair and credible," he pointed to the absence of the "two senior investigating officers" (presumably Swayze and Beaton), Danny Doyle, who made the silencers, Cody Crutcher, and Garry Anderson's brother-in-law who had helped pick up the car two days after the murder. The jury was asked to "decide whether you've had all the evidence fairly put before you that the law says that you should have."

Turning to the Crown witnesses, "the ones who did come," he suggested that the evidence of Jack Janzen was that he sold the gas to Colin in "mid-afternoon" on Tuesday when "Colin Thatcher's supposed to be in a '292' government car, out in front, conducting surveillance . . . when Mrs. Hasz says he was there."

This was a small slip. Hasz had not identified the occupant of the "292" car as Thatcher. The jury, however, picked up on this.

Anderson provided a similar conflict, Allbright said, having testified that he saw Thatcher at Caron on the afternoon before the murder.

Craig Dotson's description of the killer was not from a fleeting glimpse. "Fleeting glimpse, nothing. That man is no fool." Colin Thatcher could not disguise himself to look like Dotson's composite. "A slim face he ain't got."

Adams and Hasz: once more the point was made that the composite picture did not match Thatcher's appearance and that Mrs. Hasz may have been honestly mistaken about the car. Adding in Margaret Johannsson, Allbright stated that "nobody suggests for one minute that the man inside the car looked remotely like Colin Thatcher."

Allbright proposed another theory for the car on 20th Avenue — a break and entry and "somebody scouting the neighbourhood." Avoiding the other, obvious reasons for a waiting killer to wear gloves, he suggested that Thatcher would hardly be "afraid to leave a fingerprint" in his government car.

Coming to Tony Wilson, Allbright promised that "I don't suggest to you for one minute that Tony Wilson's a suspect," and then proceeded to do just that "as an example." He pointed out Wilson's proximity and financial motive as a beneficiary under JoAnn's will, but did not seriously put the husband forward as the explanation for the murder.

Colin Thatcher had said "Oh, really," when his assistant Chuck Guillaume had shown him the gun holster he had found in the minister's car. A guilty man, said Allbright, would have grabbed the holster out of Guillaume's hands and "gotten it out of there," not ignored it.

Seizing on the conflict between Ron Williams, who had sold Colin a .357 with a stainless steel barrel, and Garry Anderson, who had testified that the one he had was blue, Allbright tried to take it too far. If Anderson had the gun at all, he said, he would have known what colour it was.

Jim Street, Allbright emphasized, had "maximized every possible condition" to get from Regina to Moose Jaw in twenty-eight minutes. The defence counsel termed "sheer folly" the "Crown's theory that Colin Thatcher might have driven that distance in less than twenty-two, twenty-three minutes."

Dealing with Lynne Mendell, Allbright seemed to forget that it was important to his defence that she was on the telephone with Colin Thatcher at 6:24 p.m. Referring again to "Palm Springs time warp," and the two-hour time difference, he concluded that "she got calls at seven and nine o'clock [Moose Jaw time] from Saskatchewan."

"Lynne Mendell. You going to put him away for the duration, whatever, because of her evidence? I doubt it." Allbright dismissed Mendell with the accusation that she was a woman scorned: "If I can't have your name by marriage, I'll use it some other way."

Charlie Wilde got short shift as a "man who will do anything for a dollar" and who had been affected by his drug usage.

Allbright seriously overstepped himself when he came to Dick Collver. After describing him as one who "every time he has a moral dilemma, he gets a legal opinion for it," he suggested that the Crown felt its case "slipping away and decided to call Dick Collver."

It is considered an extreme discourtesy to interrupt opposing

281

counsel while he is addressing a jury, even when provoked, and Kujawa adhered to the code, restraining himself with some difficulty at this misrepresentation.

Allbright did the best he could with Garry Anderson:

> He's late for the trial because the keepers of him aren't looking after him properly. Here's a man who turns on his own benefactors. A guy who'd do what he says he'd do for a thousand bucks, what would he do for fifty thousand? Garry Anderson's evidence isn't worth the paper that we're ultimately going to record it on. It simply isn't.

Thatcher's counsel repeated the accusations he had put to Anderson when he was on the stand. The tape contained no admission or confession, he said, and the reason for that was that Anderson "couldn't say something that would get a denial because, if he did, it's all over, and Anderson's ruse is up."

"Don't convict Colin Thatcher on speculation," his counsel beseeched the jury. Allbright contended that there was no evidence of anyone having killed JoAnn "at the behest of Colin Thatcher." Either the accused performed the murder himself or he did not, he said, and he wanted a not guilty verdict if the jury could not find the first.

As he came to his closing, Allbright skimmed over his own witnesses. "Tony Merchant: You decide what you want to make of Tony Merchant's evidence." Sandra Silversides: "a scheming, devious type of person or just a twenty-two-year-old girl on the stand doing her best." Would Greg and Regan lie "if they thought their father did that to their mother? You can have differences with your mother, but she's still your mother."

Allbright thought he should address the question of Stephanie in the courtroom. "You decide if this isn't where a family belongs at this time, all the family, when this is all the family there is. You decide whether that's a ploy to gain a little sympathy from you or whether that's because the family wants to be here."

His counsel had little more to say about Colin's testimony. Giving credit to Kujawa's cross-examination, he asked the jury: "Do you know how difficult it is to take the stand when your life is in the balance; answer even the most innocuous of questions and not look a little furtive at times?"

And then Allbright stepped into more trouble. Warning the jury of making a mistake, he cited three celebrated cases as examples of error: the Donald Marshall conviction overturned in Nova Scotia; another such incident in Vancouver; and the case of Susan Nelles in Toronto.

Before Allbright's closing "May God's ultimate wisdom go with you" had sunk in, an incensed Kujawa was on his feet, asking to address the court in the absence of the jury. When the jury had left, the prosecutor listed nine objections he took to Allbright's address. Some were minor, but some were major enough to prompt Kujawa into the unusual step of asking Mr. Justice Maher to correct them immediately, instead of waiting until he charged the jury.

The gist of Kujawa's unhappiness was: Allbright's recitation of the pre-trial bail applications and the publicity; the 6:24 p.m. phone call which he had treated as evidence; the suggestion that the Crown had improperly withheld witnesses; the allegation of calling Collver to shore up the Crown case; and the references to the supposed cases of jury mistake (two of which were not).

Allbright thought Kujawa's complaints were matters between the two counsel. "If my learned friend feels that there has been, on the part of the defence, an impropriety, I take no exception to him correcting the jury in his view as to what's been improperly done." But he defended himself to Mr. Justice Maher on each one of the Crown's concerns except the pre-trial matters he had introduced. On that aspect he agreed that Mr. Justice Maher "ought to direct the jury that that is not available to them" and suggested that "you might wish to consider a mistrial."

The trial judge had no intention of aborting nearly three weeks of trial. He agreed with Kujawa and told Allbright that his reference to the Marshall and other cases was "very, very improper." Correcting the defence counsel to the jury other than in his charge was another matter, however, and, after considering the question, he reluctantly agreed to only two corrections at that time.

Recalling the jury, Mr. Justice Maher gave them the correct version of the calling of Dick Collver and straightened out the allegation of missing witnesses. Telling the jury that their evidence was of doubtful admissibility and that the Crown is not obliged to call every witness, he referred to Kujawa and Johnston as "not only competent, but men of integrity," who could be trusted to bring forth all the proper evidence.

It was an unpleasant episode for Gerry Allbright. Straining to do the utmost for his client, he had, as Mr. Justice Maher said the next day, allowed himself to "exceed the bounds within which he should confine himself." Worse, he had suffered some loss of stature with the jury and would suffer more when Mr. Justice Maher addressed them and completed the corrections he had reserved until then.

Allbright had spoken to the jury for an hour and a half. The debate over his excesses had consumed more than another hour, so that it was almost five o'clock when Kujawa's turn came. That late in the day he would have difficulty keeping their attention for long.

In contrast to the dramatic flair of Allbright, the Crown seemed dull and mechanical as it swiftly reviewed the consistencies in the prosecution's case. Kujawa had been truly angered by Allbright's comments, particularly those that reflected on his conduct of the Crown case. He was still upset and off stride as he addressed the jury.

Referring first to Allbright's key points, the composite drawing and the credit card slip, Kujawa reminded the jury of the limited observations of Dotson and Adams that the "picture" was based upon. If the credit card slip was "planted," whoever did so had also to arrange the brutal beating of JoAnn to "look like Colin in his great hate," get the slip to begin with, get Colin's car, put the holster in Colin's car a year before, and have the bullet in JoAnn's head the same or similar to the ammunition bought by Colin from Williams.

Lynne Mendell, he said, had shared some of the most important parts of Colin Thatcher's life for several years and no motive had been suggested for her lying. Her story was consistent, he claimed, and he gave the example of the doll shower box and the *Los Angeles Times* found in Colin's bedroom, as she had described seeing it in Palm Springs.

Garry Anderson and Charlie Wilde, Kujawa said, had not seen

each other since 1981 "and yet one story fits the other completely. Is that consistent? Could it have happened if either one was lying?"

Kujawa now put to the jury an analogy he had developed and was quite fond of. The tape, he said, was "like a transparency put over the top that fits everything underneath, and there isn't one part anywhere that it doesn't fit." The tape, he submitted, "amounts to a complete, plain, ordinary English confession of the murder by the accused."

The prosecutor asked the jury to consider the evidence of the defence witnesses according to their understanding, "as people of the world, of the situation they're in." He referred to the discrepancies in time between the affidavits and the court testimony as "a great sliding of time to fit in possibilities."

On the evidence, Kujawa suggested, the jury would have "no difficulty in deciding that the accused Colin Thatcher likely killed his ex-wife himself, but it does not exclude the possibility that he had it done. In either case, he is equally guilty."

With a few sentences about the protections of the jury system, one of those being its application to anyone, "the Prime Minister, the Chief of Police, the Chief Justice," the prosecutor was finished. He had spoken only twenty minutes.

Allbright, still recovering from the criticisms of his jury address, attempted to even the score. He complained that Kujawa had expressed opinions. Mr. Justice Maher did not understand. He had "never heard before that counsel, in addressing a jury, do not give their opinion of the evidence." Kujawa's comments, he said, were "a far cry" from Allbright's reference to the supposed cases of mistake.

The jury was not present for this complaint, but the defence closed the day looking small. Mr. Justice Maher considered his charge overnight and delivered it on Friday morning.

Kujawa and Allbright made sure that they did not encounter each other after court. They disrobed at separate times. There was real hostility between the two.

Lawyers quickly learn not to allow the contest in the courtroom to affect their personal relations. There are exceptions, however, particularly when one feels that the other has stepped over the line or been personal in his attack. There had

285

been several such occasions during the progress of the Thatcher case, the last when Allbright had produced the ammunition from Drinkwater. The defence counsel had apologized and friendly relations had been restored.

This time there would be no patching up until well after the trial was concluded. At a time when both counsel had mostly finished their functions and had little to do but wait, their professional cameraderie had vanished. It would make the waiting seem much longer.

CHAPTER 20

The Verdict

The duty of Mr. Justice John Hayes Maher was to instruct the jury on the law and the principles they should be guided by in assessing the evidence they had heard. It was also his responsibility to take them through that evidence and direct their attention to its important features, making sure they did not pay too much attention to minor inconsistencies and points of not much relevance. In doing so he could not avoid, and would not want to avoid, signalling his own views of the case.

He knew the immense subtle power he possessed to affect the jury's thinking. He would wield that power with every intention of encouraging them to reach the just decision he saw in the case, but with care and skill to ensure that the decision was theirs and not his. He must put both sides fairly to the jury and be careful to commit no excesses. He fully expected his charge to be reviewed by at least the Saskatchewan Court of Appeal and probably also the Supreme Court of Canada. He would not lightly risk the loss of a jury verdict to either a Crown or defence appeal because other judges concluded that "a miscarriage of justice" had resulted from an unfairly weighted address.

Just as the jury members would bring to the case perceptions developed by their life experiences, Mr. Justice Maher's views were affected by recollections. He had known Ross Thatcher well. It was not possible to preside over the trial of Ross's only son without some intrusion by thoughts of other times.

On Friday morning, November 2, 1984, Jack Maher was all jurist as he turned to the expectant jury. His remarks would have a flavour, but they would be carefully considered and very precise. He had been up until 2:00 a.m. writing his intended comments. Re-reading his work the next morning, he had delayed the court opening half an hour.

The flavour, however, would be heightened by the need to finish correcting Allbright's comments to the jury the day before. Impressions are considered vital in jury cases, and the impact of the negative opening comments by the trial judge was unfortunate for the defence, even if self-inflicted.

Mr. Justice Maher covered the remaining items he had accepted from Kujawa's list. One was the 6:24 p.m. telephone call which, he said, was not properly in evidence and "should be totally disregarded." Down went one of the major supports to the defence Allbright had tried to construct.

"It ill behooves Mr. Allbright" to refer to the bail applications, continued Mr. Justice Maher. The final item, the citing of the cases of supposed jury error, was described as "the most serious."

It was an opening to ruin the day of any defence lawyer. There was very little to follow that would restore Allbright's spirits.

Much of the content of jury charges is "boiler-plate," standarized instructions on law and evidence developed by judges over many cases and which have survived appellate review. Innovation can be risky.

Mr. Justice Maher passed to the jury the inherited wisdom on the likelihood of witnesses telling the truth. The human mind is frail, he reminded them, mistakes in recollection are natural, and exaggerations occur without intention. "The truth usually lies somewhere in between" is as useful a principle in a courtroom as anywhere.

To Allbright's disappointment, the jury was told that Colin Thatcher could be found guilty if they concluded that he did the act himself or, alternatively, if he helped or encouraged another to cause the death. The two-pronged indictment was accepted.

Rabbit tracks on a snow-covered lawn would support the inference that a rabbit had crossed. Colin Thatcher's guilt could be found if it was the only reasonable inference "to be drawn from the facts."

Reviewing the Crown evidence, the jurist came to the composite drawings and mentioned the "limited time and circumstances" of the Dotson, Hasz and Adams observation, "particularly important" in the case of the Dotson's "fleeting glance."

Lynne Mendell, if believed, said some things of "vital importance." The jury was referred to the consistency between her story and Garry Anderson's on the rented Mustang, as well as the doll shower box and the *Los Angeles Times* found in Colin's bedroom.

Charlie Wilde and Garry Anderson, not unexpectedly, were not of "exemplary character or lofty moral persuasion," but "the vicar or the local parish priest" would not be likely candidates for the line of work they were engaged to perform. Mr. Justice Maher had been impressed with Charlie Wilde's statement that "you do not go back to the well too often," and did not think that Charlie was suffering much brain damage from his drug usage.

Turning to the defence, the trial judge was harsh with Tony Merchant. The police burglary suggestion was "incredible," an "ill-founded suspicion" based on statements made to the court that were "inaccurate and in error."

The jury was told that the alibi evidence need only raise a reasonable doubt to succeed, but they were urged to consider the defence testimony "carefully" and keep in mind the time differences between the affidavits and the court testimony.

Colin Thatcher, who had spent two and a half days in the witness box, received scant attention on this critical day. Six sentences of the hour-and-a-half jury charge were devoted to the testimony of the accused. Three of these were warnings to weigh his evidence against that of Anderson, Wilde and Mendell.

Avoiding a review of the accused's testimony might have been a boon to the defence. It would have been difficult to say much more than Mr. Justice Maher did about Colin's testimony without getting into the tape recording. About that, perhaps the less said the better.

Mr. Justice Maher reviewed the defence "position" and came to Allbright's contention that, if the jury found that Colin Thatcher did not do the deed himself, they must find him not guilty as there was no evidence that anyone else had killed JoAnn on his behalf. Not so, said the trial judge. "I tell you as a matter of law that the fact that the Crown cannot adduce evidence that another individual or individuals actually did the act, does not preclude you from finding that the killing was done on behalf of Colin Thatcher.''

Allbright's ''key,'' the credit card slip, provoked a warning ''of the danger of speculation.''

The supports to Allbright's defence had been kicked away one by one.

First degree murder is ''planned'' and ''deliberate'' killing. If the jury found that Colin had killed JoAnn, Mr. Justice Maher suggested ''the evidence is almost overwhelming that the crime he committed is first degree murder.'' It was not only a discouragement of a finding of second degree murder, it flavoured the essential question of guilt or innocence.

There was no mistaking Mr. Justice Maher's views of the case. An Appeal Court would have to determine if he had gone too far in signalling a preference for the Crown case.

When the jury left, Kujawa and Allbright were invited to comment. The Crown thought only that the tape might have been emphasized more. On the other hand, Allbright was naturally distraught. He saw such an ''inference that the court has a preference'' for the Crown case that he did not think it could be corrected by recharging the jury. The Crown's case was highlighted and the defence testimony ignored in a manner he thought was ''highly detrimental to the defence.''

The defence counsel took ''strong personal exception'' to the comments from the bench about his jury address. The judge had, Allbright concluded, ''pointed a bit of a judicial finger at Mr. Thatcher.''

''You are entitled to your opinions, Mr. Allbright,'' was the chilly response from the bench. There would be no amendments made to the instructions he had left with the jury.

The jury came back after eight o'clock that evening with some questions. They wanted the tape and it was arranged to play it for them whenever they wished. They wanted to know what Garry Anderson said about the colour of the gun and they were interested about the times of several events. Particularly, they wanted to know when ''did Mrs. Hasz testify to seeing Colin

Thatcher on Thursday, January 20th?'' Clearly, they had been listening carefully to Allbright and had picked up on his slip. The money drop? The jury wanted to hear Jim Street's evidence of when he found the money and the Special ''O'' description of how it had been placed.

By 10:15 Friday night everyone had had enough for one day; court adjourned and the jury retired for the night. They were now sequestered and billeted in the Bessborough Hotel across the street from the courthouse. The Bessborough, a classic railroad hotel formerly owned by Canadian National Railway, was now in private hands. Management consultant Dick Collver, whose evidence the jury was considering, had been a participant in the group that had purchased the hotel from CNR.

On Saturday morning the court reassembled half an hour later than usual. Nothing new was going to happen this day and few spectators were present.

The jury listened as the court reporters read the evidence of Garry Anderson about his meetings with Colin Thatcher on Thursday and Friday, January 20 and 21, and his negotiations with Charlie Wilde. Charlie Wilde's version was also read and Lynne Mendell's testimony about her trips to Saskatchewan and the packing of the gun in the doll shower box. So, too, was Joan Hasz's description of the blue car on 20th Avenue at 4:30 p.m. on Thursday afternoon. The conflicting stories of Street, Special ''O'' and Colin Thatcher about the placing of the money were also read.

In Regina that weekend, the Thatcher trial was a hot topic of conversation at the annual NDP convention. The Queensbury Rules have never been adopted in Saskatchewan politics, and some would say neither has the Geneva Convention, but the lapel buttons being distributed by the NDP were considered a bit extreme. With a gruesome double entendre, they read ''The Tories Are Trying To Get Away With Murder.'' The buttons presaged another low point when the Thatcher case became an issue in the Saskatchewan Legislature later in the month.

A similar event was taking place in Saskatoon. The members of the press corps were placing orders for a T-shirt designed to be a memento of the trial and their common assignment. The T-shirt bore the words "Deny, Deny, Deny" on the front and "The Hamburger Helper Trial, Saskatoon, Oct. — Nov. 1984" on the back.

There was a sizeable demand. There were almost forty working journalists covering the trial and, in addition, photographers, sound and camera crews, police and prosecutors. Orders came from as far away as Winnipeg.

In the courtroom the reading of the testimony was completed at 2:30 in the afternoon and the jury retired. The court remained on standby.

Colin Thatcher had become seriously interested in the tenets of the Christian faith while he was in the Regina Correctional Centre. There he had met Reverend Ray Matheson of the Christian and Missionary Alliance Church who was giving him guidance in his studies of the Bible. Late Saturday afternoon, while the jury was out, Rev. Matheson visited his novitiate in the courthouse cells.

Rev. Matheson was promptly interviewed by Michael Tenszen of the *Globe and Mail* through whom he stated that Colin was now a "born-again Christian." While some questioned the sincerity of Colin's conversion, most were kind enough to hope that it was real.

At 9:30 Saturday night the jury called it a day and retired to their rooms in the Bessborough.

The jury worked all day Sunday and the court was not reconvened. Mr. Justice Maher had told the jury that he would put everyone on standby and would have the court available in an hour when they gave notice. The press corps organized a jury watch in shifts and settled into the two hotels, the Bessborough and the Renaissance. Those on duty would alert the others.

Across Canada three other trials of national interest were taking place, of financier Robert Harrison in Montreal, abortionist Dr. Henry Morgentaler in Toronto, and serial killer Clifford Olsen in British Columbia. The Thatcher trial in Saskatoon outranked all the others in national media attention.

On Monday morning the jury asked for a reading of the entire testimony of Craig Dotson. That was completed at 11:15 a.m. and again the jury returned to its deliberations.

Conventional wisdom is that a long jury is a good sign for the defence. Most juries are back the same day they go out. As the Thatcher jury wait extended, it was assumed that the odds for an acquittal, or at least a hung jury, were improving.

Gerry Allbright was confident. He felt that an acquittal was in the wind. Kujawa believed that the evidence would force the jury to a conviction, but he refuses to attempt to "second-guess" juries.

On Monday afternoon Mr. Justice Maher summoned Kujawa and Allbright to his chambers. He informed them that he had sent a note to the jury, inviting them to request further instruction on the law if it would be helpful. A reply had come, saying that the jury was working methodically, no help required, thank you.

The media, suffering from tension and news starvation as the jury deliberations continued, had become a bother to the jury members dining and sleeping in the Bessborough. On Saturday evening as the tired group entered the darkened salon where their supper was waiting, news photographers had leaped at them out of the darkness. By Monday evening the jury wanted some peace and privacy and a place with more comfort than the stark jury room where they could relax while continuing their discussions.

The matter was raised with Sheriff Bill Siemens, who took it up with Mr. Justice Maher. The two made arrangements with the Saskatoon Inn, a hotel across town near the airport. The management at the Inn guaranteed that the jury would receive relief from the intense scrutiny of the press; they would bar the media from the premises if necessary.

It was not necessary. Sheriff Siemens decoyed the press corps with an RCMP bus containing twelve members of his staff, and the reporters continued their vigil, in vain, at the Bessborough.

Whether the change of atmosphere helped or not, on Tuesday morning the jury reported that they were ready with a verdict.

It was well after 10:30 a.m. when the word went out that the jury was returning, but it spread quickly and by 10:45 the courtroom was almost full. Five minutes later Colin Thatcher, wearing a dark pinstripe suit, entered the prisoner's dock. Regan and Stephanie had returned to Moose Jaw, but Peggy, wearing a fur coat and gloves, Greg in jeans and a ski-jacket, and girlfriend Diane Stoner, also in a coat, were anxiously waiting in the family section.

293

Jurors are human. As the seven men and five women filed into the jury box and took their seats each avoided looking at Colin Thatcher who was looking very intently at them.

The proceedings were brutally swift:

(*10:53 a.m.*)

COURT CLERK: Ladies and gentlemen of the jury, answer present to your names, please.

(JURY POLLED — ALL PRESENT)

COURT CLERK: Ladies and gentlemen of the jury, have you agreed upon your verdict?

JURY FOREMAN: Yes, we have.

COURT CLERK: How say you, do you find the accused guilty or not guilty on the charge of first degree murder?

JURY FOREMAN: We find the accused guilty.

COURT CLERK: You say by your foreman that you find the accused guilty of first degree murder; so say you all?

JURORS: Mhmm. Yes. Yes.

THE COURT: I propose to proceed to sentencing, Mr. Allbright. Would you stand, Mr. Thatcher? The jury, having found you guilty of first degree murder, the sentence I must pronounce is mandatory. You will be imprisoned in a Federal Penitentiary for life, without eligibility for parole until you have served twenty-five years of that sentence. You may sit down.

Ladies and gentlemen of the jury, the Court wishes to express its thanks and appreciation for your diligence and the obvious dedication to the task you were required by law to perform. You are now excused from further attendance at this Court and you are free to go.

(THE JURY LEAVES THE COURT ROOM)

THE COURT: This Court will stand adjourned.

(*10:55 a.m.*)

Colin Thatcher, holding what appeared to be a bible, accepted both verdict and sentence stoically. After a brief few moments with his family in the basement cell area, he was whisked away to the Saskatoon Correctional Centre in a convoy of four police cars, three of them marked and with red lights flashing. At the centre, he was permitted a comment before being led inside.

"I am innocent, I didn't kill her, but it wasn't in the cards," Colin said. "No, I'm not going to appeal," he added, "It doesn't matter now."

Observers noted ironically that this was the first time Colin had publicly claimed to be innocent. "I will be exonerated," had been his prediction at earlier court appearances.

Gerry Allbright, who had promised the press a statement after the verdict, whatever it might be, was not up to his commitment. He ducked out of the courtroom and avoided reporters.

Serge Kujawa spoke to the press corps but refused to exult. His feelings were relief and sadness, he said, "It's not a happy moment for anybody." "The system works for everybody," commented Ed Swayze.

As news of the verdict flashed throughout Saskatchewan, part of the telephone system in Regina, particularly in the downtown core, collapsed under the overload of calls.

In his Regina office, Tony Merchant was shocked. He had been convinced that the jury would not convict Thatcher.

Gerry Gerrand heard the news of the verdict in the Vancouver air terminal where he was changing planes on his way to Victoria. When he arrived on the Island shortly after, he telephoned Mr. Justice M.A. MacPherson who had retired from the Bench three years before and was now living near Victoria.

The former jurist and the lawyer, who had both spent so much time on Colin Thatcher's civil litigation, got together for a drink. Both men were grimly satisfied that the Saskatoon jury had delivered what they considered a just verdict.

In Ames, Iowa, Betty Geiger, JoAnn's mother, telephoned by reporters, said that the guilty verdict came as a "tremendous relief. We feel it was a just and appropriate verdict, though there is not a great deal of happiness."

In Palm Springs, Lynne Mendell said the jury made "the right decision."

When Mendell had returned to Palm Springs at the end of the first week of the trial, she took with her a copy of the testimony given at the preliminary by pathologist Dr. J.M. Vetters. It contained a detailed description of the beating JoAnn had received.

After the trial was over and Serge Kujawa was back in his office, he received a telephone call from Lynne Mendell in Palm Springs. Lynne told the prosecutor that she had read the testimony with fascination, not having any knowledge until then of how JoAnn had suffered. The reading had provoked, she said, a remembrance of a further conversation she had had with Colin on the subject of the beating.

"You really did beat her, didn't you?" she said she had accused him.

"I wanted it to look like an Indian high on drugs had done it," she said he replied.

A few days later she called again.

"You do believe me, don't you?" she asked the prosecutor.

"Of course," Kujawa replied.

CHAPTER 21

Dénouement

I n 1976, the Liberal MLA from Thunder Creek came out squarely in favour of capital punishment. Had his side of the national debate on that issue won the day, Colin Thatcher would, in a manner of speaking, have lived to regret it.

The pros and cons of capital punishment aside, the execution of Colin Thatcher would have made the shock waves still reverberating from the hanging of Louis Riel in Saskatchewan a century earlier seem faint by comparison. Never before has a Canadian of such position been convicted of such a crime. This alone ensured that the Thatcher story would continue, on many fronts, long after the trial. The following pages recount some of those affairs as they unfolded up to August 1985.

Colin Thatcher, although a convicted murderer, was still the Member of the Legislative Assembly for Thunder Creek and a member of the governing party.

The day following Thatcher's conviction, Premier Devine took it upon himself to divorce the Conservative party from the political liability in the Saskatoon Correctional Centre. The premier announced that he had directed that Thatcher be asked to resign from the party and stated that, if the MLA refused, he would be "stripped" of his membership.

Dealing with Thatcher's status as an MLA was a more difficult matter. It would be a decision for the Legislature which, in the process of unseating the MLA, sank to a very low ebb in stature.

The Criminal Code provides that "an office under the Crown or public employment" held by any person sentenced to more than five years imprisonment is vacated. Minister of Justice Gary Lane concluded that this provision probably did not apply to an MLA and there was nothing in the Saskatchewan Legislative Assembly Act to cover the problem. New legislation would be required.

The Legislature would resume sitting on November 22 after the summer recess. The government adjourned the planned throne speech for a week to enable the House to deal with an amendment to The Legislative Assembly Act which would expel convicted felons from the Legislature. The government hoped that it would be dealt with expeditiously and delicately. Neither hope was attained.

The source of the government's difficulty was placed in the maximum security wing of the Saskatoon Correctional Centre after his conviction, following the institutional policy for life termers. There Colin Thatcher was allowed out of his cell only two hours a day. He promptly went on a hunger strike in protest. Correctional Centre officials assured the public that they would not be swayed by the MLA's protest.

The Correctional Centre regarded Thatcher as a high-risk prisoner with ''escape potential.'' An internal memo, entitled ''Colin Thatcher: Security Concerns,'' stated: ''Thatcher has interpersonal skills, and has the ability of manipulating people with cooperative and pleasant behaviour.'' He was suspected of having tried to persuade other prisoners to disobey prison routine.

Three days after the trial ended, one hundred supporters of Colin Thatcher met in the Legion Hall at Caron to establish a defence fund. A week later, four hundred attended at Moose Jaw's Exhibition Building where donations were taken. The Thatcher Defence Fund eventually reached $15,000.

Before the week of his conviction was out, Thatcher changed his mind about not appealing. Gerry Allbright announced that he had been instructed to file an appeal and would be doing so shortly.

On November 20, two days before the Legislature met to deal with his status, the Thunder Creek MLA issued a statement through Allbright asking to be allowed to keep his seat until his appeal was determined. If he lost in the Court of Appeal,

Thatcher would then resign, Allbright said, even if he appealed further to the Supreme Court.

On behalf of Thatcher, Allbright thanked the hundreds of people who he said had shown support for him by way of letters to the MLA and to his family, as well as donating to the defence fund.

On Thursday, November 22, when Thatcher's fellow MLAs assembled to decide his political fate, Premier Devine and his government ran into a totally unexpected assault. The NDP leader and former premier, Allan Blakeney, rose and asked of Premier Devine: "Did you at any time hear conversations in the cabinet chamber by which Mr. Thatcher talked freely about the murder of his ex-wife?" Mr. Blakeney referred to press reports stating that, at a cabinet meeting, Energy Minister Thatcher had said, "Why do I have to pay the settlement when a bullet only costs a dollar?" Colin's remark to some fellow MLAs, after a caucus meeting in the summer of 1982, had been elevated to conversation around the cabinet table.

The NDP attempt to score against the government on the Thatcher affair went further. Pointing out that Colin had been invited to join the cabinet just a year after the first shooting of JoAnn, and might well have been a police suspect, the premier was asked if he "had any investigation done prior to the appointment of Mr. Thatcher to cabinet?"

Stunned by the enormity of the accusation that his government was guilty of complicity to murder, Premier Devine fell back upon cabinet confidentiality. "I can't, and I won't talk about anything that was discussed in cabinet."

The next day, however, the premier made a statement to the House in which he denied that he or his cabinet had ever discussed "the Wilson incident." Since his government had not taken office until a year after the attempted murder, he turned the matter back to Mr. Blakeney somewhat. "At no time did the former premier [Blakeney] give me any information about the Wilson incident, or its investigation during his administration."

Many Saskatchewanites, seasoned to heavy politics, were shocked at the performance in the House. Colin Thatcher had left his final mark upon the Legislature.

In spite of a filibuster by the lone Liberal MLA in the House, a defector from the Conservatives, the amendment was passed on November 28, and Colin Thatcher ceased to be the member from Thunder Creek. The Conservative party had already revoked his membership. Thus, after forty years of almost uninterrupted elected office, there was no Thatcher in any elected position in Saskatchewan. Ross Thatcher went from CCF to Liberal to the premier's office. Colin Thatcher went from Liberal to Conservative to the cabinet and then out of cabinet, out of caucus and out of office.

Ten days after being removed from his seat, the former MLA was transferred to the federal maximum security prison near Edmonton. Cody Crutcher was still in Edmonton Max and, some weeks later, hearing that Thatcher had been approaching his until then un-met accomplice, Regina police prevailed upon prison officials to move Crutcher.

Within a month of Thatcher's conviction, Tony Wilson, as executor of JoAnn's estate, seeking to enforce payment of the balance of the $500,000 to be paid under the settlement agreement, commenced foreclosure proceedings against the land upon which Colin had secured the monies. Wilson's lawyers said that, in spite of the $150,000 paid initially, with penalties and nearly two years' interest, $470,000 was owing.

The Wilson action had to wait. To provide relief for the province's farmers, drought stricken and hard pressed to meet their mortgages, the Devine government enacted legislation forestalling farm foreclosure actions for one year from January 1, 1985. Colin Thatcher became an unwitting beneficiary of the new law as the Wilson action became suspended. The Moose Jaw Credit Union foreclosure, also caught by the legislation, was already in abeyance due to arrangements worked out with the Thatchers.

In Palm Springs, the lawsuit brought against Colin Thatcher by Bob Gustav and the other condominium joint venture partners had been slated for trial in June 1984. Pre-empted by Colin's arrest and detention the month before, the action was adjourned until December and then again and again. It was then rescheduled for September 1985. Filed in support of the requests for adjournment until after the appeal is decided was a letter from Gerry Allbright to Thatcher's American attorney stating, "I believe the chances of succeeding on the appeal and having a new trial ordered on Mr. Thatcher's behalf are excellent.''

The mischief charges against Colin Thatcher and Tony Merchant arising out of the taking of Stephanie the day following the murder were still before the courts when the murder trial was over. Because of Colin's conviction for murder, the charge against him was dropped, but Merchant's case continued. Because Colin is expected to be a witness for the defence, it was adjourned until the fall of 1985 on the understanding it would be proceeded with once the Thatcher appeal is determined.

Sandra Silversides' suit against the Regina police for false arrest and imprisonment has not been resolved. Efforts made by Gerry Gerrand, acting for the police, to examine Silversides for discovery before the criminal trial were strongly resisted. Usually parties to civil litigation, particularly plaintiffs who have initiated the action, willingly submit to this standard pre-trial procedure. Gerrand had to make an application to the Court of Appeal to have a date fixed for the examination of Silversides. When, in December, Sandra appeared under oath, she admitted having cashed several thousands of dollars of cheques in her name for Colin in November and December 1980 and January 1981. The cash, some of it American, was provided to Colin. She also admitted having purchased a gallon of acid for Colin — the acid Wally Beaton thought might have been used to dissolve a gun — but recollected that it was at a time far removed from the murder. Sandra denied, as she had at the trial, having seen the Mustang car at Redland Avenue in May 1981, or having seen a rifle in Colin's truck, although she acknowledged seeing the bullets in the truck cab. The Thatcher housekeeper also denied most of the recollections of her former boyfriend, Blaine Mathieson, and any knowledge of conversation about murder planning around the Redland Avenue home.

The new year brought the news that the Regina Police Department had totalled up the cost of the investigation of the murder of JoAnn Wilson: $790,000 worth of time and ''operational and investigational expenses'' had been consumed in 1983 and 1984.

The department had been in turmoil at the executive level since the early summer of 1984, as the Thatcher case was moving from the preliminary to trial. The disruption continued until the spring of 1985. Chief Vern New was having a dispute with the Regina Board of Police Commissioners that finally terminated with the chief's resignation in April. Much of the dispute had to do with Ed Swayze.

In a competition to fill one of the two deputy chief positions on the Regina force, the Board of Police Commissioners chose to select Inspector Swayze, the junior candidate, for whom it was a double promotion. Chief New resisted, to the point of complaining to the Saskatchewan Police Commission about the Regina board's "inappropriate exercise of authority." The power struggle engaged Regina City Council, which split along factional lines, and D.K. MacPherson, QC, a member of the Board of Police Commissioners, resigned over the issue. Swayze's suitability for the deputy position was not questioned by either side, the issue being the authority to make the appointment. For months the department and the board teetered on the edge of a public investigation as demands for inquiries were considered by the Ministers of Justice and Urban Affairs and even by the courts. Although Swayze was appointed deputy chief in September, in the middle of the contest, the chief investigator of the Wilson murder had much to distract him as the case was prepared for trial.

Upon Chief New's resignation, former deputy chief Tom Savage was appointed chief and calm was restored to the department.

While Swayze stepped up in the department, Staff Sergeant Al Lyons followed Wally Beaton into retirement at the end of 1984. Both continued to live in Regina. Sergeants Jim Street, Bob Murton and Gene Stusek carried on with the department. Street chafing in uniform, is looking forward two years hence to his retirement to the frontier farm he is developing next to the bush in north-east Saskatchewan.

But the Thatcher case did not disappear from the concerns of the Crown and the Regina police. As the trial transcripts became available in January, the Crown acknowledged that it was studying the defence testimony to determine if charges of perjury were warranted with respect to the alibi witnesses. No charges were laid.

In February, a charge against Charlie Wilde for breaking and entry of a Winnipeg drugstore was stayed by the Crown. Serge Kujawa stated that the decision was not part of any deal made with the witness.

The allocation of the $50,000 reward posted a few days following the murder has not been determined. Recommended for shares are Wilde, Garry Anderson, Lynne Mendell, Cody Crutcher and the young son of the deceased Gloria Debolt, who provided Ed Swayze with the first usable lead in the case. The proposed participation in the reward by three who were accomplices to crime has raised concerns of public policy.

No trace of the weapons used in the two assaults upon JoAnn Wilson has been found, not the rifle which first shot her, the pistol which killed her, or the instrument (if there was one) used to beat her. Police scuba divers with metal detectors scoured every body of water between and around Regina and Moose Jaw. Mostly these were sloughs or dugouts. Nothing was recovered.

On March 27, Thunder Creek elected a new MLA. Once again the contest was all over with the Tory nominating convention, where Rick Swenson, son of Colin Thatcher's 1978 protagonist Don Swenson, narrowly defeated Thatcher supporter Lyle Stewart. Swenson was sent to the Legislature with almost 43 per cent of the vote and a 950-vote edge over the NDP and Liberals, nearly tied for second place. Campaign workers found the Thatcher trial to be a tender and volatile issue in several areas of the large, rural riding.

On April 30, Tony Merchant revised a libel suit on behalf of Colin Thatcher against Southam News and several Saskatchewan newspapers and radio stations. The original suit, launched in July 1984, had complained of a story that was carried shortly after Thatcher's arrest. The report cited certain alleged expense account irregularities of the former Energy Minister as having contributed to his dismissal from the cabinet. When the story was repeated following the trial, and other stories printed concerning Thatcher's personal life, the lawsuit was expanded to include reporters Peter Calamai, Don Sellar and Heather Bird. Tony Merchant applied to have the case heard in Saskatchewan, although the articles were published outside the province.

While it was the reportage around the time of the trial that concerned Merchant, the commentary in the editorial and letters columns of periodicals both national and provincial carried on long after, and in more heated style. It was here that the public zeal for theorizing about the case and criticizing its disposition was given vent.

Passing judgment on the Thatcher case had become something of a provincial sport. The armchair jurors outside the courtroom, basing their analyses on media reports of the evidence, seemed reluctant to concede to the actual jurors any advantage in assessing all the testimony, and in having heard it directly from the witnesses. The length of time spent in reaching a verdict was assumed by many to be proof that the decision was reached only with difficulty, and that unanimity was evasive.

The conduct of the Crown drew most of the fire. The form of the indictment bothered many trial-watchers, as it had Gerry Allbright. A *Globe and Mail* editorial asked: "Did part of the jury convict Mr. Thatcher for committing the crime and part for inciting it? Is that a unanimous verdict?"

The editorial writer went on to suggest that the jury had been, in effect, told: " 'If you don't think there is enough evidence to convict the accused of committing the murder personally, you may consider whether he hired someone to do it; you may put the two collections of evidence together.' Yet how can both be true? Is there not here a question of double jeopardy?"

Other and less moderate criticism came forth from a vocal cross-section of the Saskatchewan public. Colin Thatcher was nearly prosecuted for criminal libel because of comments he made following his civil proceedings. His remarks were mild in comparison to much of the public criticism of his criminal trial. The Department of Justice refrained from laying libel charges, reasoning that such action would increase the furor and give credibility to the critics.

"Dark Day for Justice" was the headline chosen by Ray Zalowsky, publisher of the weekly newspapers at Fort Qu'Appelle and Balcarres, for the story he wrote a week after the verdict. "Justice did not prevail," he wrote. "By finding the man guilty — the jury has made a mockery out of our justice system." Accusing the police and prosecution of overdramatization, Zalowsky may have lost his point with readers when he charged that Kujawa had polished his balding head for the trial "because it gave him a halo effect."

Perhaps due to the Crown's inaction, by the spring of 1985 the bounds of restraint seemed to have disappeared entirely. In its May 9 edition, the United Grain Growers publication *Grainews* carried a full-page commentary under the headline: "Colin Thatcher's Conviction Wasn't a Rational Decision." Written by regular contributor David Bryan, a farmer from Central Butte in the Thunder Creek constituency, the column witheringly attacked everyone involved in the prosecution, from the "Attorney-General" to the jury. Bryan stated that the prosecution was made for political reasons and theorized that the "Attorney-General" and the Regina police were "intimidated" by the real killer into "framing" Thatcher. The conviction, he suggested, was due to "error and bias on the part of the judge, overdramatization and bias by the prosecution and the media, and gullibility and bias by the jury."

The Crown lawyers, when considering prosecuting Thatcher himself for criminal libel, had concluded that "the Department simply cannot ignore those kinds of remarks and fulfill its mandate to protect the integrity of the courts in the province." Yet, they have been reluctant to proceed against *Grainews,* somehow being fearful of becoming embroiled in a publicity circus.

In the flood of commentary following the trial, the media itself was condemned for having whetted the public's appetite and for prejudicing Thatcher's right to a fair trial. Less than two weeks after the trial ended, the University of Regina's Centre for Investigative Journalism sponsored a panel discussion on the balance between the public's right to know and the accused's right to a fair trial. The group of journalists and lawyers from the trial generally agreed that Thatcher had, if anything, benefited from the storm of publicity. Panelist Al Johnston, Assistant Crown Prosecutor, stated: "I don't see how the news media or anyone else can prevent the public from making inferences."

Other lawyers publicly worried that excessive coverage of matters before the courts can distort perceptions, regardless of the actual evidence. Open trials were introduced in the English system of justice to protect the accused from the perils of being dealt with behind closed doors. Permitting public attendance in the courtroom is somewhat different from ensuring adequate media coverage when it follows that the trial expands out of the courtroom.

The media predictably responded to the charge of influencing the trial by contending that they were merely meeting the public demand for news of the trial. The Regina *Leader Post* claimed: "The story deserved treatment in a detailed, complete and sometimes graphic fashion. The alternative would have been to open the gates even more widely to the rumour-mongering and unsubstantiated speculation that became the currency of much casual conversation in recent weeks."

As the court date for Colin Thatcher's appeal approached, the *Leader Post* received an anonymous shipment containing a hatchet and a supposed confession that had been printed on a duplicating machine. The "confessor" claimed to have been a lover of JoAnn's who had lost patience with her. The hatchet, of course, was represented as the missing weapon. Police have been unable to locate the sender. Presumably intended to provoke wide publicity and perhaps influence the appeal, the shipment received no coverage at all.

Colin Thatcher's appeal was heard in Regina on May 27 and 28, 1985.

Shortly after the trial another alibi witness had surfaced, one who, unlike the others, had the virtue of not being in any way connected with Colin Thatcher, though he did have a prodigious memory. Fred Jenner, a Moose Jaw businessman, remembered, when Thatcher was arrested in May 1984, that he had seen him driving on the highway west of Moose Jaw at "eighteen minutes to six" on the day of the murder fifteen months before. Jenner said he had telephoned that information to the Regina police and had assumed that he would be called as a witness.

Gerry Allbright took an affidavit from Jenner and, at the appeal, asked for a new trial so that this new evidence could be heard. The Regina police had checked their tapes and the SaskTel records for Jenner's telephone and the Crown countered with affidavits that no such call had been made.

306

The courtroom employed by the Saskatchewan Court of Appeal has limited seating and on May 27 and 28 again there was a contest for accommodation between the media and the public. A proposal to televise the proceedings into an adjoining courtroom was vetoed by Thatcher and Allbright.

A five-member panel of the Court of Appeal — usual only in important cases — was elected to hear the Thatcher appeal. Chief Justice E.D. Bayda presided, joined by Justices R.L. Brownridge, R.N. Hall, C.F. Tallis and W.J. Vancise. Colin Thatcher, looking tanned and in good spirits, sat quietly through the hearing, as did Peggy and Greg Thatcher, and Colin's girlfriend Diane Stoner.

Gerry Allbright spent the five sitting hours of the first day of the appeal presenting his arguments for a new trial. He raised the matter of the 6:24 p.m. telephone call, contending that the Crown should have put it into evidence, and complained of the calling of Dick Collver. The thrust of his argument, however, was the form of the indictment and the jury charge of Mr. Justice Maher.

The charge, Allbright contended, was "virtually impossible" to defend against. "The Crown had two half-baked theories and, since they couldn't prove either one, then they threw the two together and came up with an either/or situation." Mr. Justice Maher's comments the lawyer submitted, "impugned the defence witnesses and even myself." There had been no meaningful review of the defence testimony, he said, and no adequate explanation of "reasonable doubt." The Thatcher case, according to Allbright, was more "trial by judge" than trial by jury.

With the same contrast as at the trial, Kujawa consumed less than the morning of the second day of the hearing in rebuttal of the defence arguments and in support of the verdict. It was natural, he said, that Mr. Justice Maher spent more time reviewing the Crown case than he did the defence; the Crown evidence was far more lengthy and complex. Viewing the evidence as a whole, the Crown submitted, the only rational and reasonable conclusion open to the jury was that Colin Thatcher was responsible for the death of JoAnn Wilson.

The justices of appeal appeared sympathetic to some aspects of the defence's concerns. Chief Justice Bayda wondered if the jury had not been left with the impression that they had to choose which to believe, the Crown or the defence, instead of understanding that the defence need only raise a reasonable doubt in their minds. Mr. Justice Vancise pointed out that three and a half pages of the trial judge's charge "damned the evidence of Tony Merchant" but only a paragraph reviewed the evidence of five defence witnesses. The inference, the justice suggested, was that the evidence "is not worthy of consideration."

Mr. Justice Hall suggested that the Crown had initially contended at the trial that Thatcher had committed the murder himself, but later admitted that someone else might have done so, and had perhaps confused the jury.

The justices of appeal retired to consider their decision as to whether the jury's verdict was "unreasonable or cannot be supported by the evidence" or based on a wrong decision on a question of law. Even if they found error on the part of Mr. Justice Maher, they would likely not disturb the verdict if they were "of the opinion that no substantial wrong or miscarriage of justice has occurred."

No decision had been made by August. In any event, it is likely that the case of Her Majesty The Queen against W. Colin Thatcher will not be finally determined until it has been reviewed by the Supreme Court of Canada.

At 1116 Redland Avenue, Moose Jaw, the three Thatcher children, Greg, Regan and Stephanie, carry on under the supervision of their grandmother, Peggy, who visits regularly. Sandra Silversides is no longer with the family. Greg manages the ranch and handles the complex legal affairs which still beset the family. In July he was appointed the guardian of Stephanie's modest financial assets.

What effect the trial had on the children remains to be seen. Child psychologists in Saskatchewan publicly worried that the extreme exposure given to the Thatcher case would cause children of other broken marriages to suffer undue fear that their parents might face similar fates. The members of a Sunday school class in a small southern Saskatchewan town chose a photo of Thatcher to illustrate "evil" in a word exercise.

Tony Wilson carries on with his life and his work at IPSCO. The house on Albert Street has been for sale since the trial.

In Palm Springs, Lynne Mendell, now a full-time artist specializing in collage, is preparing for her first showing. She and her husband have moved into a larger condominium that provides studio space.

Dick Collver continues to live in Arizona. Turning his consulting talents to the problems of growing medicare costs, in the spring of 1985 he made a proposal to the Saskatchewan government that he alleged would provide new efficiency in health care administration.

Serge Kujawa has returned to his normal routine as Associate Deputy Minister of Justice but now finds that he is often the centre of attraction at legal conferences across Canada.

Charlie Wilde enjoys a new identity but has not entirely given up his old friends.

Garry Anderson lives "somewhere in Western Canada" under a new identity. He stays in occasional contact with Ed Swayze and Bill Gardner.

Colin Thatcher remains in Edmonton Max. In January he made another trip to hospital by ambulance. The explanation was that he had choked on a bay leaf. Prison officials have acknowledged his abilities and communication skills. At Christmas he was the prison Santa Claus. He has been assigned to instruct a course in elementary computer usage. Over the winter he wrote a book on the inside story of Saskatchewan politics. Entitled *Backrooms*, it will detail Thatcher's understanding of what he calls "the roughest game in the world."

Transported to Regina in May for the hearing of his appeal, Colin gave some indication that he still expected special treatment. Given more freedom than convicts usually enjoy in such circumstances, he complained to the RCMP that there was no radio in his detention quarters, and was unhappy at their refusal to drive him out to Caron to look at his crops. Colin calls Gerry Allbright daily, if only to chat. It is not known whether his interest in the Christian faith has abated or not.

In Saskatchewan the debate continues, only somewhat diminished by the jury's verdict and the passage of time: did Colin

Thatcher really do murder in the Wilson garage? What follows is one interpretation of the facts.

Garry Anderson's meeting with Colin Thatcher at Caron on January 20, 1983, the day before the murder, was pure coincidence. The police, who had determined that Anderson had telephoned Colin's office on January 10 and twice on Monday the 17, took some convincing on this, but it turned out that Anderson had not reached Thatcher. Anderson had been calling about a better job. The closest he got to the Energy Minister was executive assistant Chuck Guillaume, who told Anderson on Monday afternoon that Thatcher was no longer in the cabinet.

When they met again at Caron on the morning of the day of the murder, Thatcher told Anderson that he had been stalking JoAnn for a week and had, in fact, been in the Wilson garage the night before. They agreed to meet again at one o'clock on Henleaze Avenue in Moose Jaw, four blocks west of Redland. Colin would be jogging, he told Anderson.

The jogging is interesting. Although it seems that Colin was a sometime jogger, he did little, if any, from home and his neighbours were surprised to learn, after the murder, that he was a runner. They had never seen him running on Redland Avenue.

Colin testified that about 7:30 p.m., after dinner and after learning of JoAnn's death, he put on his jogging clothes and went for a run. The Redland Avenue home was under surveillance from 7:10 p.m., and Colin said he saw the police cars. But the police did not see Colin leave. A possible explanation for this contradiction lies in Colin's earlier statement to Garry Anderson that he had a way of getting into his house without being observed. The police did not have the back of the house covered in their surveillance. Perhaps Colin, knowing how likely it was that someone had seen him running home from Henleaze Avenue, concluded that he had best invent some real jogging for his activities in that early evening.

Colin was not jogging when Anderson met him on Henleaze Avenue at one o'clock. He was walking, dressed in jeans and jacket. Were the jogging clothes underneath?

Colin dropped Anderson off at the Moose Jaw bus depot and took his car, the 1974 Mercury with a 400 cubic-inch engine, two-barrel carburetor and full gas tank.

310

Anderson kept a dental appointment, did some visiting, had an early supper at the Modern Cafe, dropped in at the Moose Jaw AA office, said hello to some friends at the Grant Hall Hotel, and caught the 7:45 bus to Regina where he spent the weekend with a girlfriend. Wally Beaton had confirmed all this after speaking to Anderson a few days after the murder.

On Sunday, January 23, Anderson had recovered his car from the agreed location on Henleaze Avenue. In it were the jacket and jeans Colin had been wearing, some heavy work socks, he thought, as well as a pair of sunglasses and some incidentals. The gas tank was nearly empty.

There is no positive proof of Colin Thatcher's movements from the time he left Garry Anderson early in the afternoon on the day of the murder until his return to Redland Avenue, whenever that was.

Had he driven Anderson's big car to Regina, parked in front of 2865 Angus Street as had been done on May 17, 1981, done murder in the Wilson garage, ducked up the alley as seen by Craig Dotson, cut through the houses to the car and raced back to Moose Jaw? Then had he parked on Henleaze, stripped off the jacket and jeans down to his jogging clothes, and run back through the streets to Redland Avenue and his alibi?

Jim Street did all that in twenty-eight minutes, although he had not taken time to remove clothing.

When would that have put Colin back in his home? When was the actual killing? Reported at 6:05 p.m., how long had Craig Dotson spent trying to raise the neighbours and alerting the Wilson household? Allow five to ten minutes, and the murder took place at 5:55 to 6:00 p.m. Colin, then, is home at 6:30 p.m. or slightly before. That is in time for him to receive Tony Merchant's telephone call, when it was likely made. Merchant initially estimated the time of his call as "some time before 6:30 p.m."

But what about the 6:24 p.m. telephone call from Lynne Dally in Palm Springs? Was Colin Thatcher at home talking to Lynne at 6:24 p.m.?

The police reconstruction of the long distance telephone records show a total of five calls on January 21, 1983, between the two phones at 1116 Redland and Lynne Dally's telephones in

311

Palm Springs. Because the information was gleaned from several sources, including American, it varies in the precision with which the times are shown. The outgoing calls are identified only according to the hour in which they were made; the incoming calls, including the critical one, are precise to the minute:

12:00 p.m.: (the hour) a one-minute call to Dally's number
 1:00 p.m.: (the hour) a three-minute call to Dally's number
 6:24 p.m.: (the minute) a five-minute call to Redland
 9:00 p.m.: (the hour) a nine-minute call to Dally's number
10:15 p.m.: (the minute) a thirteen-minute call to Redland

Lynne Mendell cannot remember the times of the calls with any precision and, with reference to the fact of the 6:24 p.m. call, cannot remember whether or not she spoke to Colin himself at that time. It might just as easily have been Greg or Regan, she suggests. Notably, the two calls preceding the one at 6:24, and the call following it, were made *from* Redland, but the one key to the alibi was not.

The 6:24 phone call does not prove Colin Thatcher was at home at that time. Nor does it show that he wasn't.

What about the testimony of those who say Colin was in his home at 6:00 p.m., never mind 6:24 p.m.? Those whom Colin had told Garry Anderson before the murder would verify his presence at home? The recollections of these and the other alibi witnesses all had become clearer with the passage of time. Apart from this, Sandra Hammond discovered some time after the murder that one of the clocks in the Thatcher home was running half an hour behind, just enough to turn 6:30 into 6:00.

But what about the gun, or the other weapon if there was one? A .357 magnum is a large gun but it could be held by the barrel and tucked up the loose sleeve of a jogging suit. The time estimates do not provide for time to dispose of a gun, but it could have been temporarily ditched in a pre-selected spot near home. In any event, a murder weapon was never produced by the police, who did not search the Redland Avenue home until the arrest, fifteen months after the murder.

And we are left as well with the Dotson description of the man leaving the Wilson garage, based upon a fleeting glance, to be sure, but still of a figure clearly dissimilar to Colin Thatcher.

312

And, improved with the passage of time or not, the alibi testimony is still there. Sandra Silversides and Colin's two sons testified that he was at home during the crucial hour. Two others put him far from the murder scene.

The debate must continue. There is no definite conclusion yet available to the question of whether Colin Thatcher was in the Wilson garage in Regina shortly before 6:00 p.m. on January 21, 1983.

Epilogue

On Friday, November 23, 1984, the investigators and prosecutors who had gathered on the week of Colin Thatcher's arrest, assembled again in the same boardroom, this time to commemorate the conclusion of the judicial process. Joined on this occasion by several who had retired during the investigation and others who had become involved since the arrest, the group now numbered more than thirty. There was no air of celebration over the conviction of Colin Thatcher, only the quiet satisfaction of a job well done.

In the Saskatchewan Legislature that day, and the day before, there had been vicious debate over the Thunder Creek MLA and former Energy Minister.

Gerald L. Gerrand, QC, rose and proposed a toast.

> We're here this evening marking an event that has touched the lives of all of us, some more than others, but all of us in some way, just as it has really touched everyone in this province. We have seen a tragedy, a tragedy that has exposed failures in the civil justice system, failures in the criminal justice system, and yesterday we heard accusations that those failures had perhaps extended into our government.
>
> I would like to propose a toast tonight to two ladies. One of those ladies was a lovely person who wanted very little for herself, who wanted only to live her life, design offices, continue to love her family, love and be loved. She was denied those simple wants.
>
> The other lady bears an affliction. She knows nothing of power, or money, age or beauty or colour of skin. She knows nothing of these things because she is blind to all of them. I speak, of course, of our lady of justice.
>
> Please rise with me and drink a toast to those two great ladies — JoAnn Wilson and Justice — Justice who has finally triumphed over evil.

"Amen," responded Serge Kujawa, QC, and Deputy Chief of Police Edward Swayze.

There is no single factor that caused the Thatcher tragedy. But features of laws and the actions of individuals interacted in ways that did have a bearing on what happened. No one of these can be said to have caused the crime; nor could any one person involved have foreseen the consequences.

Saskatchewan's Matrimonial Property Act was certainly one of the elements in this volatile mix of people and law.

The case of *Thatcher v. Thatcher* merely applied the law as written by the act, broke no legal ground of its own, and is of little jurisprudential value. But it focused so much public attention upon the new fifty-fifty division of matrimonial property that it must be credited with contributing greatly to proposals to amend the legislation which came forward in 1984.

The Saskatchewan Law Reform Commission began to look at how the new law was operating in 1980 and published its "Tentative Proposals for Reform of The Matrimonial Property Act" in September 1984, just as Colin Thatcher was going to trial for the murder of JoAnn. The commission's report noted "that a substantial part of the value of many farms is a result of the increase in land prices. . ." and that "A matrimonial property order can destroy the viability of a farm or business carried on by one of the spouses." Two of the most provocative proposals were the suggested exemptions from division of the appreciated value of property brought into marriage and gifts or inheritances unless intended for both spouses.

A year later the government of Saskatchewan had not accepted the report or made any change to The Matrimonial Property Act. But Colin Thatcher must have quickly calculated that just the two proposals mentioned, if they had been in effect when *Thatcher v. Thatcher* was tried, would have exempted from division more than $600,000 worth of property and reduced JoAnn's award by at least $300,000.

The legislation that Colin Thatcher himself had supported in the spring of 1979 likely was one of the factors which contributed to the final tragic result.

315

In 1973 a Toronto real estate developer named Peter Demeter was charged and convicted of the murder of his wife Christine by "having a person or persons unknown kill the said Christine Demeter." It has never been established who actually killed Christine Demeter. The guilty verdict, and the form of indictment, were upheld by the Ontario Court of Appeal and the Supreme Court of Canada.

This was the case Ed Swayze had studied at Toronto's Centre of Forensic Sciences and which he had found so useful when planning the taping of Colin Thatcher. Serge Kujawa had studied other aspects of the Demeter case, particularly the form of indictment employed in a situation where the actual killer could not be identified. When he looked at the evidence the Regina police had garnered against Colin Thatcher, Kujawa could see no clear choice between charging JoAnn's ex-husband with the actual killing or with arranging her death. Either way was murder in the first degree. He settled for a simple charge that alleged that Colin Thatcher "did unlawfully cause the death of JoAnn Wilson and did thereby commit first degree murder." With this phrasing, the method would not matter.

Little did Kujawa suspect that such a succinct legal phrase would become a matter of public debate.

The indictment caused little concern among the Saskatchewan legal fraternity. That it became at all a public issue is indicative of the continuing attitude that Colin Thatcher was to be given the benefit of every possible doubt. With another accused it might well have been said, "JoAnn is dead. He is charged with bringing about her death. It matters not how he accomplished it."

Serge Kujawa had told the Regina police in the spring of 1984, before the taping of Thatcher's conversation with Anderson, that they did not have enough evidence to bring about the conviction of such a prominent accused. Harsh reality dictates that, equality before the law notwithstanding, a person of achievement and position is the beneficiary of a somewhat larger doubt than the mythical "average man." Colin Thatcher received the advantage of that "larger doubt" in almost every one of his many encounters with the justice system and, in the minds of many, remained entitled to it after his conviction for murder.

Because of the apparent leniency with which Colin Thatcher was treated in his brushes with the law prior to the murder, the Saskatchewan justice system has come under criticism. If he had been given his just desserts on those earlier occasions, the critics say, Thatcher would have been less tempted to carry on with his course of conduct.

Colin's acquittal on the assault charge might not have come about, or be allowed to stand, if he had not been an MLA. He was not prosecuted on what was considered to be a clear case of criminal libel when he criticized the civil courts. The $6,000 fine for the contempt finding arising out of Regan's disappearance was, perhaps, a modest penalty for one of Thatcher's wealth. A non-member of the Legislature would clearly have been jailed, but Colin was the beneficiary of a privilege originally instituted to protect the independence of legislatures.

Even though each one of these affairs can be justified in isolation, the collective result may well have been to reinforce Colin Thatcher's belief that he could disregard the law with impunity.

Colin Thatcher was also the beneficiary of the reluctance of a long list of people to speak up about behaviour that was at least suspicious and usually incriminating. Whether they were motivated by fear or a desire to protect, the result was that Colin walked secure behind a shield of silence for at least the three years between the first shooting of JoAnn and his arrest.

Dick Collver, who had learned of Colin's intentions in early 1980, Lynne Mendell, who knew in 1981, and Blaine Mathieson, who saw suspicious happenings in May 1981, each for entirely different reasons said nothing. Chuck Guillaume and other staff members said nothing about the Energy Minister's packing a gun holster. Girlfriends who had heard strange revelations remained silent. Sandra Hammond (Silversides) stayed mum. Individually, no one person could have foreseen or prevented what eventually happened, but Colin Thatcher benefitted from the unwitting, collective deferral of action by this group of people. Others — Garry Anderson, Charlie Wilde and Cody Crutcher — had different reasons for saying nothing.

In fairness to the justice system, it can be said that police investigators were up against a difficult adversary surrounded by a wall of silence.

The criticism of the Saskatchewan justice system extended to the legal profession. The revelation by Dick Collver in his testimony that, long before the killing, he had made his lawyers aware of Colin Thatcher's murderous intentions towards JoAnn and that the information had been protected, caused many to question the legal ethics involved.

Following the conviction, Harlan Geiger, JoAnn's father, was publicly quoted as saying: "I think the legal profession ought to take a look at moral as well as legal responsibility. If they had, JoAnn might have been alive today."

MacPherson, Leslie & Tyerman, the prestigious Regina law firm retained by Collver, had maintained as confidential the information he gave them. In doing so they were adhering to the ethical requirements of the profession.

The confidentiality, or privilege, accorded to information given by a client to his lawyer, is regarded as one of the cornerstones of our adversary system of justice. Without such protection, it is felt, the defence lawyer becomes the agent for the state and the client loses his right not to incriminate himself and remain innocent until proven guilty. The privilege is the client's, not the lawyer's, and the lawyer who abuses it may be subject to disbarment.

The Code of Professional Conduct of the Canadian Bar Association is unequivocal: "Where legal advice of any kind is sought from a professional legal adviser in his capacity as such, the communications relating to that purpose, made in confidence by the client, are at his instance permanently protected from disclosure by himself or by the legal adviser, except if the protection be waived."

The code provides exceptions, of course, and one is that the disclosure of information necessary to prevent a crime will be justified if the lawyer has reasonable grounds for believing that a crime is likely to be committed. Few lawyers in private practice have not experienced a bitter spouse fondly contemplating the

318

murder of his or her mate. When is it reasonable to believe that a crime is likely to be committed?

Colin Thatcher was not the client of MacPherson, Leslie & Tyerman; Dick Collver was. Such information as the law firm had was second-hand.

The propriety and application of the confidentiality requirement in the circumstances revealed by Dick Collver provoked debate in Saskatchewan's legal fraternity. The question arose spontaneously at a February meeting of the Saskatchewan members of the Canadian Bar Association in Saskatoon. There was no unanimity on the question, and no resolution was achieved. Some members thought that an anonymous tip might satisfy both the ethical and the moral concerns.

Collver testified that he had called his lawyers for advice three times, once in January 1980, shortly after Colin spoke to him, once more following the May 1981 wounding, and a third time after the murder. The law firm's records disclose only the last two communications.

The advice Dick Collver had received from his lawyers, that he was under no legal obligation to reveal the intentions Colin Thatcher had disclosed to him, was legally correct and Collver chose to follow it. The moral decision was his.

After the first shooting of JoAnn, Colin's statements to Collver could no longer be taken as idle threats. Should he have come forward then? Would it have done any good if he had? It would have come as no surprise to JoAnn that Colin had designs upon her life; the attempt, she said, could have been caused by "no one else." Does it matter that disclosure might have changed nothing?

As they drove back together to Regina from Saskatoon after listening to Dick Collver testify, Gerry Gerrand had made Ron Barclay of MacPherson, Leslie & Tyerman very aware that he was incensed on another front. W.M. Elliott of the firm, who had been retained to act as mediator between Gerrand and Merchant and had achieved the settlement of the property dispute, had made no disclosure of his knowledge of the intentions Thatcher had revealed to Collver. A normal solicitor-client relationship would have required either disclosure or a refusal to act because of a conflict of interest due to the possession of the special knowledge. But Elliott was acting as a mediator. Gerrand suggested to Barclay that the matter should perhaps be referred to the Law Society of Saskatchewan. MacPherson, Leslie & Tyerman decided to retain J.J. Robinette, QC, of Toronto, the dean of Canadian lawyers, to review and advise upon their conduct in the entire matter.

The Law Society did become involved. The Discipline Committee, chaired by Elton Gritzfeld, QC, a prominent Regina barrister, concluded that MacPherson, Leslie & Tyerman had not acted improperly. The law firm has revealed that Mr. Robinette advised them that his opinion on the propriety of their conduct was "favourable."

It was not the first time that the ethical requirement of client confidentiality has placed a lawyer in an uncomfortable position. It is understandable that Harlan Geiger would feel that his daughter's life might have been saved but for a rule that might seem to be in existence only to protect criminals. In fact, although it may also be in need of modernization, it is at least as soundly based as the privilege against incarceration afforded legislators in session. Once again, a perfectly legitimate privilege worked to the benefit of Colin Thatcher.

If the justice system did stumble in its early encounters with Colin Thatcher, it recovered following his arrest on the murder charge. On the initial bail application clearly Thatcher and his counsel, Tony Merchant, felt that special treatment was in order. Another murder accused would hesitate to suggest that he be entitled to continue to visit Palm Springs, California. Although Thatcher actually had good reason to be in Palm Springs, with the Gustav lawsuit a month away, it was not thought necessary to mention that to the court.

With the eyes of the province upon it, the justice system prevailed and Colin Thatcher did not receive bail. From then on, with one or two modest exceptions such as the special seating at the trial, Colin Thatcher was tried like any other accused — except, perhaps, for the publicity which, if anything, probably worked for this accused. If it was otherwise, it is hard to see what might have been done to correct this problem: wealth and position have their disadvantages as well as their privileges.

The continuing public concern over the trial and conviction of Colin Thatcher may be evidence of a still-existing sentiment that sordid crime is inconsistent with the character of those who achieve prominence and public office. Perhaps, having created our own icons, we resist their destruction.

The national image of Saskatchewan suffered from the Colin Thatcher case, perhaps losing an innocence that can never be regained. The hardworking homesteader, the drought-defying dirt farmer and the agrarian socialist reformer all gave way in the public eye to the millionaire jet-set rancher who considered himself above the law.

As the Thatcher saga enters the realm of popular history, destined to become one of the touchstones of the Eighties, it trails a number of loose ends, some of which will stretch into the Nineties. Colin Thatcher's years before the courts, culminating in his challenge of the ultimate crime — murder — exposed weaknesses that will long remain of concern.

It is fascinating to contemplate the life of this man as he juggled his increasingly contradictory activities. Father one minute, legislator the next, murder plotter the next, then rancher, lover, litigator, financial schemer, he must have attended to his affairs like a harried bigamist. How often did he sit in the councils of government with his mind on matters that would have stunned those about him?

Who was this man, son of a premier, cabinet minister in his own right, product of at least two generations of high ethic, charged with a course of conduct far beyond civilized contemplation? A man who could, and did, explain the predicament of his murder indictment as simply an act of political vengeance on the part of the province's Minister of Justice, retribution for his having out-manoeuvred Gary Lane in Thunder Creek ten years before?

Some look to the father for the answer. Certainly Colin Thatcher had suffered severely under Ross's harsh dominance, had been given little or no acknowledgement of his own worth, and had been left with an ego both swollen and too fragile to stand the disavowal of his wife. But he had been his own man for ten years before the rifle was centred on JoAnn's back as she stood in her kitchen in May 1981. He was then forty-two years old. When does a man cease to be his father's son?

There was not a touch of evil in the makeup of Ross Thatcher. Seemingly uncaring, he was actually emotionally timid; he avoided facing many sensitive duties or disguised his true feelings behind a mask of callousness. Ross was honest and seldom able to lie, even in political matters where it is often a necessity. He took his losses like a man, and carried no grudges.

Colin was none of these things. The father alone does not explain the son.

When Colin Thatcher returned to Saskatchewan from Palm Springs in January 1983, he seemed to have brought with him a resolve to take some action against JoAnn. He had made arrangements with Lynne Dally for regular telephone calling and he promptly arranged for an additional car, the CVA blue Oldsmobile KDW 292. But the previous October he had secured a car from Garry Anderson with some purpose in mind and nothing had happened.

Almost immediately upon Colin's arrival back in Saskatchewan, he was struck with a series of blows that not only would have stiffened any resolve he was developing; they attacked the very foundation of his existence. The loss of his cabinet position, the launching of the foreclosure action against his lands, both highly publicized, and the reminder of the large payment due to JoAnn, all hit within a few days. All of these were repercussions of Colin's own actions. He was reaping what he'd sown. And it was just too much.

Maps

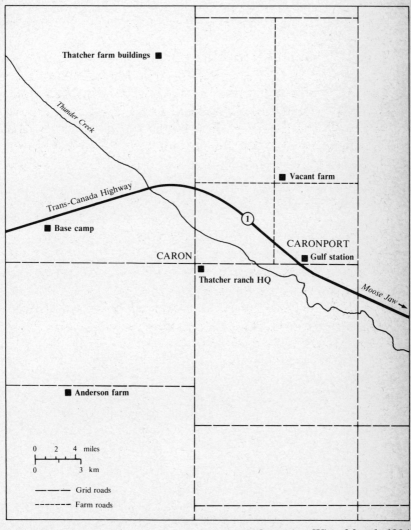

Thatcher farm buildings ■

Thunder Creek

Trans-Canada Highway

■ Base camp

■ Vacant farm

①

CARON

CARONPORT
■ Gulf station

■
Thatcher ranch HQ

Moose Jaw →

■ Anderson farm

0	2	4	miles
0		3	km

— — — Grid roads

------ Farm roads

Operation Wire: May 1, 1984

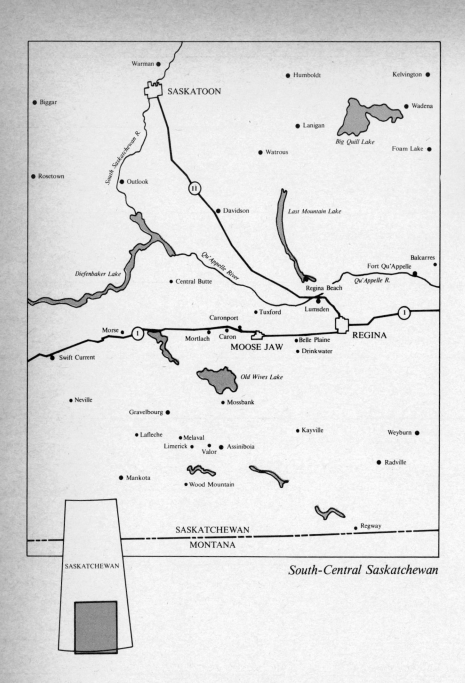

South-Central Saskatchewan

324

Chronology
1977-1985

1977

Winter/Spring	Colin and JoAnn Thatcher buy Palm Springs condominium.
24 June	Colin Thatcher leaves Liberals for Conservative caucus.
Summer	Colin and Ron Graham on first annual "bachelor holiday."
	JoAnn begins freelance work for Ron Graham.

1978

June	Colin and Ron Graham on second bachelor holiday.
Summer	JoAnn and Ron Graham meet in Des Moines.
18 October	Colin re-elected, as Conservative.
November	Colin bluffs to JoAnn that he has seen a lawyer about divorce.

1979

Easter	JoAnn and Ron Graham meet again in Des Moines.
24 July	JoAnn visits Brampton to arrange move.
9 August	Colin and Ron Graham leave on third bachelor holiday.
13 August	JoAnn leaves Colin, taking Stephanie and Regan.
11 September	Colin takes back Stephanie and Regan.
27 November	Custody of Stephanie and Regan granted to JoAnn (Colin appeals; custody order stayed until spring).

10 November	Grant Devine elected Conservative leader.
7 December	JoAnn makes property settlement application.

1980

1 January	Colin visits Dick Collver in Arizona.
	New Matrimonial Property Act in effect.
1 February	Colin commits $420,000 to Palm Springs condominium project.
13 March	Colin buys $425,000 worth of land for sons.
Spring	JoAnn meets Tony Wilson.
8 May	Colin's custody appeal dismissed; custody of Regan and Stephanie given to JoAnn.
17 May	Altercation at Redland Ave.; Colin charged with assault.
June	Divorce and property trial begins.
17 July	Decree nisi handed down.
11 August	Custody decision favouring JoAnn reaffirmed.
16 August	Regan disappears in Moose Jaw; later reappears in Palm Springs.
20 October	Property decision handed down: Colin to pay JoAnn $820,000.
October	Colin meets Lynne Dally in Palm Springs.
Fall	Colin begins looking for contract killer; meetings with Garry Anderson.
4 November	Colin acquitted on assault charge.
November	Lynne Dally's first trip to Saskatchewan.
December	Anderson, Charlie Wilde and Cody Crutcher make deal at Sheraton Hotel in Regina.
22 December	Decree absolute issued.

1981

3 January	JoAnn marries Tony Wilson.
5 February	Colin found guilty of contempt for refusing to disclose Regan's whereabouts.
March	Colin meets Charlie Wilde at abandoned farm; and again in Regina.
28 April	Colin loses contempt appeal; fined $6,000.
13 May	Anderson secures car for Colin.
15 May	Colin speaks in Legislature on his custody bill.

17 May	JoAnn wounded by gunshot.
25 May	Meeting between Colin Thatcher and Tony Wilson.
13 July	JoAnn gives up custody battle for Regan.
21 July	Chief Justice asks Attorney General Roy Romanow to act on Colin's contempt.
September	Attorney General's Department begins contempt proceedings.
13 November	Roy Romanow delays contempt proceedings against Colin.

1982

29 January	Colin buys handgun in Palm Springs.
19 February	Property settlement negotiated down to $500,000; Colin makes first payment ($150,000) to JoAnn.
Feb.-March	Colin's condominium project foundering.
2 March	Attorney General's office closes file on contempt motion against Colin.
4 April	Condominium partners sue Colin.
26 April	Conservatives win provincial election.
8 May	Colin named to cabinet; appoints Tony Merchant as Crown corporation counsel.
June	Colin transfers handgun from Palm Springs to Moose Jaw.
July	Lynne Dally attempts suicide in Moose Jaw.
August	Credit Union moves to foreclose on Colin.
October	Colin obtains second car from Garry Anderson.
October	Colin and Lynne Dally travel to Europe.

1983

10 January	Colin obtains Central Vehicle Agency car.
14 January	Colin leaves cabinet.
21 January	JoAnn murdered.
	Foreclosure on Thatcher property approved.
22 January	Colin and Tony Merchant arrested for abduction of Stephanie.
1 February	Colin's second payment to JoAnn due.
	Colin files further application for custody of Stephanie.
August	Tony Wilson withdraws claim for custody of Stephanie.

327

1984

29 February	Garry Anderson gives statement to police.
9 March	Charlie Wilde and Cody Crutcher give statements to police.
1 May	"Operation Wire" at abandoned farm.
4 May	Colin drops off money at abandoned farm.
7 May	Colin arrested.
8 May	Bail refused (subsequent appeal and second hearing unsuccessful).
10 June	Lynne (Dally) Mendell agrees to testify.
25-28 June	Preliminary inquiry.
July	Tony Wilson applies for interim custody of Stephanie until murder charge resolved (refused).
July	Libel actions against media launched on Colin's behalf.
12 October	Proposals for revising Matrimonial Property Act released.
15 October	Thatcher murder trial begins.
6 November	Colin found guilty of first degree murder.
9 November	Thatcher defence fund created.
15 November	Mischief charge against Colin (for taking Stephanie) dropped.
23 November	Colin's PC party membership revoked.
28 November	Legislature passes motion vacating Thunder Creek seat.
Late November	JoAnn Wilson estate lawyers launch foreclosure action against portion of Thatcher lands.
December 6	Colin transferred to Edmonton Max.

1985

5 February	Manitoba stays break and entry charges against Charlie Wilde.
27 March	Thunder Creek by-election won by Conservatives.
27-28 May	Appeal hearing in Regina.

Operation Wire Transcript*

THATCHER: Been having truck trouble. I had to — Let's get in this car and go for a ride.

ANDERSON: I'd prefer to stay around. I just — I only wanted to be a couple of minutes.

THATCHER: All right.

ANDERSON: Just so we can . . . So, I haven't seen you around, how you been keeping?

THATCHER: Fine. I thought I saw you from a distance.

ANDERSON: Yeah, well . . .

THATCHER: Have to be awfully cautious, one never knows . . . Is everything okay with you?

ANDERSON: Yeah, not bad, I guess.

THATCHER: How long are you around for?

ANDERSON: Friday. How does the — you guys getting ready to start seeding?

THATCHER: Well, I've been away. I just got back last night.

ANDERSON: Uhuh.

THATCHER: I haven't seen and I couldn't get the truck started this morning, and when you pulled out of the yard, but —

ANDERSON: Land's dry.

THATCHER: Yeah, it is. It's really down at this end, this is where Evan Thally used to dump his manure. Well, everything is — let's walk over this way. Everything is — there's no problem, have you been hassled?

ANDERSON: Well, they came once and talked to me and just asked me about the Chev car, and that was about it. Other than that, nothing at all. How about you?

*The first few minutes of the recording, during which Garry Anderson describes his movements for the record, and he and Colin Thatcher agree to meet at the vacant farm, are not reproduced here. The remainder of the transcript, beginning at the start of the meeting, is reproduced in its entirety.

THATCHER: Just the once, the day after, and that was — they — no question, there's been some attempts to put us together and we should not be seen together.

ANDERSON: Okay.

THATCHER: They've pulled some — I'll tell you, they've pulled some cheap stunts. Well, for instance, pulled a stunt like the — Wayne's sister-in-law, once last summer they came to her, they went to the door of his barn, there, and asked for you. You know, just to see what her reaction. Of course, and that never —

ANDERSON: Yeah.

THATCHER: — never heard of you.

ANDERSON: Yeah.

THATCHER: You know, you hear all sorts of wild rumors, but . . .

ANDERSON: Well, I've been out of circulation.

THATCHER: Where you been?

ANDERSON: Up north.

THATCHER: What — were you — did you have a government job?

ANDERSON: Yup.

THATCHER: Who with?

ANDERSON: DNS.

THATCHER: DNS. Well they spent some time trying to connect me, getting you up — getting you that job.

ANDERSON: Hmm.

THATCHER: Are you working for them now?

ANDERSON: No, I'm on holidays.

THATCHER: Right.

ANDERSON: I took some time off.

THATCHER: But I mean, you've still got a job with them, have you?

ANDERSON: Yeah, but — everything's — it's on a contract, eh, you know?

THATCHER: Uhuh.

ANDERSON: Terminated on a day's notice, two day's notice. Whatever they hell — whatever the hell they feel like, so. Everything went okay though, eh?

THATCHER: Yeah, there's no connection back. I saw Jane Graham, in California, about a week ago, and they were up — well it sounded like they were trying to hang something onto him, because Beaton's who's handled the investigation, was in Calgary, seeing him on April the 11th.

ANDERSON: Mhmm.

THATCHER: Jane wasn't supposed to know about it. Well, you know, they're up to that. I can't figure it out, I don't know.

330

ANDERSON: I got rid of the stuff out of the car.

THATCHER: Good.

ANDERSON: You kind of give me a scare there with — I found the stuff laying in there and then I wondered what the hell — I didn't know where the hell you — what the hell you'd done with the gun?

THATCHER: Don't even talk like that, don't — don't even — walk out this way a little, away from the car. Now, there are no loose ends, at all, and, you know, they've gone at — every which direction. Was there anyway a loose end from a couple of years ago can ever resurface, from some of the guys that — discussing some business with, is there anyway there'd ever be a problem surface from them?

ANDERSON: You mean from Vancouver and Winnipeg? I located one of them.

THATCHER: The one that I met, or the other one?

ANDERSON: The other one.

THATCHER: Son of a bitch.

ANDERSON: Well, it's up to you.

THATCHER: Is he in — he's not in jail now, is he, or in any trouble?

ANDERSON: Not to my knowledge.

THATCHER: Is he about to cause any problems?

ANDERSON: I don't know. He didn't exactly recognize me.

THATCHER: Oh, okay.

ANDERSON: Like, I know who he is, but I don't think he has — knows who I am or has connected me.

THATCHER: Okay, I'll — I'm going to tell you something my lawyer told me, and he had heard this on a real rumor basis. There's just a rumor, and of course, there's been fifty thousand rumors. I heard this oh, almost a year ago, and this is from Merchant.

ANDERSON: Mhmm.

THATCHER: Some guy in Alberta, by the name of Eddie Johnson, on a plea bargain, said, "I got the answer to the Thatcher thing."

ANDERSON: Mhmm.

THATCHER: And as the story — and he told this bizarre story of a meeting in the LaSalle Hotel, with Harry Kangles, and me, Tony Merchant.

ANDERSON: Mhmm.

THATCHER: Somebody else, and the killer. The killer was never identified. They apparently took it very seriously and they even pulled Kangles in and —

ANDERSON: Mhmm.

THATCHER: — gave a lie detector. I mean, everybody laughed at the

331

story, including me, but does any of that have any familiarity to you at all?

ANDERSON: Nothing at all.

THATCHER: I think there's been some crap, like, what gets them going. I think somebody gets made for something —

ANDERSON: Mhmm.

THATCHER: And then I think, you know, as they say, "I know what happened," and he'll make up sort of a fabrication and they'll, you know, start running around. Do you need some bread?

ANDERSON: Yeah, I can use some. I can use some for that car.

THATCHER: Okay.

ANDERSON: How about Friday, in the afternoon?

THATCHER: Yeah.

ANDERSON: Pick a time, later in the afternoon the better.

THATCHER: Okay, I'll . . . Okay, now there's — we got wild oats coming. We got no problem. There is no problem. You and I have any distance — keep a distance. We've got to be very careful around Caronport because Royden is the mouth there.

ANDERSON: Mhmm.

THATCHER: I know they've been to see him.

ANDERSON: Mhmm.

THATCHER: A multitude of times, and I know they'd love to just catch you and I conversing. So, I'll tell you what I'll do, I'll round some up. I'm really strapped right now, but I'll round some up. And what I'd prefer to do is leave it somewhere, and I don't think we should even converse again for a good number of months.

ANDERSON: Okay. Any idea where? Do you want to leave it here?

THATCHER: I can leave it —

ANDERSON: Hey, hey, why don't you just leave it, why don't you take it and throw it in a plastic bag, in an envelope, and throw it in the coulee back there.

THATCHER: Well —

ANDERSON: Hey, I don't have to get out of a vehicle and drive in, just — I don't want to be seen here with my vehicle. This is last trip I want to come in with it. I just — you know as well as I do it — like you said, we don't want to be seen. What was I going to ask you — Okay . . .

THATCHER: I always have a great fear of those parabolic mikes that they have.

ANDERSON: Yeah. Well, I'd prefer it in the open. Okay, is there — okay — let me see — okay — yeah. Okay, is there anything else that you want to . . .

332

THATCHER: No, just — remember that car, that orange car that you use to have, has it disappeared?

ANDERSON: Which one? Orange one?

THATCHER: Yeah.

ANDERSON: You mean the brown one.

THATCHER: The brown one, yeah. Whichever — the stuff that was left, you know.

ANDERSON: You mean the jacket and that? I got rid of that.

THATCHER: The car, too?

ANDERSON: The car was cleaned and sold.

THATCHER: Okay.

ANDERSON: That really screwed me because I'd — like at that time I needed that money.

THATCHER: Yeah. Okay, you — he's just driving slow there.

ANDERSON: Let's walk.

THATCHER: What?

ANDERSON: Let's walk over to here. Let's get in behind the barn.

THATCHER: You go back there, I'll walk over here.

ANDERSON: Okay.

THATCHER: There is no question my phones are bugged. They probably always will be. I'm just wondering — tell you what, how about I just leave a garbage bag stuck right there?

ANDERSON: Okay.

THATCHER: Okay. And — did they hassle you at all?

ANDERSON: Just to the point of they asked about the Chevy. That was about it.

THATCHER: Yeah.

ANDERSON: You know they haven't — you say hassle. I'm assuming, you know, haul you into a room and beat you with a rubber hose, or something, no.

THATCHER: Well, remember you don't — remember your rights, you don't even have talk to them.

ANDERSON: Yeah, but what do I do for a lawyer if I'm strapped, who do I get? I'm — this should never come, I mean, you can't very well go for a legal aid lawyer.

THATCHER: Why?

ANDERSON: There isn't any good ones.

THATCHER: Oh well, don't worry about that, but I mean, it ain't coming to that. It ain't coming to that 'cause they have no way of — there's only two places to put the connection together, and they got zero else. They've got zero else, and I mean you know what there is to put together and it ain't possible, and it ain't coming from me. I

333

mean, just always remember that if you were ever to say that I said this or that, it's a crock of garbage. It's just always deny, deny, deny.

ANDERSON: Mhmm.

THATCHER: Because no matter what it was, you know. And, you know, I was just lucky that night. I was home with four people. Four people, pretty solid, and that's pretty hard. What about you, are you covered at the time?

ANDERSON: Yup.

THATCHER: Well, then there's, you know, that's — I didn't know about you, but —

ANDERSON: Yeah, but, under questioning or if something ever happens, would they ever crack those — your witnesses?

THATCHER: No. Never.

ANDERSON: Never?

THATCHER: Never.

ANDERSON: No?

THATCHER: Never, never, never. They tried. They worked on Sandra, they showed her a variety of photographs. They showed her one of you, and one of Larry, and anybody that had a beard about that time, they showed photographs. They were showing photographs of a young guy. I never saw him, but they were flashing them around Caronport. I never — they never showed them to me. They, you know, they're trick is, their style was they — somebody that they're talking to, their style is, "Well, listen, we know that he did it, and we're close to it, and we know that you know," something like this. And then they'll start showing these pictures. When, in fact, they don't. They — you know, I mean, they're just fishing.

ANDERSON: Mhmm.

THATCHER: And, like — oh, they tried to — they tried to crack Sandra, and there was just . . .

ANDERSON: Oh, I had a hell of a time to clean the car out.

THATCHER: Is that right?

ANDERSON: Yeah. I had a bitch of time getting the blood and stuff off.

THATCHER: Yeah. Is there no chance that it can ever surface. There is a chance it can surface?

ANDERSON: No, I don't — no.

THATCHER: Okay.

ANDERSON: The car was cleaned.

THATCHER: Okay.

ANDERSON: I didn't burn it, but it was cleaned.

THATCHER: All right. They — as I say, the only — the only link that they've got — when you want to see me just — like this again — just give me that — I'd have gone right up there, I was out of gas.

ANDERSON: Okay, the next — if we should ever, ever, ever have to meet again, okay?

THATCHER: Well, we will.

ANDERSON: Okay, we'll meet at the other abandoned place.

THATCHER: Okay.

ANDERSON: Over by Hous's.

THATCHER: Okay.

ANDERSON: And then you can — well it's just away from here, because I don't want to be back in here again.

THATCHER: Okay, okay. Are we — is that the only — that is the only connection and the only other one is those one's that we're talking business with over two — almost two years ago. Unless one of those — the other guy, the one was here, is he still in — is he still in Manitoba?

ANDERSON: I'm assuming. I'm close to coming on to that, but I haven't had the opportunity to really get into it. I just happened to run into the other one by very, very — quite by accident. I was asking some people and just sort of checking around and I found him. He doesn't know me.

THATCHER: You know, should go just visit that son of a bitch some day, but not right now, not right. Now, there is no problem, there are no other loose ends, eh, I mean, you know what the ends were and obviously I ain't a loose end and you're not, and there's nothing — there's nothing to come to. I mean, I think they've done a lot of speculating and a lot of guessing, but, you know, if — they originally got eighteen guys on it and they're down to — well I don't know whether anybody's on it all the time, but I do know that Beaton was up in — talking to Graham two weeks ago — well that's, you know. That tells you —

ANDERSON: Mhmm.

THATCHER: — something. I mean.

ANDERSON: What's Beaton like?

THATCHER: Oh, he's a nice guy, but they're all — I don't trust any of them, they're, you know. I think what happens is I think the thing just sits dormant and then I think some guy that's an umpteen time loser tries to make a plea bargain or something, and makes up a cock and —

ANDERSON: Mhmm.

THATCHER: — bull story that he knows something, and of course it goes on the channels and they start running around again. That's sort of my guess. Because they — incidentally, Friday afternoon, I won't — I'll put the stuff here, sometime on Friday. You're leaving on Friday, are you?

ANDERSON: Mhmm.

THATCHER: All right, I'll put the stuff there sometime on Friday and I'll put as much as I can get there without suspicion. Slip back, you know, a little bit, you know, in a couple of months if you have to. There — as long as there's nobody — we just don't want to be seen, but the next time, meet you on the road.

ANDERSON: Mhmm.

THATCHER: If you go like that with your hand.

ANDERSON: Mhmm, mhmm.

THATCHER: I know what you mean, five minutes up in that spot, and —

ANDERSON: Okay.

THATCHER: If I'm, you know, unless I'm with somebody or something, if I'm not there within five minutes, I mean, it will be as fast as I can get rid of whose ever with me. Okay?

ANDERSON: Okay.

THATCHER: If I'm by myself, I'll go right there. But, you know, there's no problem unless something stupid's done, now, and I'll pull what I safely can, and, but I just don't want to do something stupid in this stage of the game. But, next time, slip back, give me that — don't drive in my yard again though. There's no problem, I know, I know, I saw you and I couldn't come because I thought I was going to run out of gas any minute.

ANDERSON: Oh.

THATCHER: And, I would have.

ANDERSON: That's — I didn't stick around, I just — in and out.

THATCHER: Okay, and just remember there are no — there's no problems and there won't be unless they trip over something and I got no intention of giving them anything to trip on. There are no loose ends like, you know, there's nothing for them to find, you know.

ANDERSON: It's all been taken care of.

THATCHER: All, sure. Heavens yes, heavens yes. I still don't trust the bastards for bugs, I mean, I don't know whether there's any possibility that that — that's why when we talk, just assume the bastards are listening.

ANDERSON: Okay.

THATCHER: Don't give them any information. You taught me that. Remember, they got that one guy three years later.

336

ANDERSON: Mhmm.

THATCHER: And certainly never call, okay, on the telephone. But no question, no question, I'm bugged.

ANDERSON: No. What am I going to do if you change parties?

THATCHER: I'm not changing parties. I ain't changing parties.

ANDERSON: You like where you sit, eh?

THATCHER: Well, I'll tell you, they're getting into a little bit of trouble now, with Sveinson, and then those two guys this morning that went to the Liberals. All of a sudden Devine likes to talk to an old pro again there.

ANDERSON: Does he?

THATCHER: Yes, all of a sudden, yeah, it's — yeah, he called me in California and —

ANDERSON: Maybe he wants your seat?

THATCHER: No, no, no. I don't think that, no. You know, he can't have that. And — no, things are slipping away from him and I think he's starting to know it, so —

ANDERSON: Mhmm.

THATCHER: I'm falling back into favour again, even though I really don't care one way or the other. Sort of like it where I'm sitting right now. Okay I'll . . .

ANDERSON: Well, like . . .

THATCHER: Like I say, there ain't . . . I've been curious to know whether or not they hassled you or not, because no question, your name came up when they talked to Greg. And, you know, they just slipped it in and Greg, oh yeah, sure. They've been through me with a fine-tooth comb.

ANDERSON: Could I — if I had to get a lawyer, could I get Merchant?

THATCHER: Oh, I think so.

ANDERSON: Is he familiar on . . .

THATCHER: Nope.

ANDERSON: No?

THATCHER: Zero. Knows zero. But it ain't coming to that.

ANDERSON: Well . . .

THATCHER: Do you have some feeling it is?

ANDERSON: Not really, but it's like everything else. We went second — well, basically went one step further, you know, really.

THATCHER: Well, it ain't coming to that because, you know, you're covered that night. No question. Like they're not . . . As long as you're covered that night there's not a hell of a lot they can do. Are you covered good?

ANDERSON: Mhmm.

337

THATCHER: Well, then . . .

ANDERSON: I was . . . Well, I'm covered.

THATCHER: Don't even tell me. But if you're covered good that night, there isn't anything. And they got no interest in you anyway. It's me.

ANDERSON: Mhmm.

THATCHER: Just only as a . . . You know, and then one of the great rights that you get in this country is they have to give you . . . And you don't have to take a Legal Aid lawyer. But for instance, if you haven't got the cash for it, they're, you know, you get the chance to get a hell of a lawyer and the court pays for it. That's one of the things that . . . I mean, that's the least of your problems.

ANDERSON: Yeah.

THATCHER: You can almost name who it is. Oh yeah, that is the least of your problems. But just remember, it's, you know, deny, deny deny. Sure, you know me as a constituent. Sure, you've rented some land. Now they've never asked about me, but, you know, sure, I've rented some land from him, and, yeah, sure, they did ask my office about, like, that you had a government job. They pedalled to Royden and he said, "Well you know, we know he got him a government job." I didn't get you any DNS one. Of course I'd given your name to SMDC.

ANDERSON: Mhmm.

THATCHER: But, you know, they were just pulling through everything. But, you know, if they ever come up to you, sure, you know, just tell them the general stuff.

ANDERSON: Mhmm.

THATCHER: Sure, had coffee with him at Caronport. Now I haven't seen him for a year and a half or two years.

ANDERSON: Mhmm.

THATCHER: Well, there's . . . If nothing's happening with you, you would have the feeling, because nothing is happening with me. Like I say, I think they get in . . . I think some guy that's bucked to go up the river makes a cock and bull story up to get them running again . . .

ANDERSON: Mhmm.

THATCHER: . . . running around. But if they ain't hassling you then there's nothing going on. I didn't know how heavy they'd leaned on you.

ANDERSON: What . . . Okay. Well, I'm glad it went down.

THATCHER: Yeah. If they ain't leaned on you, then they, well, then they're . . .

338

ANDERSON: I'm glad it's over.

THATCHER: Yeah.

ANDERSON: You know.

THATCHER: So am I. Well, if they like, if they haven't been leaning on you and they were in Alberta two weeks ago, I mean, what's that tell you?

ANDERSON: They're still fishing.

THATCHER: Sure they are. Totally. Totally. Totally. In fact, it sounds, Janie thought were looking hard at her husband. Couldn't care less.

ANDERSON: Still got visions of him?

THATCHER: Not particularly.

ANDERSON: How's your feelings with your old buddy Gerry . . .

THATCHER: (Laughter).

ANDERSON: . . . Gerry Gerrand.

THATCHER: Well . . .

ANDERSON: Kind of mellow to him?

THATCHER: No. A guy I could do. That guy I could do. Yeah, it's . . . Oh, I'll tell you, they've tried every goddam gimmick in the world on me. They have tried set-ups, like a guy from Ontario had to see me at the Leg.

ANDERSON: Mhmm.

THATCHER: You know, it's the story about: "I'm in the same situation you are: can you give me a name, can you give me a phone number?"

ANDERSON: (Laughter).

THATCHER: Didn't know whether to laugh or cry. So I played out the role and I said, "I don't know what you're talking about." And I said, "Even if I did know what you're talking about, which I haven't the slightest idea, obviously I couldn't, and I don't believe you're who you say you are." He said, "Well check me out." I said, "No, I ain't going to check you out."

ANDERSON: Mhmm.

THATCHER: Anyway, it was the crudest set-up. But you know, they tried garbage like this. And they'll, you know, like when they come in and they started leading up to, "We know this and we know that and we know this," when they really don't, they're fishing.

ANDERSON: Well I hadn't heard a hell of a lot, just what you read and see in the papers.

THATCHER: Well I didn't know how things have changed.

ANDERSON: That fucking car story went from so many fucking different extremes I didn't know if they were coming or going. And they didn't know if it was green, black, purple, orange, pink.

THATCHER: Well they sure went on a shopping mission on for green Cordobas that night in Regina. But for about a month afterwards there, if you owned a green Cordoba they would knock on your door. It was . . . Yeah, it was really bizarre.

ANDERSON: I think . . .

THATCHER: However, Let's not push it. I think we should move on.

ANDERSON: Okay.

THATCHER: Well, I'll tell you what, I'll put her in a garbage bag and I'll dump her here. Next time I see you, just give me that same sign and there is no problem unless you do something stupid.

ANDERSON: Okay.

THATCHER: Okay?

ANDERSON: Yeah. I'm glad you got her.

THATCHER: Okay.

ANDERSON: See you.

THATCHER: You bet.

Also from
James Lorimer & Company

The Life and Death of Anna Mae Aquash
Johanna Brand

Who killed Anna Mae Aquash and why? The startling story of a Canadian victim in the secret war involving the FBI, the RCMP and the American Indian Movement.

"This book should force the government to insist on a full-scale investigation." — *Toronto Star*.

Sweethearts
The Builders, the Mob and the Men
Catherine Wismer

In this study of organized crime involvement in legitimate business, Catherine Wismer zeroes in on the mobsters, extortionists, hit men and builders who moved in on Toronto's thriving highrise apartment business during the 1960s.

"A very human chronicle of a shabby period in modern Toronto labour history." — *Globe and Mail*.

"A real-life tale of violence and union corruption — Wismer excells in describing the social and political atmosphere of Toronto . . . and in explaining why the city was ripe for development at such a breakneck pace." — *Toronto Star*.

The Flying Bandit
Heather Robertson

The Flying Bandit is a fast-paced account of the life and times of one of Canada's most notorious and best-loved bank robbers. Based on Ken Leishman's private journals, Robertson's book brings back to life all his legendary front-page exploits and spectacular heists.

"Entertaining and highly readable." — *Winnipeg Free Press*.

"A fabulous story." — *The Windsor Star*.